ADAPTED EXERCISES FOR THE DISABLED ADULT:

A Training Manual

(2nd Edition)

Peggy Lasko - McCarthey, Ph.D.
San Diego State University

Karl G. Knopf, Ed.D.
Division Assistant of Special Education
Foothill College

eddie bowers publishing company
2600 JACKSON STREET
DUBUQUE, IOWA 52001

eddie bowers publishing company
2600 JACKSON STREET
DUBUQUE, IA 52001

ISBN 0-912855-84-3

Printed in the United States of America.

9 8 7 6 5 4 3 2

This training manual was developed for the use of program directors, instructors, and assistants involved in Adapted Physical Education programs for disabled adults. Very few comprehensive books exist on Adapted Physical Education for the post-secondary level. Even fewer manuals exist on how to train assistants in these programs. Since the success of an individualized exercise program depends upon the skills of the assistants, thorough training is essential. It is the intent of this manual to guide and supplement the instructor's efforts in this enormous task.

We would like to acknowledge the following people for volunteering as models in the photographs: Rick Lasko, Wendy Borgerd, and Dory Cox (Chapter 4); (cover) Jennifer Quin and Michael Lung. We would like to thank Kristen and Karen Webb for assisting with the final copy of the manuscript.

Gratitude is expressed to Sam Britten, Ph.D., and Margie Corbett (California State University, Northridge) for their extensive contributions in adapted exercise programs for the disabled adult. Their influence is present throughout the manual.

We would like to extend our heartfelt thanks to the many disabled adults and student assistants who have participated in our programs over the years. They have provided the impetus for this manual and have significantly influenced its contents. We sincerely hope that our exercise programs have enriched their lives, and will continue to, as much as it has ours.

Peggy M. Lasko
Karl G. Knopf

TABLE OF CONTENTS

CHAPTER I: INTRODUCTION   1

CHAPTER 2:   BASICS IN KINESIOLOGY   5

Anatomical Directions   5
Anatomical Planes   7
Anatomical Movements   9
Spinal Nerves and Their Somatic Distribution   17
Muscles   19
Study Questions   32

CHAPTER 3:   CONTRAINDICATED EXERCISES   33

Study Questions   43

CHAPTER 4:   HOW TO DEVELOP AN ADAPTIVE PHYSICAL EDUCATION
               PROGRAM   45

Transfers   55
Body Positions   60
Lower Extremity Orthotics   63
Ambulation Aids   66
Study Questions   70

CHAPTER 5:   TEACHING METHODOLOGIES   71

Accommodating Different Learning Style Preferences   73
Characteristic Behaviors of Effective Teachers   74
Instructional Strategies   74
Assistant Behavior   76
Study Questions   77

CHAPTER 6:   ASSESSMENT AND PROGRAMMING FOR MUSCULAR STRENGTH
               AND ENDURANCE   79

Assessment of Muscular Strength and Endurance   80
Programming for Muscular Strength and Endurance   84
The Exercise Program Card   92
Exercises for Developing Muscular Strength and Endurance   93
Study Questions   122

CHAPTER 7:   ASSESSMENT AND PROGRAMMING FOR FLEXIBILITY   123

Assessment of Flexibility   123
Stretching   128
Study Questions   140

CHAPTER 8:   ASSESSMENT AND PROGRAMMING FOR CARDIOVASCULAR
               ENDURANCE   141

Assessment of Cardiovascular Endurance   141
Arm and Leg Bicycle Ergometers - Submaximal Exercise Test   144
Assessment of Cardiovascular Endurance in Ambulatory Persons   146
Techniques in Training for Cardiovascular Endurance   146
Study Questions   151

CHAPTER 9:   ASSESSMENT AND PROGRAMMING FOR GAIT   153

Assessment of Gait   153
Techniques in Gait Training   159
Study Questions   163

CHAPTER 10:   ASSESSMENT AND PROGRAMMING OF PERCEPTUAL-MOTOR
              SKILLS.. 165

    Perceptual-Motor Checklist 167
    Perceptual-Motor Skill Progressions 168
    Activities for Developing Static and Dynamic Balance 169
    Activities for Developing Kinesthetic Awareness 173
    Perceptual-Motor Games 175
    Fine Motor Tasks 176
    Study Questions 177

CHAPTER 11:   ASSESSMENT AND PROGRAMMING FOR POSTURE 179

    Assessment of Posture 179
    Procedures for Spinal Screening 184
    Posture Exercises 185
    Study Questions 192

CHAPTER 12:   ASSESSMENT AND PROGRAMMING FOR ADAPTED AQUATICS 193

    Adapted Aquatics - Hydrogymnastics 193
    Therapeutic Aquatic Exercises 196
    Adapted Aquatics Evaluation Sheet 199
    Hydrogymnastics Assessment Tool 203
    Definition of Test Items on Hydrogymnastic Assessment Tool 204
    Study Questions 204

CHAPTER 13:   SPECIFIC DISABILITIES 205

    Acquired Brain Injury 205
    Amputations 213
    Arthritis 214
    Asthma 221
    Cerebral Palsy 222
    Diabetes 224
    Epilepsy 228
    Gerontology 230
    Hearing Disorders 232
    Learning Disabilities 236
    Multiple Sclerosis 240
    Spinal Cord Injury 242
    Visual Impairments 249

CHAPTER 14:   SPORTS PARTICIPATION 253

    Stroke Technique for Wheelchair Sports 253
    Teaching Progression 253
    The Characteristics of a Sports Wheelchair 254
    Wheelchair Basketball 255
    Wheelchair Tennis 259
    Goalball for Visually Impaired Students 261
    Weight Routines 264

CHAPTER 15:   EMERGENCY PROCEDURES 267

    First Aid 268
    Contraindications to Exercise Testing 268
    Indications for Termination of an Exercise or a Graded Exercise Test 268
    Medications 270

APPENDIX: A) Abbreviations 273
           B) Summary of Muscles Involved in Anatomical Movement 276
           C) Posture Grid 280
           D) Sit-and-Reach Apparatus 281
           E) Quad Gloves 282
           F) Anecdotal Record for the Student with Epilepsy 283

ABOUT THE AUTHORS

PEGGY LASKO - McCARTHY, Ph.D. is currently Assistant Professor of Adapted Physical Education and Motor Development at San Diego State University. She is also Research Director of the Fitness Clinic for the physically disabled at San Diego State University. Dr. Lasko has presented numerous research papers on the effects of cardiovascular training for the spinal cord injured person. Her research focus is in exercise physiology for the spinal cord injured adult.

KARL G. KNOPF, Ed.D. is the Division Assistant of Special Education at Foothill College. Dr. Knopf has had extensive experience with disabled adults in the field of Adaptive Physical Education. He has lectured at several state and national conferences on Physical Education for the Head Injured Adult as well as the effects of controversial exercises on the older adult. He has served as consultant to the California Community Colleges Chancellor's office on matters such as Program Evaluation and Adaptive PE credentials.

CHAPTER 1

INTRODUCTION

A teacher who makes little or no allowance for individual differences in the classroom is an individual who makes little or no difference in the lives of his/her students.
-William A. Ward

Physical Education implies the full involvement of the students mind and body in concert. From time to time the idea arises that one can educate the mind and ignore the body. It has been stated that "to develop the mind and neglect the body is analogous to developing a powerful jet engine without a fuselage to carry it." Yet, many times well-meaning rehabilitation counselors and special education teacher tell the disabled to develop their cerebral qualities at the expense of their physical potential. By ignoring the body the deleterious effects of a sedentary lifestyle will manifest themselves.

Education through the "physical" has become a principle of both education and rehabilitation. One of the many encouraging developments of recent years has been the realization that physical education for the disabled can make a major contribution in the lives of the disabled. Being physically competent enhances a persons self-image, and self-confidence which are important in social and intellectual growth. As Julian Stein said about the disabled "give me pride; give me substance; give me a life of my own and I'll stop feeding off of yours."

Prior to the 20th Century the attitude towards the disabled were those of pity and sympathy. Today fortunately attitudes towards the disabled are improving. As one disabled person said: "I can think of ways to deal with architectural barriers but attitudinal barriers are far more difficult." As educators who work with the disabled we must remember that the disabled person is an individual first who happens to have a disability.

The 20th century has seen many strides attained for the rights of the disabled. Within the past fifteen years vast improvements have been made in improving the services and programs for the disabled within our society. Many laws have been enacted to assist the disabled. Some of these legislative changes involving the disabled are Public Law 94-142, Rehabilitation Act of 1973, and in California Assembly Bill 77. These laws provided the impetus for the physical educator and special educator to work together to assure quality education for the disabled. The general theme of these laws and others were that education for the disabled should be free and appropriate.

Adaptive Physical Education is a diversified psychomotor and educational experience in which the teaching styles and activities are modified to insure success for each individual adult. In addition, it should provide the opportunity for interactions which develop appropriate social skills. Adaptive Physical Education differs from regular Physical Education in that it features individualized programs of instruction. Adaptive Physical Education at the post-secondary level may vary from clinical habilitation programs to those that provide modified sports and games. Adaptive Physical Education programs should focus on developing and maintaining muscular strength and endurance, cardiovascular fitness, flexibility, posture, balance, perceptual-motor skills, and gross and fine motor skills. The Adaptive Physical Education program should always be designed in conjunction with medical consultation and recommendations from physicians. Lastly, Adaptive Physical Educators should coordinate their efforts with those of physical, occupational, and corrective therapists in order to provide the most comprehensive and beneficial treatment for the disabled adult.

Adaptive physical educators work "with", not "on", the disabled individuals. Typically, students involved in a Adaptive Physical Education Program at the post-secondary level have acquired disabilities such as post-stroke, spinal cord injuries, visual impairment, neuromuscular diseases, to name but a few. The focus of an Adaptive Physical Education Program for these types of individuals should be to develop and maintain psycho-motor fitness and posture.

KEY POINTS

Adaptive Physical Education (APE) is medically approved physical education. APE is designed to be therapeutic as well as educational. APE uses many of the tools of physical medicine in an educational environment. The focus of APE is to increase the disabled individuals psycho-motor skills and allow them the opportunity to maximize their greatest potential

A sound Adaptive Physical Education Program should address the major components of physical and motor fitness. These are muscular strength , muscular endurance, cardiovascular endurance, flexibility, body composition, agility, balance, neuromuscular coordination, power and speed.

STUDY QUESTIONS

1. What do the words handicapped, disabled, crippled make you think of?

2. If you became disabled, what changes, in your career, hobbies, friends, the way you go to school, would occur?

3. What is your attitude towards the disabled?

4. How do you think the students respond to individualized exercise programs?

CHAPTER 2

BASICS IN KINESIOLOGY

It is critical to the development of an individualized exercise program that the assistant understand at least the rudiments of basic kinesiology. This chapter will attempt to provide a basic foundation for those who have never taken Anatomy and Physiology and to serve as a refresher for those who have.

ANATOMICAL DIRECTIONS (see Figure 2-1)

1. Anterior/ventral: Towards the front of the body.

2. Posterior/dorsal: Towards the back of the body.

3. Superior/cranial/cephalic/rostral: Toward the head; one body part above another.

4. Inferior/caudal: Toward the feet; one body part below another.

5. Medial: Toward the midline of the body.

6. Lateral: Away from the midline of the body.

7. Proximal: A position nearest the source or midline.

8. Distal: Position farthest from the source.

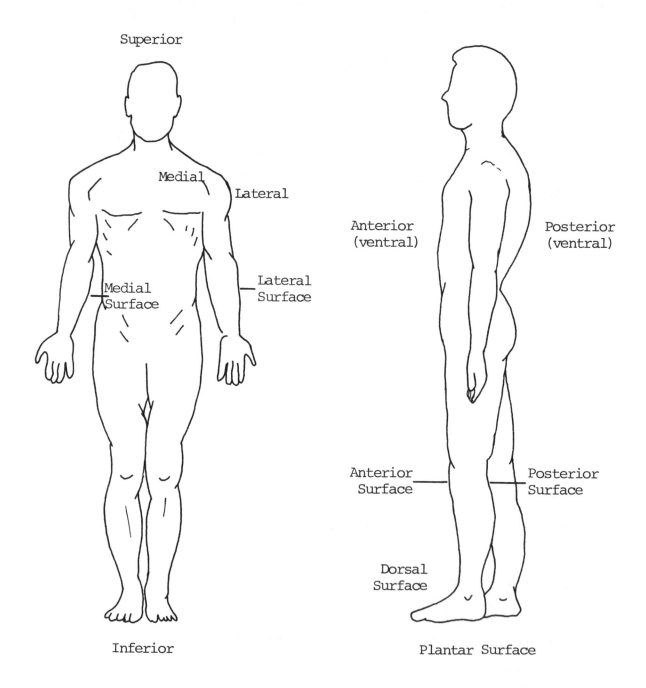

FIGURE 2-1. Anatomical Frame of References.

ANATOMICAL PLANES

Sagittal Plane (see Figure 2-2)

Definition:	The sagittal plane passes through the body from front to back, dividing the body into right and left segments.
Anatomical Movement:	1. flexion
	2. extension
	3. hyperextension

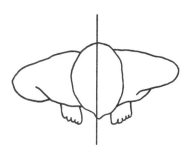

FIGURE 2-2. Sagittal Plane.

Frontal Plane (see Figure 2-3)

Definition:	The frontal plane passes through the body dividing it into anterior (front) and posterior (back) segments. Movement of the limbs must be toward or away from the axial skeleton (midline of the body). The axial skeleton can flex to the right or left side.
Anatomical Movement:	1. abduction
	2. adduction
	3. lateral flexion

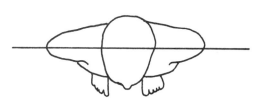

FIGURE 2-3. Frontal Plane.

Transverse Plane (see Figure 2-4)

Definition: The transverse plane passes through the body dividing it into upper (superior) and lower (inferior) segments. The axial skeleton can be rotated to the right or left, and the limbs can be rotated toward or away from the midline of the body.

Anatomical Movement:
1. external (or outward) rotation
2. internal (or inward) rotation
3. supination
4. pronation
5. eversion
6. inversion
7. rotation right or left (axial skeleton movement)

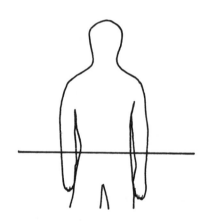

FIGURE 2-4. Transverse Plane.

ANATOMICAL MOVEMENTS

Anatomical movements are always described in reference to the "anatomical position". This is a position where the individual stands erect with the arms at the sides and the palms facing forward.

Abduction
  Movement away from the midline of the body.
Adduction
  Movement toward or beyond the midline of the body.
Anterior Tilt
  Forward tilt of the pelvic girdle (present in lordosis).
Circumduction
  A combination of flexion, extension, abduction, adduction; movement describing a circle (e.g., hip and shoulder).
Depression
  Downward movement of a part (shoulder and pelvic girdles).
Dorsiflexion
  Flexion of the foot (ankle joint) upward.
Downward rotation
  Movement of scapula as the arms are lowered. Superior border of the scapula moves away from the spine. Rotation of the scapula clockwise.
Elevation
  Upward movement of a part (shoulder and pelvic girdles).
Eversion
  Raising the lateral border of the foot.
Extension
  Movement resulting in the increase of a joint angle. Return from flexion to anatomical position.
External (outward) rotation
  Rotation of a bone in a counterclockwise direction away from the midline.
Flexion
  Movement resulting in a decrease of a joint angle.
Horizontal Abduction
  With the shoulders flexed at 90 degrees (elbows extended), the arms move horizontally to the side of the body.
Horizontal Adduction
  With the shoulders abducted at 90 degrees (elbows extended), the arms move horizontally to the front of the body.
Hyperextension
  Movement beyond the position of extension.

Inversion
  The medial border of the foot is raised up.
Lateral Flexion
  Flexing the trunk or the neck to the left or the right in the frontal plane.
Medial (inward) Rotation
  Rotation of a bone in clockwise direction away from the midline.
Plantar Flexion
  Pointing or extending the foot (ankle joint) downward.
Posterior Tilt
  Backward tilt of the pelvis.
Pronation
  Foot -- eversion combined with abduction of the forefoot.
  Forearm -- turning the palms back from anatomical position.
Protraction
  Forward movement of a part (shoulder girdle).
Radial Deviation
  Movement of the wrist toward the radius.
Retraction
  Backward movement of a part (shoulder girdle).
Rotation
  Movement of a bone about its long axis.
Supination
  Foot -- inversion combined with adduction of the forefoot.
  Forearm -- palms facing forward in anatomical positions.
Ulnar Deviation
  Movement of the wrist toward the ulna.
Upward rotation
  Movement of the scapula when raising the arms.

SHORT HAND FOR ANATOMICAL MOVEMENTS

Name	Short Hand
Abduction	$\longrightarrow$
Adduction	$\longleftarrow$
Flexion	$\vee$
Extension	$\diagup$
Hyperextension	H $\diagup$
Internal rotation	$\longrightarrow$ ⋀⋀⋀⋀
External rotation	$\longleftarrow$ ⋀⋀⋀

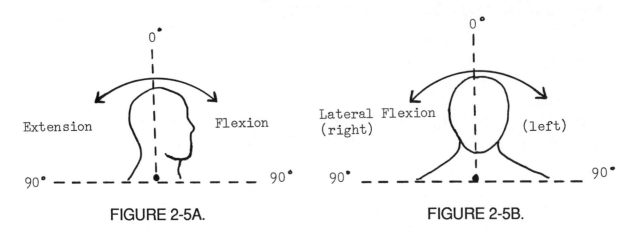

FIGURE 2-5A.　　　　　　　FIGURE 2-5B.

FIGURE 2-5. CERVICAL SPINE - NECK

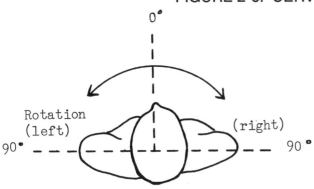

FIGURE 2-6. CERVICAL SPINE - NECK

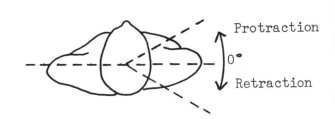

FIGURE 2-7. SHOULDER GIRDLE

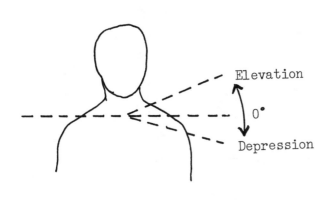

FIGURE 2-8. SHOULDER GIRDLE

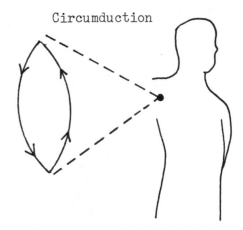

FIGURE 2-9. SHOULDER

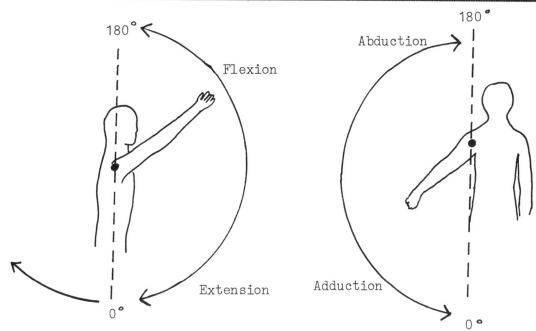

Figure 2-10A.   Figure 2-10B.

FIGURE 2-10. SHOULDER

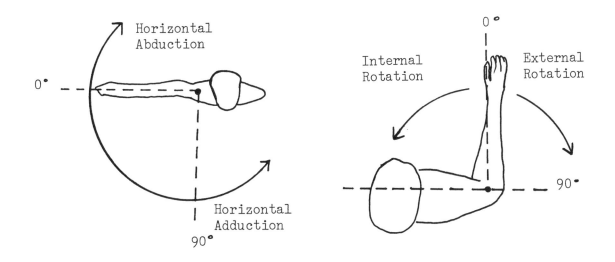

Figure 2-11A.   Figure 2-11B.

FIGURE 2-11. SHOULDER

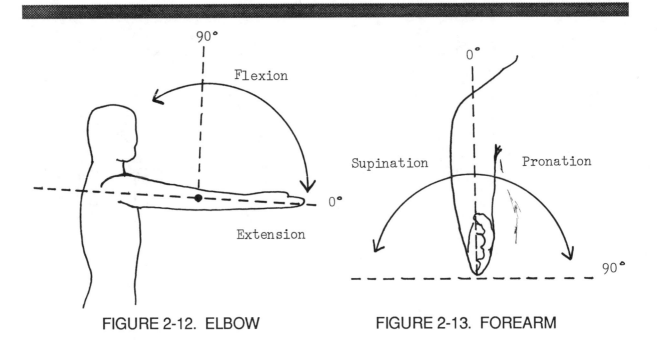

FIGURE 2-12. ELBOW

FIGURE 2-13. FOREARM

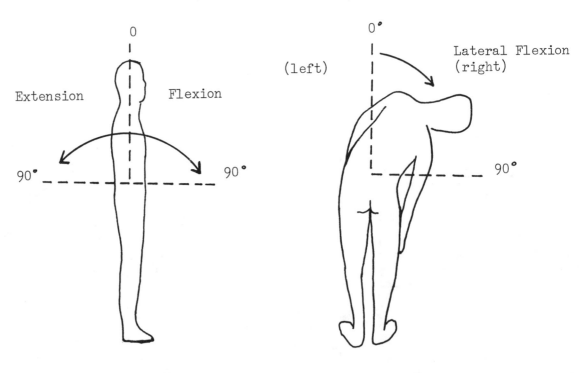

Figure 2-14A.

Figure 2-14B.

FIGURE 2-14. SPINE

14

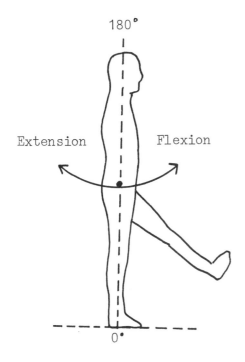

FIGURE 2-15. HIP

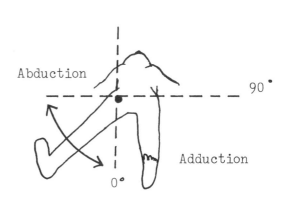

FIGURE 2-16. HIP

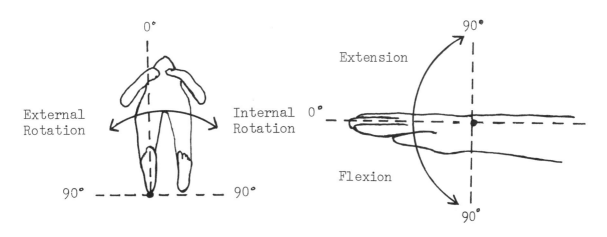

FIGURE 2-17. HIP

FIGURE 2-18. WRIST

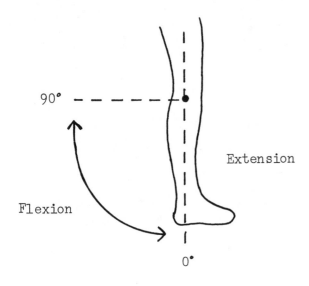

FIGURE 2-19. KNEE

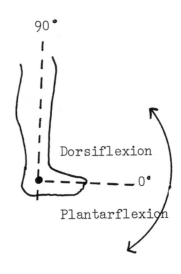

FIGURE 2-20. ANKLE

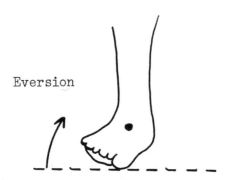

Figure 2-21A.

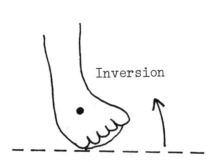

Figure 2-21B.

FIGURE 2-21. ANKLE

(redrawn from Joint Motion. American Academy
of Orthopedic Surgeons, Chicago, 1965.)

SPINAL NERVES AND THEIR SOMATIC DISTRIBUTION

There are 31 pairs (right and left) of spinal nerves. Each spinal nerve exits between two adjacent vertebrae through the intervertebral foramen. There are eight cervical (C), 12 thoracic (T), five lumbar (L), five sacral (S), and one coccygeal (Cx) pair of spinal nerves. Each spinal nerve is identified according to its exit zone (C, T, L, S, or Cx) and its number in the area. For example, spinal nerve T-9 exits through the intervertebral foramen formed by thoracic vertebrae 9 and 10 (Smith, 1974).

"While there are eight nerves that exit the cervical spine, there are only seven cervical vertebrae. The first through the seventh nerves exit above the cervical vertebra and above the first thoracic vertebra. The first thoracic nerve then exits below the first thoracic vertebra." (Hoppenfeld, 1976)

TABLE 2-1. Spinal Nerves and Their Somatic Distribution
(adapted from Smith, 1974)

Spinal Nerves	Plexus	Somatic Distribution
C-1	———	Some muscles of the head and throat.
2		
3	Cervical Plexus	Some muscles of the throat, neck, and shoulder joint.
4		
5		
6		
7	Brachial Plexus	Muscles of the shoulder girdle and shoulder joint.
8		
T-1		Muscles of the upper extremity.
T-2 - T-11	No Plexus	Muscles of the trunk.
T-12		Muscles of the hip joint.
L-1		
2	Lumbar Plexus	Anterior and medial muscles of the hip and knee joints.
3		
4		
5		
S-1	Sacral Plexus	Muscles of the knee and ankle joints and the foot.
2		
3		

MUSCLES

Definition

A bundle of contractile fibers held together by a sheath of connective tissue and attaches to bone by means of a tendon.

A muscle can be stretched and then return to its normal resting length. Therefore, it is commonly said that muscles have extensibility and elastic properties. Muscles also have the capability to contract, because they respond to irritability and conductivity. It must be remembered that muscles are a neuromuscular unit and that without neurological innervation, movement cannot occur and atrophy will follow.

JOINT STABILITY

Basically, three factors account for the stability of a joint.

1. Muscles - such as in glenohumeral joint.
2. Shape of articular surface - such as in the hip joint
3. Ligaments - such as in the knee area
    a. Ligaments are tough and practically non-elastic (*point to remember)
    b. Ligaments hold bone to bone
    c. Ligaments generally found where joints stability is needed
    d. Ligaments restrain undesirable motion, e.g.: side-side motion of knee
    e. Ligaments will yield to continuous regular stretching - thus the adage, "structure follows function". This is why full squats are controversial.

ROLES IN WHICH MUSCLE MAY RESPOND

Muscles can only do two things:

1. Develop tension or
2. Relax

It is important to remember that muscles can function solely or as a member of a team.

Mover/Agonist	Is the muscle responsible for concentric contractions. Mover/Agonist muscles are often subclassified as prime movers or as assistant, or secondary movers for a given action.
Prime Mover	Is a muscle primarily responsible for eliciting a specific joint action.

Assistant Mover	Is that muscle which aids the prime mover to effect a joint movement.
Antagonist	Is a muscle that produces an action which is exactly the opposite of an agonist. An example of this is that the biceps brachii is an antagonist of the triceps brachii with respect to elbow extension, and vice-versa with regard to elbow flexion.
Fixator/Stabilizer	Is a muscle which anchors, steadies or supports a bone or body part to enable another muscle to have a firm base upon which to pull.
Synergist	Is a muscle which acts along with some other muscle(s) as part of a team.
"Helping Synergist"	Two muscles that contract each other's undesired secondary action.
"True Synergy"	Occurs when one muscle contracts statically to prevent any action in one of the joints transversed by the contracting of the two or multi-joint muscles.
Neutralizer	Is a muscle which contracts in order to counteract, "rule out", or neutralize an undesired action of another muscle which is acting upon that joint. This term is probably better than helping synergist or true synergist, because it avoids the various meanings attached to "synergist".

TYPES OF MUSCULAR CONTRACTIONS

In kinesiology, the term "contraction" refers to the development of tension within a muscle. It does not imply that any noticeable shortening or movement occurs at the joint.

Static/Isometric Contraction	Occurs when a muscle does not develop enough tension to cause movement; thus, the length of the muscle remains unchanged. Technically, no internal shortening of the contractile components occur because the muscle remains the at the same length.
Concentric Contraction	Is when a muscle develops sufficient tension to overcome a resistance, resulting in visible movement and shortening of the muscle (e.g., bringing your hand to your face is an example of a concentric contraction of the biceps brachii).
Eccentric Contraction	Is when a resistance overcomes the muscle tension so that the muscle actually lengthens.

REASONS FOR THE NAMES OF MUSCLES

Muscles get their names from various reasons.

1. Action (e.g.,adductor longus)
2. Direction of fibers (e.g., transverse abdominus)
3. Location (e.g., anterior tibialis)
4. Number of Divisions Comprising a Muscle (e.g., biceps, triceps)
5. Shape (e.g., trapezius, quadratus)
6. Point of Attachment (e.g., sternocleidomastoid)

MUSCLES USED IN BREATHING

Diaphragm
Origin	Xiphoid process, costal cartilages of last six ribs and lumbar vertebrae
Insertion	Central tendon
Nerve Innervation	Phrenic nerve
Action	Increase vertical length of thorax during inspiration
Exercise	Breathing exercises to point where belly enlarges

Intercostals
Origin	External: inferior border of rib
	Internal: superior border of rib
Insertion	External: superior border of rib
	Internal: inferior border of rib
Nerve Innervation	Intercostal nerve
Action	External: elevate ribs during inspiration
	Internal: assist in forced expiration
Exercise	Deep forced breathing inhalation and exhalation

MUSCLES OF THE NECK ANTERIOR

Sternocleidomastoid
Origin	Sternum and clavicle
Insertion	Mastoid process of temporal bone
Nerve Innervation	Accessory nerve
	C2-C3
Action	Contraction of one muscle rotates face toward side opposite contracting muscle
Exercise	Watching tennis match exercise looking to the left, then to the right

MUSCLES THAT MOVE THE VERTEBRAL COLUMN
Anterior
Rectus Abdominis
Origin	Publc crest and symphysis pubis
Insertion	Cartilage of fifth to seventh ribs and xiphoid process
Nerve Innervation	Branches of 7-12 intercostal nerves
Action	Flexes vertebral column
Exercise	Bent knee sit-ups

External Obliques
Origin	Lower eight ribs
Insertion	Iliac crest; linea alba
Nerve Innervation	Ranches of 8-12 intercostal muscles, iliohypogastic and ilioinguinal nerve
Action	Literally flexes vertebral column
Exercise	Side bends, twisting sit-up (right elbow to left knee etc.)

Posterior
Sacrospinalis (Erector Spinae)

This muscle consists of the following muscles:

Iliocostalis Lumborum (lateral section)
Origin	Iliac crest
Insertion	Lower six ribs
Nerve Innervation	Dorsal rami of thoracic nerve
Action	Extends lumbar, maintain erect posture
Exercise	Hyperextension of back - In prone position, arch back

(Note: This could be contraindicated. See chapter on Controversial Exercises)

Longissimus thoracis
Origin	Transverse process of lumbar vertebrae
Insertion	Transverse process of all thoracic and upper lumbar vertebrae and ninth and tenth ribs
Nerve Innervation	Dorsal rami of spinal nerves
Action	Extends thoracic portion of vertebral column
Exercise	See iliocostalis

Spinalis thoracis
Origin	Spines of the upper lumbar and lower thoracis vertebrae
Insertion	Spines of upper thoracic vertebrae
Nerve Innervation	Dorsal rami of spinal nerves
Action	Internal flexion - extends vertebral column
Exercise	See iliocostalis

MUSCLES OF THE SHOULDER GIRDLE

Serratus Anterior
Origin	Outer portion of upper nine ribs
Insertion	Anterior portion of vertebral border of scapula
Nerve Innervation	Thoracic nerve
Action	Scapula abduction
	Scapula lateral rotation
Exercise	Exercises for winged scapula

Trapezius
Origin	Occipital bone, spinous processes of 7th cervical and all thoracic vertebrae
Insertion	Posterior portion of lateral aspect of clavicle, top of acromion process, upper border of spine of scapula
Nerve Innervation	Spinal accessory nerve
	C3-C4
Action	Elevation of clavicle
	Upward rotation
	Adduction of scapula
	Elevation of scapula or
	Depression of scapula
Exercise	Shoulder shrugs with barbells (elevation) raise shoulders up

Rhomboids
Lie beneath trapezius muscle (consists of major and minor; for this text, classified as one)
Origin	Major: spines of second to fifth vertebrae
	Minor: spines of the seventh cervical and first thoracic vertebrae
Insertion	Major: vertebral border of scapula
	Minor: superior angle of scapula
Nerve Innervation	Dorsal scapular nerve
Action	Adduction of scapula
Exercise	Shoulder retraction - Facing pulleys, grasp shoulder height handles toward chest pinching shoulder blades together.

MUSCLES THAT MOVE THE ARM

Deltoid -Shoulder Muscle
   Anterior Portion

Origin	Anterior border of clavicle
Insertion	Lateral aspect of humerus
Nerve Innervation	Axillary
Action	Humeral flexion
	Horizontal adduction
	Inward rotation
Exercise	Lateral raises with D.B. or pulleys (humeral flexion)

   Middle Portion

Origin	Acromion process and outer end of clavicle
Insertion	Lateral aspect of humerus
Nerve Innervation	Axillary
Action	Humeral abduction
Exercise	Lateral raises with D.B. (humeral abduction)

   Posterior Portion

Origin	Lower margin of spine of scapula
Insertion	Lateral aspect of humerus near midpoint
Nerve Innervation	Axillary
Action	Humeral horizontal abduction
	Humeral extension
	Humeral outward rotation
Exercise	Shoulder retractions at pulleys

Subscapularis — A protector of glenohumeral joint

Origin	Anterior surface of scapula
Insertion	Lesser tuberosity of humerus
Nerve Innervation	Subscapular nerve
Action	Inward rotation
Exercise	Arm wrestling exercise with resistance - increasing strength of this muscle may present dislocations at shoulder joint.

Supraspinatus — A protector of glenohumeral joint

Origin	Medial two thirds of supraspinator fossa
Insertion	Superior portion of greater tuberosity of humerus
Nerve Innervation	Suprascapular nerve
Action	Humeral abduction
Exercise	Lateral raises with D.B. - standing or seated, starting with D.B. weight in hand, raise arm above shoulder while keeping arm straight.

Infraspinatus and Teres Minor

These two muscles are protectors of the glenohumeral joint. They both share a common origin and insertion.

Origin	Axillary border and inferior border of scapula spine
Insertion	Greater tuberosity of humerus
Nerve Innervation	Suprascapular and axillary nerve
Action	Outward rotation
	Horizontal extension
Exercise	Parallel pulls - Facing pulley machine, grasp handles (upper) and pulls straight back keeping arms parallel with floor.

Teres Major

This muscle assists the latissimus dorsi muscle.

Origin	Inferior angle of scapula at lateral border
Insertion	Bicipital groove of humerus
Nerve Innervation	Subscapular nerve
Action	Humeral adduction
	Humeral extension and hyperextension
	Inward rotation
Exercise	Adductions - With body at side of pulley, grasp top handles and pull down towards your hip.

Pectoralis Major

A large fan shaped muscle that makes up what is generally referred to as the chest muscle.

Origin	Clavicular and sternal head
Insertion	Lateral surface of humerus at outer border of bicipital groove
Nerve Innervation	Anterior thoracic
Action	Humeral adduction
	Horizontal humeral adduction
	Humeral inward rotation
	Humeral flexion
Exercise	Cross-chest fly - horizontal adduction with pulleys bench press

ARM MUSCLES

Anterior

Biceps Brachii

	Has two heads
Origin	Long head: upper portion of glenoid fossa
	Short head: coracoid process of scapula
Insertion	Tuberosity of radius
Nerve Innervation	Musculocutaneous nerve

Action	Elbow flexion
	Forearm supination
Exercise	Arm curls with weights
	D.B. supination exercise

Brachialis
Origin	Anterior surface of lower portion of humerus
Insertion	Tuberosity of ulna below coronoid process
Nerve Innervation	Musculocutaneous, radial and medial nerve
Action	Elbow flexion
Exercise	Arm curls with weights
	Bringing palm towards shoulder with weights

Brachioradialis   Large muscle of forearm
Origin	Upper section of lateral supracondyloid ridge of humerus
Insertion	Styloid process of radius
Nerve Innervation	Radial
Action	Elbow flexion
Exercise	Reverse curls, curls done with hands in pronated position on curling bar

Posterior

Triceps   Named because it has three heads
Origin	Long head: infraglenoid tuberosity
	Lateral head: posterior and lateral surface of upper half of humerus
	Medial head: posterior surface of lower two-thirds of humerus
Insertion	Olecranon process of ulna
Nerve Innervation	Radial nerve
Action	Elbow extension, extends forearm
Exercise	Tri ext - can be done with D.B. or lateral bar
	The key to this exercise is to extend the lower arm against a resistance slowly and completely.

MUSCLES OF THE UPPER LEG

Adductor Brevis (brevis = short)
Origin	Inferior ramus of pubis
Insertion	Linea aspera of femur
Nerve Innervation	Obturator nerve
Action	Adducts, rotates, and flexes thigh
Exercise	See adductor longus

<u>Adductor Magnus</u> (magnus = large)

Origin	Inferior ramus of pubis, ischium to ischial tuberosity
Insertion	Linea aspera of femur
Nerve Innervation	Obturator nerve
Action	Adducts, flexes, and extends thigh (anterior part flexes, posterior part extends)
Exercise	See adductor longus

<u>Tensor fasciae latae</u> (tensor = to make tense; fascia = band; latus = wide)

Origin	Iliac crest
Insertion	Tibia by way of the iliotibial tract
Nerve Innervation	Superior gluteral nerve
Action	Flexes and abducts thigh
Exercise	Adduction exercise at pulleys; move leg towards mid-line of body, or in side-lying position, raise lower leg up

<u>Adductor Longus</u> (longus = long)

Origin	Pubic crest and symphysis pubis
Insertion	Linea aspera of femur
Nerve innervation	Obturator nerve
Action	Adducts, flexes and rotates high
Exercise	Adduction exercise at pulleys; move leg towards mid-line of body, or in side-lying position, raise lower leg up

<u>HAMSTRINGS</u>   Three muscles make up the hamstring group (posterior side)

<u>Biceps Femoris</u>

Origin	Long head: arises from ischial tuberosity short head: arises from linea aspera of femur
Insertion	Head of fibula and lateral condyle of tibia
Nerve Innervation	See Semimembranosus
Action	See Semimembranosus
Exercise	See Semimembranosus

<u>Semitendinosus</u>

Origin	Ischial tuberosity
Insertion	Proximal aspect of medial surface of body of tibia
Nerve Innervation	See Semimembranosus
Action	See Semimembranosus
Exercise	See Semimembranosus

<u>Semimembranosus</u>

Origin	Ischial tuberosity
Insertion	Medial condyle of tibia

Nerve Innervation	Tibial nerve from sciatic nerve
Action	Flexes lower leg and extends thigh
Exercise	Leg curls; student brings the heel towards the buttock; PRE can be applied

Gracilis

Origin	Symphysis pubis and pubic arch
Insertion	Medial surface of tibia
Nerve Innervation	Obturator nerve
Action	Flexes and adducts leg
Exercise	Adduction exercise with pulleys attached at ankle. Student brings leg toward midline of body

Gluteus Maximus

Origin	Iliac crest, sacrum, coccyx and aponeurosis of sacrospinalis
Insertion	Iliotibial tract of fascia lata and gluteal tuberosity of femur
Nerve Innervation	Inferior gluteal nerve
Action	Extends and rotates thigh laterally
Exercise	In prone position, elevate leg; or while facing pulley machine, move whole leg straight backwards

MUSCLES OF THE PELVIC GIRDLE

Anterior

ILIOPSOAS	Made up of the psoas and iliac muscles

Psoas

Origin	Transverse processes and lumbar bodies of lumbar vertebrae
Insertion	Lesser trochanter of femur
Nerve Innervation	L2-L3
Action	Flexes and rotates thigh laterally; flexes vertebral column
Exercise	Straight leg sit-ups

Iliacus

Origin	Iliac fossa
Insertion	Tendon of psoas major
Nerve Innervation	Femoral nerve
Action	Flexes and rotates thigh laterally; slight flexion of vertebral column
Exercise	Leg turns, moving leg laterally

QUADRICEPS	Comprised of four muscles

Rectus Femoris

Origin	Anterior portion of inferior iliac spine

Vastus Lateralis

Origin	Superior portion of intertrochanteric line medial aspect of linea aspera

Vastus Medialis

Origin	Inferior portion of intertrochanteric line medial aspect of linea aspera

Vastus Intermedius

Origin	Anterior and lateral aspects of upper portion of femur
Insertion	Tendon of each muscle unites to form the quadriceps, attaching to patella and tibial tuberosity by way of patella ligament
Nerve Innervation	Femoral
Action	Extension of lower leg
Exercise	Leg extension on universal gym apparatus or similar equipment

Sartorius

Origin	Anterior superior spine of ilium
Insertion	Medial surface of tibia
Nerve Innervation	Femoral nerve
Action	Flexes leg; flexes thigh and rotates it laterally, thus crossing leg position
Exercise	Any exercise that employs above actions

LOWER LEG MUSCLES

Anterior

Tibialis Anterior: The muscle that runs alongside your shin and you feel it when you dorsiflex your foot.

Origin	Lateral condyle and upper portion of lateral surface of tibia
Insertion	Plantar surface of first metatarsal and medial surface of first cuneiform
Nerve Innervation	Deep peroneal
Action	Ankle dorsiflexion
	Foot inversion
Exercise	With foot resting off table edge, with weight on top of foot, point toe to head

Posterior

Gastrocnemius

Origin	Posterior portion of femoral condyle
Insertion	Posterior portion of calcaneus at calcaneal (Achilles) tendon
Nerve Innervation	Tibial
Action	Ankle plantar flexion Knee flexion
Exercise	Toe raises - coming up (plantar flexing) on your toes weight can be added

Soleus

Origin	Posterior portion of head of fibula; popiteal line and medial border of tibia
Insertion	Posterior surface of calcaneas by caleaneal tendon
Nerve Innervation	Tibial
Action	Plantar flexion of ankle
Exercise	Toe raises

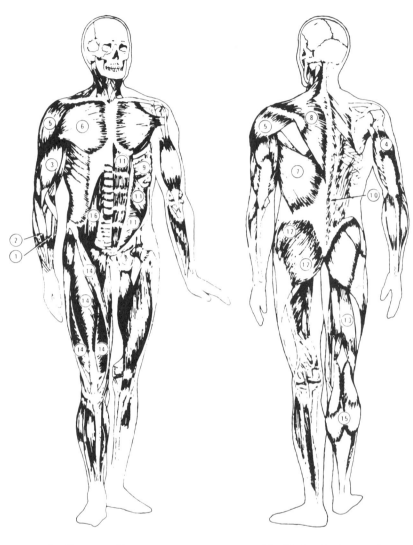

1. Forearm flexors
2. Brachioradialis
3. Biceps
4. Triceps
5. Deltoid
6. Pectoral muscles
7. Latissimus Dorsi
8. Trapezius
9. Serratus anterior
10. Erector spinae
    (spinal extensors)
11. Abdominal muscles
    a. Internal and external
       obliques
    b. Rectus abdominis
    c. Transversalis
12. Gluteal muscles
13. Hamstrings
14. Quadriceps muscles
15. Gastrocnemius, soleus
    muscles
16. Iliopsoas (under
    abdominal muscles)

FIGURE 2.22. Major Muscles of the Body.

STUDY QUESTIONS

1. When you drink a glass of water what muscles do you use?

2. An eccentric contraction of the biceps results in _____.

3. What anatomical movements and muscle groups are used in wheelchair propulsion? (or transfers)

4. What muscles are commonly referred to as the S.I.T.T.s muscle group?

5. A T-12 spinal cord injury would result in what dysfunctions?

6. Be able to identify the following muscles:

   a. Biceps

   b. Latissimus Dorsi

   c. Hamstrings

REFERENCES

Hoppenfeld, S. (1976). Physical Examination of the Spine and Extremities. New York: Appleton-Century-Crofts.

Smith, J. C. (1974). Laboratory Manual for Human Neuromuscular Anatomy. University of California, Los Angeles.

CHAPTER 3

CONTRAINDICATED EXERCISES

The purpose of this chapter is to present the kinesiological or physiological rational which make certain popular exercise and techniques contraindicated for many students. Where appropriate, alternative exercises or techniques have been provided.

1. Circumduction/hyperextension of the cervical spine ("head circles" or "rolls").

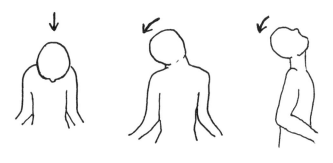

FIGURE 3-1.

Rational: Strains the supporting ligaments which maintain stability in the cervical spine. Causes compression of the intervertebral disk and impingement of the spinous processes. When combined with the degenerative changes that occur with aging (loss of synovial fluid, osteoporosis), the individual is more susceptible to neck injury.

Alternative: Perform isometric exercises for cervical flexion and rotation right and left to strengthen the muscles about the cervical spine.

2. Trunk Circling

FIGURE 3-2.

Rational: Hyperextension of the lumbar spine reinforces lordosis, especially for
               those with weak abdominals. Flexing the spine from a standing
               position with straight legs dramatically increases the intervertebral
               disc pressure in the lumbar area. Both directions compress the
               intervertebral disc which thin with age, creating a greater
               suspectibility to herniation of the nucleus pulposus. Lateral flexion
               usually results in an inadvertent rounding of the upper back and a
               relaxed abdomen.
Alternative: Omit flexion and hyperextension. During lateral flexion. Use a
               diagonal reach with the heel, buttocks, low back upper back and head
               pressed against a wall (Stevenson 1983). This requires a pelvic tilt or
               contraction of the abdomen. Performing the stretch in a sitting
               position further eliminates any uncontrolled hyperextension of the
               lumbar spine (include pelvic tilt).

3. Shoulder Stand

FIGURE 3-3.

Figure 3-3A.   Figure 3-3B.

Rational: Strains the muscles and ligaments of the cervical and thoracic spine and reinforces the postures of toward head and kyphosis.
Alternative: Exercises which stretch the hamstrings and low back from a long sitting or supine-lying position.

4. Prone spine and hyperextensions ("prone trunk raises")

FIGURE 3-4.

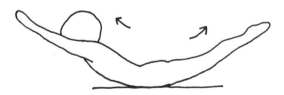

Rational: Compresses the lumbar intervertebral discs, stretches the abdominal muscles, and encourages the posture of lordosis. The purpose of this exercise is to strengthen the low back muscles; yet, weakness is seldom encountered in the general population, with the exception of paralytic conditions and flat back posture.

Alternative: To strengthen the hip extensors, assume a four-point position, resting on the elbows instead of the hands. Extend one leg and lift it up and down, keeping the abdominals contracted and being careful not to hyperextend the spine or hip. If the extensor muscles of the spine require strengthening (polio, trunk paralysis), the individual should assume the prone-lying position with arms extended out to the sides (palms down). The shoulders and arms should be raised slightly off the mat, pinching the shoulder blades together and rotating the thumbs up toward the ceiling.

If the individual has strength in the hip extensors, a hook-lying position can be assumed. The individual then lifts the hips off the mat (contracting the extensor muscles of the spine and hip).

5. Standing toe touches with straight legs

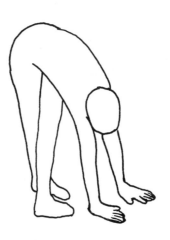

FIGURE 3-5.

Rational: Hyperextends the posterior joint capsule and ligaments of the knee. Increases intervertebral disc pressure in lumbar are during flexion. May strain soft tissue structures in the low back due to gravity-assisted during the straight leg stretch is also contraindicated for the same reasons. In addition, rounding of the upper back is encouraged from this posture.

Alternative: Hamstring stretches from a long-sitting or supine position.

6. Bilateral straight leg raises

FIGURE 3-6.

Rational: The prime mover is this exercise is the iliopsoas group (iliacus and psoas combined) which attaches to the vertebrae in the low back (twelfth thoracic and all lumbar) and femur. This exercise hyperextends spine and may strain soft tissue in the lumbar area, especially when the abdominals are weak. The abdominals only serve to stabilize the trunk and pelvis during hip flexion.

Alternative: Abdominal curls from a supine-hook position. The trunk should be raised only high enough for the scapula to clear the floor.

7. Sit-up with feet held/hands behind head

Rational: Holding the feet during sit-ups increases the use of the hip flexors, rather than the abdominal muscles, to pull the trunk up. This technique encourages a hyperextended posture of the low back (lordosis) and may cause strain.

Holding the hands behind the head may contribute to forward head and kyphosis, as well as cause pressure on the nerve rootless in the cervical area.

In addition, do not use an incline plane. This also places a strain on the low back, due to the extra work required of the hip flexors.

Alternative: Abdominal curls from a supine-hook position without the feet held. Hands should be placed across the chest or at the side of the head with the elbows out (do not interlock the fingers at the back of the head).

8. Sit-ups with straight legs

Rational: This exercise primarily involves the hip flexors; thus, the same mechanical stresses result that are described in exercise #6.

Alternative: See strength exercises for abdominals in Chapter 3.

9. Ballistic stretching
   Rational: Rapid "bounce" stretching of muscles will activate the muscle spindles, thus eliciting the stretch reflex. This relation causes the stretched muscle to contract and may induce strain or micro-tears of muscle fibers.
   Alternative: See chapter on Assessment and Programming for Flexibility.

10. Trunk twists from a standing position
    Rational: Strains the lumbar area and possibly the knee. Torque generated by the trunk must be absorbed in the knee. Never allow an individual to flex forward and then twist the trunk.
    Alternative: Perform the trunk twist very slowly in a sitting position. The knee can better absorb the torque of the knee when flexed because of its greater capacity for rotation in a sitting position.

11. Isometric exercises
    Rational: Contraindicated for individuals over 40 years old or those with a history of cardiovascular pathology, especially high blood pressure. Has a tendency to raise the systolic blood pressure to high risk levels, especially with isometric arm exercises.

12. Full flexion of the knee joint from a standing position (deep knee bends or "squats")
    Rational: Creates excessive stretch on the collateral and cruciate of the knee joint and may pinch the joint cartilage. Lengthening of the ligaments leads to instability of the knee joint.
    Alternative: Squat no more than half the distance to full flexion (thighs are parallel to the floor).

13. Bench press performed with the feet on the floor

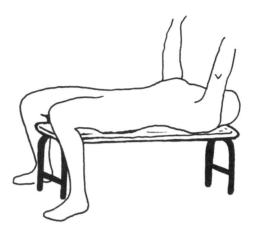

FIGURE 3-7.

Rational: Creates hyperextension of the lumbar spine which reinforces lordosis. During the press, intervertebral disc pressure increases dramatically, predisposing one to low back injury.

Alternative: Place the feet on the bench (hook-lying position) or against a wall so that the hips and knees are flexed to 90 degrees. This flattens the lumbar spine by removing the pull of the iliopsoas upon the vertebra.

FIGURE 3-8.

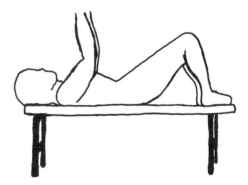

39

14. Hip flexor stretches

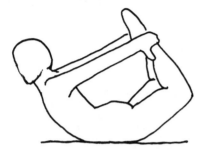

FIGURE 3-9.

FIGURE 3-10.

Rational: These particular stretches compress the intervertebral lumbar disks and reinforce the posture of lordosis. Hyperextension of the cervical disks may occur.

Alternative: See hip flexor stretches provided in the chapter on Assessment and Programming for Flexibility.

15. Hurdle stretch

FIGURE 3-11.

Rational: Strains the medial collateral ligament of the knee inwardly rotated and flexed knee, especially when the Iliotibial band is limited in flexibility.

Alternative: Externally rotate the flexed knee to remove the strain.

16. Holding the breath during exercise

Rational: Decreases venous return of blood to the heart, possibly resulting in dizziness or fainting.

Alternative: Breath rythmically; exhale with the lift or effort; inhale with the lowering of the weight. Breathe naturally during workout; do not force the exhale.

17. Wearing rubberized suits during workout
    Rational: Prevents the normal physiologic mechanisms of body cooling from functioning (i.e., evaporation, conduction). May lead to a rise in body temperature.

18. Immediate rest after intense exercise
    Rational: Prevents adequate venous return of blood. Blood lactate is not recycled.
    Alternative: Continue with low aerobic exercise (e.g., walking) to encourage venous return and recycle blood lactate.

19. Military Press

FIGURE 3-12.

    Rational: Individual often hyperextends spine during lift, causing excessive compression of the intervertebral lumbar disks. This posture is more likely to occur when the shoulders are limited in flexibility.
    Alternative: Pointing the chin down during the lift will help reduce excessive lumbar curve.
                 Perform Upright Rows from a standing position. See chapter on Assessment and Programming for Strength.

20. Prone flies from a standing position (shoulder horizontal abduction)

FIGURE 3-13.

Rational: Compression forces to the L-4 and L-5 intervertebral disks increase
             approximately 3 1/2 times when an individual assumes this straight
             leg position (without weights!). Exercises with or without weights
             should never be performed in this "7" position.
Alternative: Assume a prone position on bench. Long extensor muscles of the
             back will be relaxed and will not assist in lifting from this position.

FIGURE 3-14.

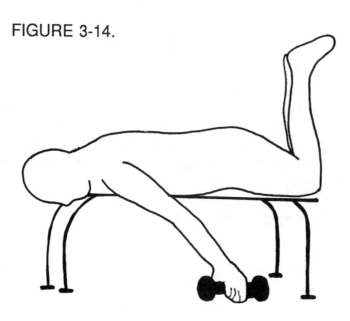

STUDY QUESTIONS

1. What exercises have you done in the past that would now be considered contraindicated?

2. Which is easier: abdominal curls with feet held or without the feet held?

3. Why should the knees and hips be flexed for any exercise performed in the supine position?

REFERENCES

Allsop, K.G. (1977). Potential hazards of abdominal exercises. Journal of Health, Physical Education, Recreation, and Dance, 45, 89-91.

Rasch, P.J. and Burke, R.K. (1971). Kinesiology and Applied Anatomy (4th ed.). Philadelphia: Saunders Co.

Stevenson, E. (1973). Physique Magic. Sacramento: California State University.

CHAPTER 4

HOW TO DEVELOP AN ADAPTIVE PHYSICAL EDUCATION PROGRAM

The time spent in the developmental or reassessing stages is time well spent. When developing or reassessing an Adaptive Physical Education Program much deliberation must be taken. A philosophy statement should be made of what direction do you want the program to go i.e. clinical or modified sports. The question needs to be asked is your philosophy for the program consistent with the department's general philosophy. Now is also an excellent time to see what type of facilities are available and what equipment is needed to attain your philosophy statement. Also, ask yourself will the equipment I purchase today interface well with equipment I plan to purchase 1-3-5 years down the road.

Another series of questions you need to ask yourself are:
1. Am I going to use assistants; if so how will I train them?
2. How can I augment my budget (i.e., fundraisers and grants)?
3. How will I publicize my program?
   a. Make a video.
   b. Make brochures.
   c. Speak at service clubs.
   d. Communicate with therapists and doctors in my area.

This chapter is designed to answer some of the many questions involved in developing an Adaptive Physical Education Program.

TRAINING ASSISTANTS

As stated earlier the success of your program depends on how well the assistants are trained many large programs offer Introduction to Adapted Physical Education courses. These courses generally include didactic material and practical application. Many smaller programs do not have this luxury. Therefore, orientation sessions for assistants should be scheduled prior to the first class meeting.

ORIENTATION SESSIONS

Send a letter to all prospective assistants regarding the orientation schedule and the materials to be covered. A sample content of the orientation sessions is provided below:

1. Introductions
2. Grading and Expectations
3. Instructional Strategies
4. Emergency Procedures
5. General Program Procedures
6. Assistant Duties
7. Equipment Care
8. Techniques in strength training, cardiovascular training, flexibility, balance, posture, gait training and transfers.
9. Medical histories of disabled students
10. Practice sessions

Several orientation sessions may be required to cover all of the material presented above. It is suggested that each session last no more than three hours in duration. Allow the assistants sufficient time to practice techniques acquired in the sessions. Using a competency checklist allows the instructor to screen assistants before assigning them to disabled students.

In addition to the orientations, it is suggested that an open house be scheduled prior to the program to allow the disabled community to view the facility and meet the assistants.

TERMINOLOGY

The following section is a simple dictionary containing a list of terms frequently used in Adapted Physical Education. The short definition of these words should be of assistance when reading medical reports, attending meetings, and talking with specialist who have contact with your disabled student. Also, the reader should be familiar with most of the abbreviations found in Appendix A.

Achilles Flare
A bowing of the Achilles tendon toward the midline (Helbing's sign) which is associated with eversion or pronation of the foot.

Activities of Daily Living

Self-care activities performed on a daily basis in order to maintain health and well-being (e.g. getting in and out of bed, personal hygiene, eating, performing manual tasks, ambulating or using a wheelchair).

Adam's Position

From a standing position with the feet together, flex forward at the hips while allowing the trunk to relax and arms to hang down with the palms together. Used to determine structural scoliosis.

Adaptive Behavior

Behavior that aids the individual in effective, age- appropriate social interactions, mobility, and independence.

Afferent

Carrying impulses to a center (input) such as the central nervous system. Refers to sensory neurons.

Affective

Pertains to feelings or emotions.

Amputee

Congenital or acquired loss of an extremity or portion thereof.

Anomalies

Congenital deformity or abnormal development of organ, tissue or bone.

Aphasia

An inability to interpret or execute spoken language (receptive and expressive, respectively) which is not related to diseases of the vocal cords or ears.

Apraxia

Inability to motor plan (i.e., execute a series of movements in a coordinated and efficient manner). Probably related to poor input from the tactile, vestibular and proprioceptive systems.

Arteriosclerosis

Thickening or hardening of the walls of the blood vessels, particularly the arteries.

Articular

The area of a bone where it is joined together with another bone as a joint.

Ataxia

Difficulties with balance; reflected in gait by a wide base of support. A type of cerebral palsy in which balance is affected.

Atherosclerosis

A build up of plaque in the arteries.

Athetosis

A type of cerebral palsy which is characterized by rotary, involuntary movements (basal ganglia affected).

Auditory Discrimination
  The ability to detect subtle differences among sounds in words (e.g., tap-cap, then-than).
Behavior Modification
  A procedure that is based on the assumption that all behaviors are learned and depend upon consequences. Therefore, behavior can be changed through a methodically applied system of rewards and punishments.
Behavioral Objectives
  Objectives which are written to describe what a student will be able to do as a result of some planned instruction. These are usually written as objectives that can be measured in some definitive or quantitative way.
Bilateral Coordination
  A lack of coordination between the two sides of the body. An inability to use the two hands and/or legs together in a coordinated fashion. If unable to cross the midline of the body, the individual may appear ambidextrous (using the left hand on the left side only and vice-versa)
Blindisms
  Mannerisms or movements characteristic of some blind individuals.
Body Awareness
  The ability to locate and identify body parts. Also includes an awareness of the relationship of the body parts to each other and to the environment. The development of the body scheme is based on receiving accurate sensory information from the skin, muscles, and joints (i.e., proprioception).
Brain Stem
  Consists of the medulla, pons, and midbrain.
Cardiac
  Pertaining to the heart.
Catheter
  A tube used for evacuating fluid from the bladder or brain. In the case of the bladder, the catheter may be in-dwelling or external..
Cauda Equina
  The terminal portion of the spinal cord (conus medullaris) and roots of the spinal nerves below the first lumbar nerve.
Central Nervous System
  Consists of the spinal cord, brain stem, cerebellum, and cerebrum.
Coordination, Fine Motor
  Pertains to usage of small muscle groups (e.g., writing, cutting).
Coordination, Gross Motor: Pertains to usage of large muscle groups (e.g., jumping, running).

Diplegia
   Paralysis/paresis of all four extremities, with more sever involvement of the lower extremities.

Directionality
   The ability to determine directions and locations in the environment (left, right, up, down, over, under, across, through, etc.). The concept of moving right or left.

Down Syndrome
   A form of mental retardation presenting a specific set of mental and physical symptoms due to a chromosomal defect.

Dysfunction
   Difficult function, improper function, or non-function.

Efferent
   Carrying impulses away from a center (output) such as the central nervous system. Refers to motorneurons.

Equilibrium Reactions
   The automatic movements which keep one balanced during static and dynamic postures. Involves automatic responses of the head, trunk and limbs.

Etiology
   The cause of disease.

Grand Mal (Tonic-Clonic)
   One of the more serious forms of epilepsy which involves convulsions of the body.

Habilitation
   Maximizing the potential of an individual who is disabled from birth.

Hemiplegia
   Paralysis of one side of the body.

Intelligence Tests
   A standardized series of questions and/or tasks designed to measure mental abilities (i.e., how a person thinks, reasons, solves problems, remembers, learns new information). Many intelligence tests rely heavily on the use or understanding of spoken language.

Kinesthesis
   The ability to perceive the position or movement of body parts and the amount of force exerted by the muscles.

Laterality
   The awareness of the sides of the body (i.e., right, left, front, back, side, top, and bottom).

Lordosis
   Exaggeration of the lumbar curve (hyperextension).

Lumbar
   The area of the low back.

Monoplegia

Paralysis of one extremity only.

Muscle Substitution

The employment of a different muscle or muscle group to replace a muscle that can no longer be used.

Osteoarthritis

A chronic disease involving inflammation of the joints.

Paralysis

Lack of innervation resulting in loss of voluntary motion.

Paresis

Muscular weakness.

Paraplegia

Paralysis of the lower extremities only.

Perseveration

Inability to stop responding to a stimulus or a directive.

Pronation

Eversion combined with abduction of the foot.

Prone

Lying in a face-down position.

Proprioception

Sensory feedback concerning movement and position of the body, occurring chiefly in the muscles (spindles), tendons (Golgi tendon organs), and joint receptors.

Psychomotor

Pertaining to movement (both fine and gross motor).

Pulmonary

Pertaining to lung function, heart valve function, or the pulmonary artery.

Quadriplegia

Paralysis affecting all four limbs.

Range of Motion

Degree of movement possible about a joint.

Scoliosis

An abnormal lateral curvature of the spine.

Seizure

Electrical disturbance of the brain.

Sensory Integration

The neurological process of organizing information from one or more sensory channels.

Spasticity

A neurological disorder of the upper motorneuron, resulting in hyperactive muscle spindles and abnormal stretch reflexes.

Spatial Awareness/Orientation

The awareness of one's position in space and the location of objects in relation to self and other objects. Includes judgments of distance, depth and directionality.

Tactile

Pertaining to the sense of touch; discrimination of texture and shape; detention of pressure, heat, and pain.

METHODS TO ENHANCE YOUR ADAPTIVE PHYSICAL EDUCATION BUDGET

When the program budget is severely limited, there exist other avenues by which to acquire equipment. In fact, these avenues should be explored in order to avoid any unnecessary purchases out of the limited program budget.

1. Federal, state, and local grants. Check both public (government) and private (foundations) grant opportunities. Most colleges house a grants office where you can obtain the names and addresses of funding sources.
2. Donations. Mail letters to your local community organizations requesting equipment donations and/or money. Local businesses may be willing to donate items such as carpets and mirrors to your program.
3. Homemade equipment. A student assistant may be able to build/sew certain pieces of equipment (e.g., treatment tables, tilt boards, bean bags, quad gloves) at a dramatically reduced cost.
4. Loan/sharing. The P. E. department within your school may be willing to loan a piece of equipment for a limited time (i.e., assessment tools) or share.
5. Fundraisers; i.e., t-shirt sales with APE logo on it.
6. Use of community/private facilities. Check in your area on the availability of recreation centers, municipal pools, bowling alleys, and archery ranges.

EQUIPMENT

The following equipment list is not meant to be inclusive but to provide the basics for initiating an adapted exercise program. Since programs may vary dramatically in budget, facilities, and populations served, a universal equipment list does not exist. Due to the heterogeneous nature of the students served in these programs, equipment will be continually modified to meet the unique needs of individual students.

Considerable planning must precede the purchase of equipment for an adapted exercise program. The following is a list of factors to consider in the selection of equipment.

1. The equipment should reflect the philosophy and objectives of the program.
2. The instructor should consider what the future directions of the program are (i.e., can the equipment be modified later to accommodate changes?).
3. Is the equipment appropriate for the populations and ages served by the program?
4. Is the equipment appropriate for the developmental or skill level of the participants?
5. Is the exercise room large enough to house the equipment?
6. Is the equipment durable and washable?
7. Does the equipment have versatility?

(Equipment catalogs may also be picked up from vendors/exhibitors at professional conferences.)

Assessment Equipment

1. Physician's weight scale.
2. Posture screen/plumb line. The design for construction of a homemade posture screen is located in Appendix D.
3. Dynamometers. These measure grip and pinch strength. More sensitive dynamometers are available (usually rubber bulbs which can be squeezed) to accommodate extreme paresis or contractures in the hand.
4. Goniometers. These measure range of motion about a joint.
5. Skin fold calipers. The Lange and Harpenden calipers are perhaps the most frequently used calipers and measure skin fold thickness at specified sites to calculate percent body fat.
6. Ergometers (arm and leg bicycles). Cardiovascular endurance is measured by these devices. Monark, Bodyguard, and Fitron (Lumex) are popular brands that allow for precise testing.
7. Metronome. This device helps maintain the desired cadence (arm or leg) during ergometer tests.
8. Stopwatches. These are necessary for measuring time during testing and training, as well as for calculating resting and exercising heart rates.
9. Sphygomometer (blood pressure cuff). Resting and exercising blood pressures should always be taken during an ergometer test.
10. Stethoscope. This is used in conjunction with the blood pressure cuff.
11. Orthotron/Cybex (Lumex). Both dynamometers are used in assessing isokinetic strength in the major joints of the body. The former is considerably less expensive than the latter but is less precise in measurement and less sensitive. Both devices are utilized for training purposes as well.

12. Spirometer. Lung volumes and flow rates are measured with this device. The values obtained are usually greatly reduced in respiratory conditions and when paralysis of the trunk muscles occurs.
13. Anthropometric tape. Limb circumferences are measured with this special tape to determine any muscular atrophy.
14. Sit and reach box. This apparatus measures the flexibility of the hamstrings and low back muscles. See Appendix E for the construction of the homemade box.

Special Adaptive Physical Education Room Equipment

1. Sliding board. This is used in supine and side-lying positions for movements performed actively (e.g., hip flexion and abduction). Covering the surface with linoleum or talc reduces friction (and thus resistance) created by the limb against the board. This term also refers to a beveled, rectangular board used for transferring an individual to another surface of equal height to the wheelchair.
2. Ankle boot. Used for strengthening the ankle.
3. Push-up blocks. Used for strengthening the shoulder and elbow muscles involved in transfers.
4. Overhead pulley with swivel hook. This self-assistive device is used for range of motion of the shoulder joints.
5. Standing frame.
6. Light dumbbells and sandbag weights.
7. Kinetron (Lumex). This isokinetic device is used for developing strength and coordination of the leg muscles involved in walking.
8. Shoulder wheel.
9. Freedom Machine (Olympic Enterprises). This four-sided machine was designed to strengthen the upper extremities of paraplegics or quadriplegics.
10. Parallel bars and ambulation stairs.
11. Therapy mat/table.

Perceptual-Motor Equipment

1. Balls: nerf, bean bags, balloons, beach, cage (canvas), wiffle, medicine, rubber.
2. Balance beams. Widths: 2", 4", 6"
3. Tilt boards.
4. Jump ropes.

Equipment for Swimming Program

1. Portable Hoyer Lift.
2. Swim fins.
3. Snorkles.
4. Life vests (small, medium, large).
5. Kick boards.
6. Non-skid decking.
7. Rubber balls.
8. Donut inner tubes.
9. Hand paddles (paraplegics and quadriplegics).
10. Swim masks.
11. Floating basketball hoop and basketball.

Miscellaneous Equipment

1. Towels. Students should place a towel under their heads when lying on the mats. This reduces the need to frequently clean the mats and prevents the spread of illnesses.
2. Stall bars. These are used for a variety of activities such as range of motion and climbing.
3. Masking/athletic tape.
4. Ace wraps. Widths: 2", 4", 6", 8"
5. Chalk board.
6. Walking belts (small, medium, large). These facilitate transfers and reduce the chance of falling during parallel bars activities.
7. Mirrors. These are helpful with individuals who lack proprioception/body awareness.
8. Storage cabinets.
9. First aid kit.
10. Laundry hamper for towels.
11. Bulletin board.
12. Velcro tape.
13. Seat belt.
14. Styrofoam cups.
15. Refrigerator or ice machine.
16. Straws.
17. Spare wheelchair.
18. Spare crutches.
19. Fans.
20. Alcohol to clean mats.

TRANSFERS

There are basically two types of transfers: standing and sitting. Variations of these two transfers reflect the capabilities of the disabled individual and the type of surface he/she is transferring to.

GENERAL GUIDELINES FOR PERFORMING TRANSFERS

1. Reduce the distance between the transfer surfaces. Removing arm rests and detachable footrests will permit closer positioning to the transfer surface.
2. Always secure wheelchair brakes. They are essential for safety and stability.
3. Provide surfaces of equal height if possible. A sliding board may be used to eliminate the gap between the two surfaces. Be sure to stabilize the sliding board on both transfer surfaces.
4. When transferring individuals with one-sided involvement (e.g., hemiplegia), position the wheelchair alongside the transfer surface on the individual's stronger side. Provide assistance at the waist from the weaker side.
5. Keep a wide base of support. Placing one foot ahead of the other allows you to shift your weight more easily.
6. Keep your back straight while flexing at the hips and knees during the transfer. Hold the person as close as possible and lift with the thigh muscles (extending at the knees and hips), not the back.
7. If possible, allow the individual to view the surface to which he is being transferred to.
8. To increase the stability of the wheelchair, place the casters in a forward position.

PERFORMANCE REQUIREMENTS
Standing Transfers
The individual should possess partial or full weight-bearing capabilities when attempting a "stand and pivot" transfer. It is possible to perform a stand and pivot with an individual possessing complete lower extremity paralysis. However, to maximize the safety of your disabled students, it is recommended that a sitting transfer be used in the case of lower limb paralysis. If the student is overweight or evidences a great deal of spasticity, a sitting transfer should also be considered.
Sitting Transfers
1. One-man (front-facing). The individual should possess sufficient muscular strength to depress the shoulder and extend the elbow, lifting his/her body weight (innervation of C7 nerve root or lower).
2. Two-man (one man front-facing and one man back-facing). Used when the individual is overweight or lacks weight-bearing ability and upper extremity strength (e.g., quadriplegia from spinal cord injury).

114151   **55**

DESCRIPTION OF SPECIFIC TRANSFERS

1. <u>Pull to Stand in Parallel Bars</u> (see Figure 4-1):
   a. The disabled student should position the buttocks as close to the edge of the wheelchair as possible. Place your hands either underneath the buttocks or around the waist. The disabled student places his/her hands on the parallel bars (elbows extended).
   b. As the disabled student leans the trunk forward and pulls with the arms, the assistant shifts his/her own weight backward and pulls the individual to a stand.
   c. Be sure to keep the student's knees blocked until the standing position is stabilized.

Figure 4-1A.

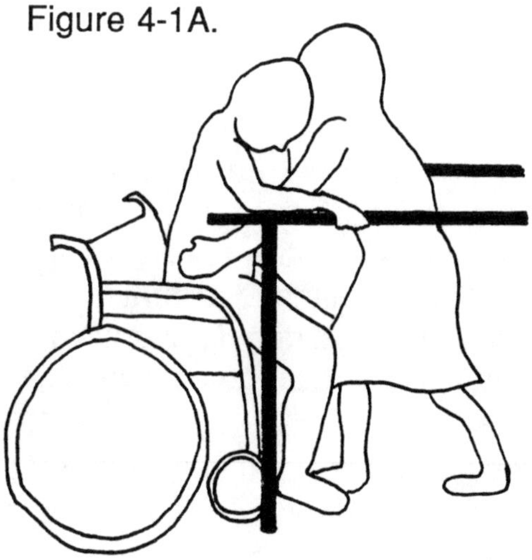

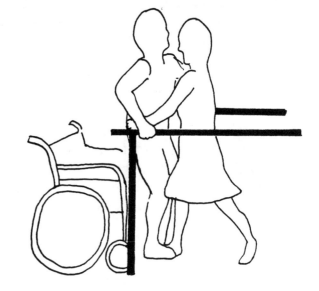

Figure 4-1C.

Figure 4-1B.

FIGURE 4-1. Pull to Stand in Parallel Bars.

2. Stand and Pivot (see Figure 4-2)

a. Slide the student forward until the buttocks are as close to the edge of the wheelchair as possible. Feet should be planted on the floor. Place your hands underneath the student's buttocks. If the student is strong enough, have him/her place the arms around your shoulders. If not, allow the arms to hang in front of the body. Block the student's feet so they do not slide out from underneath. Also squeeze or block the knees to prevent them from buckling during the transfer. Have the student hook his/her chin over your shoulder. Allow the student to view the surface he/she is being transferred to.

b. Rock the student's trunk forward and lift him/her high enough to clear the wheelchair. Pivot the student, being sure not to let his/her feel slide or the knees to buckle.

c. As you lower him/her down to the mat, slide one hand up from the buttocks to the back to stabilize the sitting position.

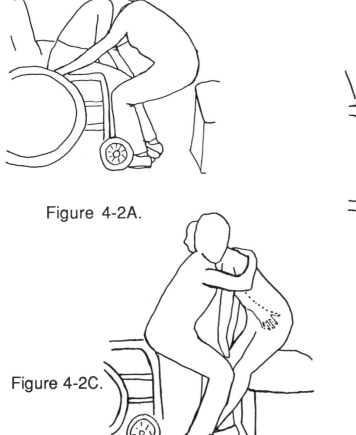

Figure 4-2A.

Figure 4-2C.

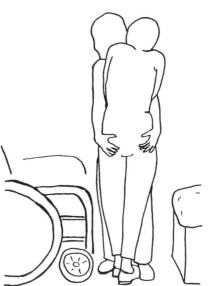

Figure 4-2B.

FIGURE 4-2.
Stand and Pivot.

3. <u>Sitting Transfer</u> (one man, front-facing) (see Figure 4-3)
   a. Place the chair approximately 45 degrees to the treatment table. Place the student's legs (extended) on the table.
   b. Place your hands around the student's waist or underneath the buttocks. Lift as the student extends his/her elbows.
   c. Swing the student over to the mat, using the feet as the pivot point.

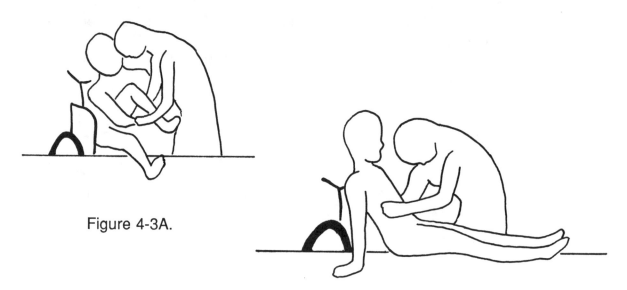

Figure 4-3A.

Figure 4-3B.

Figure 4-3C.

FIGURE 4-3. Sitting Transfer (one-man, front-facing)

58

4. <u>Sitting Transfer</u> (two-man) (see Figure 4-4)

   a. Position the wheelchair at a 45 degree angle to the treatment table. Have the student flex his/her elbows and place the forearms against the chest. Standing behind the student, bring your arms underneath the armpits and grasp the forearms. Alternative hand grip: grasp the left forearm with your right hand and vice versa. The second assistant places both hands underneath the legs in a cradle-line fashion. An alternative transfer may be indicated for a person with subluxating shoulder joints.

   b. On the count of three, both assistants lift the student to the mat. The back-facing assistant should lift by pressing the arms into the chest, rather than pulling up into the armpits. Slowly position the student on the mat to prevent spasticity from occurring.

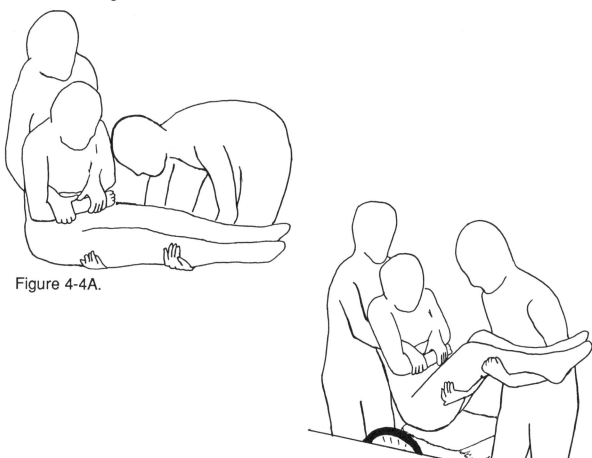

Figure 4-4A.

Figure 4-4B.

FIGURE 4-4. Sitting Transfer (two man)

BODY POSITIONS

Individualized exercise program cards should contain standard terminology whenever possible to avoid confusion when interchanging assistants with students. The following terminology relates to initial body positions for exercises and usually must be specified on the program card.

FIGURE 4-5. Cross Sitting.

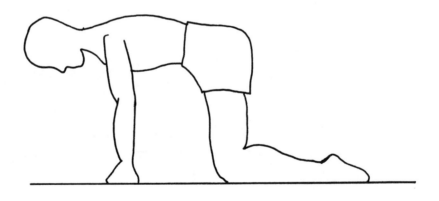

FIGURE 4-6. 4-Point (All Fours).

FIGURE 4-7. Long Sitting.

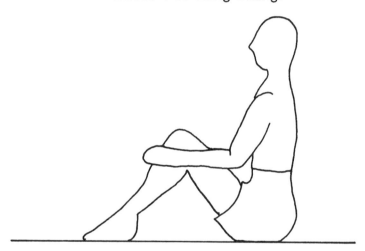

FIGURE 4-8. Hook Sitting

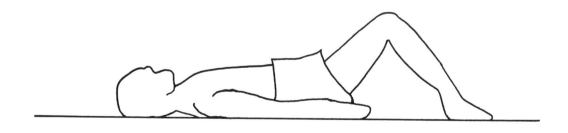

FIGURE 4-9. Hook Lying

FIGURE 4-10. Supine Lying

FIGURE 4-11. Side Lying

FIGURE 4-12. Prone Lying

LOWER EXTREMITY ORTHOTICS

Primarily three types of lower extremity braces or orthoses have been designed for assisting in ambulation: short leg braces, long leg braces, and hip braces. The purpose of these orthotics are the following (Venn, Morganstern, and Dykes, 1979):

1. To support body weight (e.g., muscular dystrophy).
2. To control involuntary movement (e.g., cerebral palsy).
3. To correct or prevent deformities (e.g., Legg-Perthea disease).

Checklists evaluating the condition of ambulation devices (lower extremity orthoses, prostheses an wheelchairs) may be obtained from an article by Venn, Morganstern and Dykes (1979).

TYPES

1. Ankle-foot orthosis (AFO) or short leg brace:
   -- Used for conditions which occur at the ankle joint (e.g., drop-foot).
   -- Controls plantarflexion, dorsiflexion, inversion, and eversion. Prevents medial/lateral instability.
   -- Consists of a metal or plastic upright bar attached to a shoe with a cuff around the calf of the leg (see Figure 4-13). Sometimes referred to as a Bi Caal brace with a t-strap.

Figure 4-13. Short Leg Brace.

2. Knee-ankle-foot orthosis (KAFO) or long leg brace:
   -- Prevents hyperextension and buckling of the knee resulting from weak quadriceps or hamstrings.
   -- Consists of an extension of the AFO with a cuff around the upper thigh (see Figure 4-14). A sliding metal lock is attached at the knee joint (locked when standing/ambulating and unlocked when sitting).

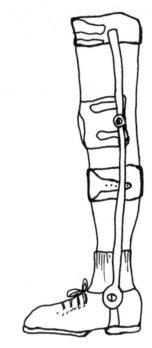

FIGURE 4-14. Long Leg Brace.

3. Hip-knee-ankle-foot orthosis (HKAFO) or long leg brace with pelvic band:
   -- Consists of an extension of the KAFO with a pelvic band attached (see Figure 4-15).
   -- Controls the six movements of the hip. Can be unlocked to allow for flexion and extension.

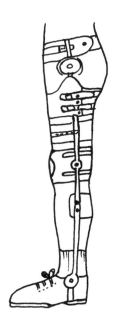

FIGURE 4-15. Long Leg Brace with Pelvic Band.

AMBULATION AIDS

People with a lower extremity disability usually require some form of assistive device during ambulation. Canes, crutches, and walkers serve as extensions which permit the upper extremities to transmit force to the floor, providing support for the lower extremities and improving balance. Because of the diversity of ambulation aids that are available, their prescription should be carefully evaluated by the physician. The ambulation aid should be fitted to the disabled person by the physician or physical therapist. The disabled person should receive instruction in their use, including proper gait pattern, ascending and descending stairs, and sitting and arising. Pre-ambulation exercises and training are often necessary for persons with severe disabilities (Jebsen, 1967).

WALKERS (see Figure 4-16)

Walkers are indicated when an individual lacks balance, strength and/or coordination (e.g., stroke, cerebral palsy). Some models can be folded up for storage or travel. During ambulation, the individual lifts the walker up and places it in front of him/her, and then walks forward between the bars. There are several different types of walkers, including some models with rollers and/or adjustable seats.

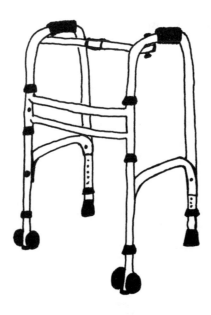

FIGURE 4-16. Walker.

Types

1. Walkerette. This model has runners attached to the bars and is pushed forward along the floor. It is not lifted by the patient like a standard walker.
2. Roller Walker. This model has wheels on the front legs so that the individual can raise the rear legs off the floor and roll the walker forward.
3. Crutch Walker. This model has crutches attached to the horizontal bars to support body weight. It also has a seat for the individual to rest on when fatigued. The crutches can be removed or draped to the sides when not in use.

CRUTCHES

The use of crutches requires more balance, strength and coordination than that of a walker. One or two crutches may be used, depending upon the extent of support needed.

Types

1. Lofstrand or axillary crutch (see Figure 4-17).
2. Canadian or Elbow Extension Crutch (see Figure 4-18). This crutch has no shoulder rest and is usually prescribed for patients who can ambulate with the four-point crutch gait and who need support for weak arm musculature.
3. Gutter Crutch (see Figure 4-19). This crutch has been designed for patients with significant flexion deformity at the elbow, a painful wrist, or very poor hand function. The forearm may be fixed to the crutch by a velcro strap or other simple release fastening.

Crutch Adjustment

The crutch height should always be adjustable. It is also preferable to use crutches in which the length and position of the arm support are also adjustable (Cash, 1976). The length of the axillary crutch should extend from a point two inches below the axilla to a point near the foot indicated in Figure 4-20. The height of the hand grip should be positioned so that the elbow is flexed between 15-30 degrees. The wrists should be hyperextended and the weight borne on the palms. When fitting axillary crutches, it is essential that the patient be instructed not to bear weight on the axillary bar. This may cause compression of the radial nerve, resulting in paralysis which may take months to resolve. The true purpose of this bar is to provide lateral stability of the crutch via pressure against the chest wall (Jebsen, 1967).

It is recommended that the crutch tips be checked regularly for worn areas, cracking, or plugging of the grooves with lint and dirt.

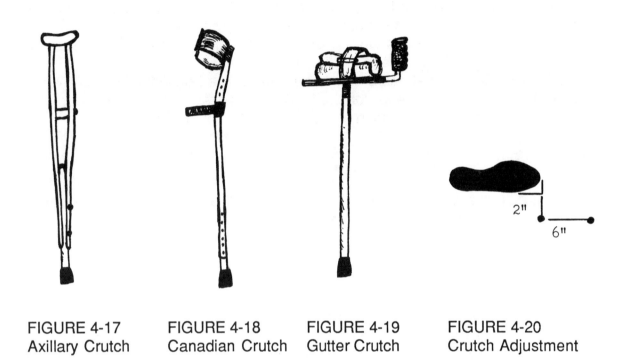

FIGURE 4-17
Axillary Crutch

FIGURE 4-18
Canadian Crutch

FIGURE 4-19
Gutter Crutch

FIGURE 4-20
Crutch Adjustment

CANES

Canes are generally prescribed when some weight bearing can be taken on the affected extremity or when mild balance difficulties exist. It is difficult for a person to develop a normal walking pattern with one cane. Since a cane supports approximately 20-25% of the body weight, the tendency is to lean the body over the cane and shorten the stride on that side.

Types

1. Standard Cane. This is made of wood or aluminum with a C-curved handle. A telescoping cane is available which can be adjusted to between 22 and 38 inches.
2. Tripod Cane. This model has three prongs at the end of the shaft with flexible rubber sockets which allow for movement of the shaft while the prongs remain in contact with the ground.
3. Quad Cane. This model has four prongs which come in contact with the floor. It is adjustable in length and provides maximum support and balance with four contact

points on the ground. This device is frequently prescribed for those with athetoid cerebral palsy.

<u>Cane Adjustment</u>

The length of the cane is determined by measuring the vertical distance from the greater trochanter to the floor. The elbow should be flexed approximately 15-30 degrees. The cane should be held in the hand opposite the affected leg. During ambulation the cane should be held fairly close to the side to avoid leaning.

WHEELCHAIRS

There are currently a wide variety of wheelchairs from which to select (heavy duty to sports models with racing tires). In addition, a variety of sizes are available such as Adult, Narrow-Adult, Tall, Junior, and Children's sizes. A physician or physical therapist familiar with the sizes, models, and components should determine a suitable chair for an individual.

An assistant of the disabled should become familiar with the basic parts of the wheelchair and their operation. The following is a description of the most basic components of a typical wheelchair.

1. Wheels. For ease of ride over outdoor terrain (soft, sandy or rough ground), pneumatic tires are recommended.
2. Handrims. Handrims are connected to the wheels to allow the user to move his wheelchair without injuring the hands. There is a variety of handrims available. Special purpose handrims consist of eight rubber-tipped vertical projections for the person who has difficulty grasping the regular handrims (e.g., quadriplegia).
3. Backrest. The height of the backrest depends on the height of the user and the degree of trunk stability. Reclining backs are available for those who need to be in a partially or fully reclined position.
4. Armrests. The variety of armrests available are either detachable or fixed. Detachable armrests easily lift off to allow the convenience of side transfers. The height of the armrests can usually be adjusted to accommodate the changes created by a wheelchair cushion.
5. Wheel-locks (brakes). These prevent the wheelchair from rolling forward or backward on inclines.
6. Casters. These are small wheels which sit towards the front of the chair. Casters are most stable when they have anti-flutter caster bearings. Casters also come in the following styles: heavy-duty, light-weight, and pneumatic (cushioned ride with a freer roll).
7. Front Rigging. This consists of a footrest or legrest. The latter is used with those

who need the legs elevated. Both types of rigging typically have a swing-away feature which allows for a close approach to transfer surfaces. Heel-loops help prevent feet from sliding off the footplate.

There are many additional accessories which can be attached to the wheelchair to enhance its effectiveness to the user.

STUDY QUESTIONS

1. What is your philosophy statement for your APE Program?

2. Write your 1-3-5 year plan on how you expect your program to develop.

3. Given $10,000 give a breakdown on how you would use the money.

4. Design an APE Room.

REFERENCES

Cash, J. E. (1976). A textbook of medical conditions for physiotherapists. Philadelphia: J. B. Lippincott Co.

Chawla, J. C., Bar., D., Creber, I., Price, J. & Andrew, B. (1980). Techniques for improving the strength and fitness of spinal cord injured patients. Paraplegia. 17, 185-190.

Hoppenfeld, S. (1976). Physical examination of the spine and extremities. New York: Appleton-Century-Crofts.

Jebsen, R. (1967). Use and abuse of ambulation aids. Journal of the American Medical Association, 199 (1), 63-65

McKenzie, T. (1984). Lecture notes from Analysis of Teaching Behavior, San Diego State University.

Smith, J. L. (1974). Laboratory Manual for Human Neuromuscular Anatomy, University of California, Los Angeles.

Thomas, C. L. (ed.) (1977). Tabers cyclopedic medical dictionary (13th ed.). Philadelphia: F. A. Davis Co.

Venn, J., Morganstern, L., Dykes, M. K. (1979). Checklists for evaluating the fit and function of orthoses, prostheses, and wheelchairs in the classroom. Teaching Exceptional Children, 11 (2), 51-56.

CHAPTER 5

TEACHING METHODOLOGIES

GENERAL INFORMATION FOR ASSISTANTS

The purpose of this class is to gain knowledge and practical experience in adapted exercise for disabled adults. By assisting one or two students with their exercise programs, you should become competent in the various techniques involved in strength, cardiovascular training, posture exercises, balance activities, and gait training. Working in the program will also provide you with the opportunity to give of yourself and to become more aware of the needs of individuals with physical disabilities.

The success and efficiency of an APE Program at the post-secondary level will to a large extent depend upon how well the assistants are trained. The assistant is faced with the challenge of facilitating learning for a group of individuals who possess various disabling conditions. The importance of the interactions between the disabled student and the assistant can not be over-emphasized.

ADULT LEARNERS

Adult learners are very different than children learners. Adult learners possess varied experiences and academic backgrounds. To teach adults as you would children would seriously impede the learning process. To foster the learning experience the assistant needs to know the characteristics of their students and what excites them.

There are numerous theories which affect the student's learning process. The teacher of adults must understand these principles if they wish to be successful and effective.

Law of Effect: People tend to accept and repeat those responses which are pleasant and satisfying and avoid those which are not.

Nothing Succeeds Like Success: Make every effort to see that your students achieve some success in each class.

Law of Primacy: First impressions are lasting. Make those initial class meeting meaningful.

Law of Practice: The more often an act is repeated the quicker the skill is established.

Law of Disuse: A skill not practiced or knowledge not used with be forgotten quickly. Important skills and concepts need to be reviewed.

Law of Vigor: A dramatic or exciting learning experience is more likely to be remembered than a routine or boring experience. Let your teaching come alive use vivid examples, and participate with your students. Remember humor is a useful teaching tool.

ACCOMMODATING DIFFERENT LEARNING STYLE PREFERENCES

We all learn in various ways and rates. This chart will help to give you an idea of whether your student is a visual, auditory or kinesthetic learner. If you teach to your student's learning style, the student will learn quicker.

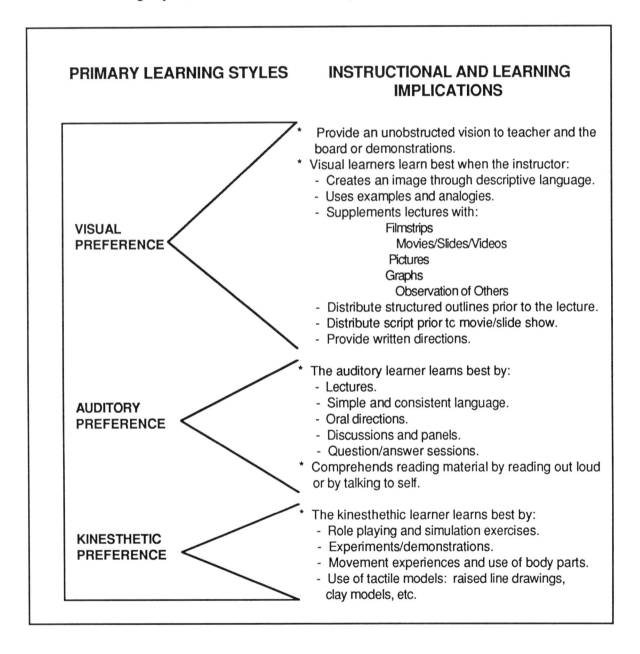

PRIMARY LEARNING STYLES | **INSTRUCTIONAL AND LEARNING IMPLICATIONS**

VISUAL PREFERENCE
* Provide an unobstructed vision to teacher and the board or demonstrations.
* Visual learners learn best when the instructor:
  - Creates an image through descriptive language.
  - Uses examples and analogies.
  - Supplements lectures with:
    - Filmstrips
    - Movies/Slides/Videos
    - Pictures
    - Graphs
    - Observation of Others
  - Distribute structured outlines prior to the lecture.
  - Distribute script prior tc movie/slide show.
  - Provide written directions.

AUDITORY PREFERENCE
* The auditory learner learns best by:
  - Lectures.
  - Simple and consistent language.
  - Oral directions.
  - Discussions and panels.
  - Question/answer sessions.
* Comprehends reading material by reading out loud or by talking to self.

KINESTHETIC PREFERENCE
* The kinesthethic learner learns best by:
  - Role playing and simulation exercises.
  - Experiments/demonstrations.
  - Movement experiences and use of body parts.
  - Use of tactile models: raised line drawings, clay models, etc.

CHARACTERISTIC BEHAVIORS OF EFFECTIVE TEACHERS

Effective teachers. . . .
1. Hold and project high expectations for student success.
2. Maximize opportunities for students to engage in learning experiences.
3. Manage their own time and organize the classroom efficiently.
4. Pace the curriculum to maximize student success.
5. Engage in active teaching with all students whether individually or in groups of varying size.
6. Work toward mastery of knowledge and skills by systematically monitoring student progress and providing feedback.
7. Are sensitive to differences in rate of learning and type of teacher-student contact required.
8. Provide a supportive learning environment that is characterized by an ambiance of warmth and personal support.

INSTRUCTIONAL STRATEGIES

Your initial attempts to teach may be a scary experience. This is normal and should not discourage you. The following is a list of teaching suggestions.

1. **Your best visual aid is yourself.**
   a. Demonstrate when possible.
   b. Assume proper posture. You are selling fitness; stand and sit like you are in shape.
   c. Maintain eye contact when speaking to your student.
2. **You're not teaching if they can't hear you.**
   a. Speak clearly and loudly.
   b. Avoid monotone and unprofessional language.
   c. Let your hearing impaired student's see your mouth or hand gestures. Do not over-exaggerate mouth movements.
3. **Be visible.**
   a. Some say that seeing is 75% of learning -- be sure everyone can see you.
   b. Tell the students what to look for in your demonstrations.
   c. Take your visually impaired students through the motions.
4. **Classroom organization.**
   a. Consider the best use of a facility -- orderly movement is the teachers' responsibility.
   b. Give directions before the class starts.
   c. Show interest and concerns for your students.

d. Keep control.
e. Think abilities -- what the student <u>can do</u> not what they <u>cannot do.</u>
f. Use a multisensory approach -- utilize all their senses.
g. Be well prepared -- know your material, know your students, and know yourself.

5. **Good teachers show concern for their students.**
   a. Give recognition and credit when and where do. Make certain all assignments relate to program objectives -- adult learners are irritated by "busy work."
   b. Knowledge of results leads to increased learning.
   c. Remember, the student's self-worth is more important than any game or activity.
   d. Be creative! Modify the exercise program until it is really individualized for the student.
   e. Respect your student's privacy! You will undoubtedly have access to information about the students' disabilities, age, medications, etc. Do not share it with your friends.
   f. Do not let your student's mood determine yours! If you have moody, depressed student, do not let it rub off on you.
   g. Use appropriate equipment and activities! Keep in mind the mental and chronological age of your student, as well as the associated disabilities.

6. **Lab Requirements.**
   a. As an assistant, you are responsible for one, or in some instances, two disabled students. These people depend on you to be there. If you are absent, they can not complete their exercise program. Please contact the instructor in advance of the class to report your absence.
   b. If your assigned student is absent, it is your responsibility to assist elsewhere during the class in any way possible.
   c. It is your responsibility to learn your student's exercise program as soon as possible. If you have any questions, see the instructor. Do not guess or skip any exercise! Never add an exercise to the program card without <u>consultation</u> and <u>approval</u> from the instructor.
   d. It is the student assistant's duty to make sure the exercise card is filled out each day, dated and placed back in the card box.

ASSISTANT BEHAVIOR

The importance of assistant/student interactions cannot be over-emphasized. The primary function of the assistant is to hasten the student's psychomotor development. Assistants should be made aware of the types of interactions which foster the student's motivation to exercise and attend on a regular basis. The following section describes appropriate assistant behavior (adapted from McKenzie, 1983).

1. **Supports.** The assistant should be ready to physically assist a student whenever needed (e.g., manual assistance which enables a student to reach full range of motion).
2. **Corrective Skill Feedback.** The assistant should provide information regarding the inadequacy of a performance attempt and how it could be corrected.
3. **Lectures, directs.** Whenever possible, the assistant should provide the student with facts or background information regarding the exercises or procedures. This also involves verbally or non-verbally directing a student to perform a task.
4. **Questions.** The assistant should remember to ask questions regarding discomfort during exercises (e.g., pain during passive range of motion; pain during cardiovascular training). This provides the assistant with feedback regarding his/her technique and alerts him/her to signs of exercise distress. The assistant should also ask questions regarding exercises or procedures with the intent of testing the student's comprehension of why he/she is performing an exercise.
5. **Listens.** The assistant should always attend to a student's questions, responses or attempts at conversation.
6. **Praises/motivates.** The assistant should utilize praise, vocal intonation, claps and gestures/expressions to activate or intensify motor performances or foster appropriate behavior. Nothing succeeds like success!
7. **Measures.** The assistant should constantly be engaged in observing a student's activity and recording the performance on the exercise program card.
8. **Professional conduct.** The assistants should always conduct themselves in a professional manner. This includes:
   a. Using appropriate language.
   b. Being punctual.
   c. Being as self-directed as possible.
   d. Refraining from unnecessary chatting with fellow assistants.
   e. Appropriate clothing.
9. **Enjoy** what you are doing and the students will probably enjoy the activity as well.
10. **Be creative!** Try to modify the exercise program (WITH APPROVAL FROM THE INSTRUCTOR) until it is really individualized for the student.

KEY POINTS

1. The importance of trainers and educators understanding the learning process cannot be over-estimated. It means the difference between poor programs and effective programs.
2. There are many characteristics, principles, and factors which must be considered when working with adult learners.
3. There are special characteristics of adult learners.
4. It is the responsibility of the teacher to develop a positive learning climate designed to motivate learners to learn.
5. Trainers and educators must continually strive to develop their own skills, knowledge and attitudes so that they will be more effective in designing and implementing programs.

STUDY QUESTIONS

1. How do you think you learn best? Explain your answer and give some examples.

2. Describe your first teaching experience. How could it be improved?

3. What are some characteristics that you think make up a good teacher?

REFERENCES

Fait, H. and Dunn, J. (1984). Special Physical Education - Adapted, Individualized and Developmental (5th ed.). San Francisco: Saunders Publishing Co.

Evans, J. R. (1980). They Have to be Carefully Taught. AAHPERD Publication, Stock Number 245-26904. 1900 Reston, VA, 22091.

McKenzie, J. (1984). Lecture notes from Analysis of Teaching Behavior. San Diego State University.

CHAPTER 6

ASSESSMENT AND PROGRAMMING FOR MUSCULAR STRENGTH AND ENDURANCE

WHY ASSESS?

Assessment is one of the more important aspects of an exercise program; yet, it is often the most neglected due to lack of evaluation tools, expertise, and time. Physical and motor assessment of a disabled student is vital to an Adapted Physical Education program for the following reasons:

1. It establishes the disabled student's current level or performance (i.e., functional ability).
2. It allows the instructor to plan individualized goals and prescribe feasible, safe, and beneficial exercises.
3. Upon post-testing, it enables the student to see the progress or maintenance which has been made (or regression).

The selection of an assessment tool is predicated on the type of disability. For example, the Manual Muscle Test is suitable for testing students with lower motorneuron lesions such as polio, but is inappropriate for any student with an upper motorneuron lesion.

In addition, the student's posture and starting position for selected activities should be considered in the assessment. It is also important to note any compensatory mechanisms or substitutions for motor performance that occur.

NOTE Before conducting any form of evaluation, please refer to Chapter six for Contraindications to Exercise Testing and Reasons for Terminating an Exercise Test.

ASSESSMENT OF MUSCULAR STRENGTH AND ENDURANCE

Developing and maintaining adequate levels of muscular strength and endurance are essential in facilitating independent living skills, preventing disuse syndromes, and avoiding acute or chronic injury (e.g., low back pain). Prior to beginning a strength training regime, some form of evaluation is necessary to determine which techniques will be used, as well as the initial amount of sets, repetitions, and load to be lifted, during a weight training regime.

DEFINITIONS

Strength   The maximal amount of force that can be elicited in a single or several voluntary contractions (Sharkey, 1979).

Endurance   The ability to exert submaximal contractions repeatedly (Sharkey, 1979).

Muscular strength and endurance are usually distinguished by the number of repetitions involved (see Figure 6-1).

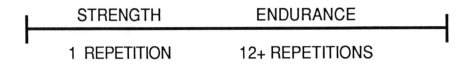

STRENGTH   ENDURANCE

1 REPETITION   12+ REPETITIONS

FIGURE 6-1.

Techniques currently used to assess muscular strength and endurance in the disabled adult includes manual muscle testing, grip force (dynamometers, cynamometers), repetition maximum with weights, static (isometric) cable tensiometry, and isokinetic measurements (Davis et al, 1981). Most of these methods are discussed below. Many other tests exist for assessing muscular strength and endurance. The reader is referred to books by Haskins (1972), Fait and Dunn (1984), and Sherrill, (1986) for additional fitness tests. Unfortunately, few norms exist for adults, especially those with disabilities.

MANUAL MUSCLE TESTING

Manual muscle testing is used by therapists, athletic trainers, and adapted physical educators to assess strength of isolated muscle (e.g., tibialis anterior) or groups of muscles (e.g., dorsiflexors). It is a valuable method because it requires no equipment other than a plinth and may be the only method for testing when paresis, contractures, or incoordination are present. However, it is a method which requires an advanced knowledge of muscles and their actions, as well as practical expertise. Therefore, it should not be attempted without rigorous training prior to its utilization. The test is inappropriate for those students with upper motorneuron lesions evidencing spasticity. Muscular strength is rated by the evaluator according to the muscle grading chart in Table 6-1 (Hoppenfeld, 1976).

TABLE 6-2. Muscle Grading Chart	
MUSCLE GRADATIONS	**CRITERIA**
5 -- Normal	Complete range of motion against gravity with full resistance.
4 -- Good	Complete range of motion against gravity with some resistance.
3 -- Fair	Complete range of motion against gravity.
2 -- Poor	Complete range of motion with gravity eliminated.
1 -- Trace	Evidence of slight contractility. No joint motion.
0 -- Zero	No evidence of contractility.

For specific details regarding the positions and procedures used in manual muscle testing, refer to the text by Daniels and Worthingham (1972) listed in the references at the end of this chapter.

Another quick version of the manual muscle test is the "break test". This technique involves placing each muscle group in its maximally shortened position and determining how much resistance is needed to "break" the student out of the position. The shortened position is used because (1) it is generally the weakest portion of the range of motion and (2) it demonstrates if the student can move through the range against gravity. .s and procedures used during this test may be found in Hoppenfeld (1976) which is listed in the references at the end of this chapter.

GENERAL GUIDELINES FOR THE BREAK TEST

1. If possible, each muscle group should be initially tested in an anti-gravity position.
2. The muscle group should be placed at the end-range (i.e., maximally shortened) position for the break test, with the exception of the elbow extensors, shoulder

flexors and abductors, and the forearm supinators and pronators. Use the mid-range position for these groups.

3. One hand of the evaluator should stabilize the joint to be tested. The remaining hand will act as the resistor.
4. The evaluator should gradually build up to the maximal resistance that the student can overcome.
5. Do not perform this test on a spastic muscle group. It will be difficult to determine actual strength if a spasm is present.
6. Compare strength bilaterally.

GRIP-STRENGTH, DYNAMOMETERS, CYNAMOMETERS

Dynamometers are hand-held devices which measure grip strength in pounds or grams of force. The individual stands or sits with the dynamometer positioned by the side of the body or above the head. The device is then squeezed as hard as possible for several seconds while exhaling. If holding the dynamometer above the head, it is brought down to the side as the maximal effort is elicited. Two trials are usually allowed and both hands are tested.

Cynamometers are devices created for those with paresis of the hands. It is a more sensitive device than the hand dynamometer and is designed to accommodate contractures of the hand. The individual squeezes a rubber bulb which comes in several sizes. Pinch strength may also be evaluated with this device.

REPETITION MAXIMUM (RM) WITH WEIGHTS

Strength may be assessed by the amount of weight that can be lifted for a certain number of repetitions (usually between one to 10 repetitions). It is recommended that a 10-RM be used for strength evaluations in adapted exercise programs. This method is based on DeLorme's Progressive Resistive Exercise technique. The following protocol is used for testing:

Warm up set	10 repetitions at 50% of 10-RM
Practice set	10 repetitions at 75% of 10-RM
Maximal set	10 repetitions at 100% of 10-RM

The purpose of the warm up set is to increase muscle irritability. The second set allows for technique practice. The third set is the maximal amount of weight that can be lifted in 10 repetitions.

Example:	
	10 repetitions at 50 lbs.
	10 repetitions at 75 lbs.
	10 repetitions at 100 lbs.

ISOKINETIC TESTING

Isokinetic equipment used for evaluating muscular strength and endurance includes the Cybex, Orthotron, and Hydragym. Due to its cost, the Cybex is usually not found within an adapted exercise program. The Orthotron is a less expensive piece of equipment which can be used for both isokinetic testing and training of the upper and lower extremities. Protocol for testing with the Orthotron is provided below.

Test Protocol for the Orthotron:
1. Warm up
   a. Stretch muscle groups to be tested (hold for 30 seconds, two times).
   b. Allow five to 10 submaximal efforts at each speed to be tested to check proper alignment, individual tolerance, and familiarize the student with the requirements of the test.
2. Positioning and Stabilization
   a. Note the height of the dynamometer head. Aligning a joint's axis of rotation with the axis of rotation of the dynamometer head has a significant effect on the accuracy of torque measurement. In the shoulder joint, the axis will change throughout the movement so a compromise must be determined.
   b. Note the distance between the seat and the edge of the lever arm.
   c. Note the length of the lever arm; i.e., the location of the tibial pad. The tibial pad should be positioned just above the ankle joint.
   d. Stabilize the thigh with the strap provided. Have the student grip the handles and keep the trunk against the seatback.
3. Test Protocol (see Table 6-3)
   a. Record the highest torque achieved (ft. lbs.) at each test speed.
   b. To perform an endurance test, use the speed setting of 7. Record the number of repetitions taken to reach one-half of the maximum (beginning) torque.

TABLE 6-3. Test Protocol				
TESTING PATTERN	**STRENGTH**		**POWER**	
	TEST SPEED	NO. MAX EFFORTS	TEST SPEED	NO. MAX EFFORTS
SHOULDER: Ext/Flex Abd/Add	3	3	7	5
KNEE: Ext/Flex	3	3	7	5
ANKLE: Plantar Dorsi Flex	2	3	5	5

HYDRAGYM

The hydragym can assess isokinetic strength and endurance, depending upon the speed setting used and the duration (number of repetitions) of the exercise.

PROGRAMMING FOR MUSCULAR STRENGTH AND ENDURANCE

Prior to embarking on any of the training programs described in this chapter, the instructor should check to see that all students have turned in the paperwork required for entrance into the program. This should include the following: (1) Medical History and (2) Medical Release (signed by a physician). The instructor should combine this information with that obtained during the assessment to design the individualized exercise prescription.
The following section will aid the instructor in selecting appropriate exercises and techniques for the development of muscular strength and endurance.

TECHNIQUES IN STRENGTH TRAINING

Strength training techniques currently available to Adapted Physical Educators include the following:

1. Active-assistive exercise
2. Active exercise
3. Isometric exercise
4. Manual resistance exercise with a partner
5. Proprioceptive Neuromuscular Facilitation (PNF)
6. Isotonic exercise
7. Isokinetic exercise

The definitions, advantages, and disadvantages of each exercise technique are presented below.

ACTIVE-ASSISTIVE EXERCISE

Active-assistive exercise is indicated when the agonist muscle group is so weak that it cannot move the limb through the range of motion without assistance from another person. The student should initiate the movement (e.g., elbow flexion), but the assistant helps overcome the "sticking point" (i.e., weight of the limb and gravity are too great to overcome) and takes the limb through the remainder of the range. This type of exercise may also be performed in an anti-gravity position. For particular muscle groups, such as the abdominals, eccentric contractions may be indicated when using active-assistive exercise. Muscles can usually accommodate more resistance with an eccentric contraction than a concentric one. For example, if a student requires a great deal of assistance to perform an abdominal curl, the assistant should bring the student to the fully curled position, but then allow the student to lower himself/herself to the mat without help. Once sufficient strength has been achieved with eccentric contractions, the student should progress to concentric contractions.

ACTIVE EXERCISE

The student contracts the agonist muscle group (e.g., elbow flexion) through the range of motion without any resistance other than the weight of the limb and gravity. Active exercise can also be performed in an anti-gravity position. When the student is able to perform one set of 10 repetitions through the entire range of motion, then he/she should progress to some form of resistive exercise.

RESISTIVE EXERCISE

During resistive exercise, the student contracts the agonist muscle group through the full range of motion against a given resistance. The amount of resistance and the number of repetitions performed will vary depending on whether the individual is working on strength or endurance.

Types of Resistive Exercise

A. Isometric Exercise

Isometric exercise involves exerting muscular force against an immovable object, thereby creating a static contraction. It may also be created by simply contracting a muscle group statically. Thus, no movement occurs (i.e., no change in the length of the muscle or in the join angle). Although tension and heat are produced, mechanical work does not occur. The force exerted may be submaximal or maximal, depending upon the purpose of the exercise. The two advantages of isometric exercise are that it requires no equipment or space to perform. It is also useful if a contracture exists. The disadvantages of isometric exercise are that: (1) it may raise the blood pressure to high levels; (2) the strength gain is specific to the angle trained at (i.e., not much strength gain for the remaining range of motion except 15 degrees to either side of the training angle); and (3) the amount of transfer to functional activities is questionable.

Isometric exercise is usually performed in sets of 10 repetitions. Each contraction is held for approximately five to 10 seconds.

B. Manual Resistive Exercise

In manual resistive (MR) exercise, the student contracts the agonist muscle group through the range of motion against a resistance applied by the assistant. This effort may be maximal or submaximal, and be performed concentrically or eccentrically. It is usually performed in sets of 10 repetitions or one continuous set to fatigue. The exercise should be performed rhythmically, and resistance can be applied in both directions or movement (e.g., flexion and extension). The advantages of MR are that (1) it requires no equipment or space; (2) it is accommodating to the student's capabilities; and (3) it is useful when contractures prevent positioning on equipment. MR is typically performed about a single joint in one plane only (e.g., elbow flexion, sagittal plane); therefore, it does not simulate functional human movement very well.

Specific MR exercises may be found under Strength Exercises in this chapter.

C. Proprioceptive Neuromuscular Facilitation (PNF)

PNF is a group of relaxation and strengthening techniques used to rehabilitate neuromuscular deficiencies. It refers to the facilitation of neuromuscular activity by stimulating proprioceptive sensory input which regulates muscle function, joint movement, locomotion, posture, and body space. Proprioceptors include the muscle spindle, Golgi Tendon Organ, and joint receptors. However, PNF takes advantage of all the senses. Additional facilitation is achieved through the use of the eyes (e.g., individual observes movement), ears (e.g., individual receives commands; posture regulated by the inner ear), and the exteroceptors of the skin (e.g., tactile input by the therapist). Treatments are directed toward the improvement of the individual's ability to perform functional activities.

The patterns of motion utilized in PNF follow spiral/diagonal pathways (e.g., shoulder flexion-adduction-internal rotation) to make use of the total muscle. The inclusion of rotation adds synergistic muscles to the movement. PNF should only be performed through the pain-free range of motion.

PNF techniques are based upon many of Sherrington's (1947) principles: (1) facilitating strong components before weak; (2) applying maximal resistance (irradiation); and (3) successive induction.

It is beyond the scope of this manual to provide a comprehensive explanation of the techniques involved in PNF. It is also a method which requires many years of practical experience in order to be competent.

Technique Components of PNF

Maximal Resistance
    Apply an amount of resistance which allows the student to move rhythmically and pain-free through the range of motion (isotonic) work within student's existing range. Isometric contractions can also be used.

Pressure/Manual Contact
    1. Guide student through pattern with resistance; hands placed on student in direction of desired movement.
    2. Do not use a circular grip on the limb.
    3. Resistance is given in the exact opposite direction of motion.
    4. Use proper body position (assistant should stand in the diagonal).
    5. Facilitory technique by pressure.
    6. Use even, lumbrical grip: MP flexion, IP extension.

Quick Stretch
    1. Facilitory in beginning of pattern.
    2. Followed by resistance (facilitory).
    3. Do not use in painful joints or joint restrictions.
    4. Triggers the stretch reflex of the muscle spindles.

Traction
1. Separation of joint structures.
2. Elongate muscle and joint capsule.
3. Muscles brought to taut position.
4. Used in anti-gravity or flexion patterns.
5. Aids in stabilizing and controlling joint motion.

Approximation
1. Joint compression through long axis of structure.
2. Cocontraction of proximal component.
3. Facilitates extension and postural reflex.
4. Used in extension patterns.
5. Most effective in lower extremities.
6. Can be maintained through the range or applied at the end range.
7. Contraindications: joint disease, osteomyelitis, non-weight bearing joints, fractures, painful joints.

Verbal Stimulation
1. Amount depends upon cognitive level.
2. Use simple, concise commands.

Visual Stimulation
Becomes important modality when tactile sensation and proprioception are deficient.

Timing
Distal to proximal or proximal to distal. Stronger muscles cause irradiation to the weaker.

Specific Techniques of PNF

1. Rhythmic Stabilization (R-S)
   Move joint to the point of limitation. Hold in the pattern isometrically until the student begins to tire. Change resistance to antagonist muscle group and hold isometrically. Move to a new point of limitation.
2. Hold-Relax (H-R)
   See description under Assessment and Programming for Flexibility.
3. Contract-Relax (C-R)
   Move joint to point of limitation. Contract isotonically with antagonist muscle group. Move to a new point of limitation. Repeat until no new further range of motion is obtainable.

4. Rhythmic Initiation (R-I)

   The assistant guides the student through the pattern until it is learned. Resistance is gradually increased as the pattern is learned.

5. Slow Reversals (S-R)

   Provide resistance in one diagonal pattern through range of motion and then reverse the pattern to the opposite direction. Perform one set to fatigue.

6. Repeated Contractions (R-C)

   Provide resistance in one diagonal pattern until a weak point is found in the range. Hold at that point and build up to a maximal isometric contraction. Pull limb back and move forward again. Repeat several times.

D. Isotonic Exercise, Progressive Exercise Resistive (PRE)

In isotonic exercise, resistance is provided by a weight such as a dumbbell, pulley, ankle/wrist weight, or Universal machine. Since the resistance remains constant throughout the movement, this form of exercise does not accommodate the changes in strength which occur as the joint angle changes (i.e., a muscle group is strongest at midrange and weaker at the end ranges). Thus, isotonic exercise may be considered submaximal when compared to MR or PNF because it cannot fully accommodate the strongest portion of the range. Some mechanical devised (e.g., Nautilus, Universal Centurion) use cams to change the amount of resistance encountered through the range of motion. This type of machine accommodates the muscle capabilities to a much greater degree than the constant resistance provided by a dumbbell or the standard Universal equipment.

Protocols using isotonic exercise vary widely. Progressive Resistance Exercise (PRE) is one technique which has been used extensively in rehabilitation and strength training programs for several decades. De Lorme and Watkins (1951) were the first to describe the technique.

PRE constitutes only one aspect of the total rehabilitation program and that is the development of absolute strength. It does not necessarily purport to develop muscular endurance or speed of movement.

PRE relies upon both concentric and eccentric contractions of the muscle. Additional muscles are utilized through static contractions to stabilize skeletal parts while primarily movement is occurring. During the eccentric contraction, the muscle is taken beyond its normal resting length, thus facilitating greater force development is the proceeding concentric contraction.

To overload the muscle for strength development, PRE prescribes the heaviest load which can be lifted through the range of motion for ten repetitions (10-RM). This is preceded by two warm up sets of ten repetitions at submaximal loads. The purpose of the warm up is to increase muscle irritability and to allow practice of the lifting technique. A forth and fifth set at the 10-RM facilitates the development of endurance.

Protocol: Establish 10-RM

              1st set --   50% of 10-RM
              2nd set --   75% of 10-RM
              3rd set -- 100% of 10-RM
              4th set -- 100% of 10-RM (optional for endurance)
              5th set -- 100% of 10-RM (optional for endurance)

Example: 1st set --   6 lbs.
              2nd set --   9 lbs.
              3rd set -- 12 lbs.

The 10-RM must be reestablished every one or two weeks initially.

E. Isokinetic Exercise

The student contracts the agonist muscle group through the range of motion against a lever a constant speed, thereby achieving a maximal effort at every point in the range. Because it accommodates the strength changes that occur as the joint angle changes, it theoretically enables one to perform more work than with isotonic methods. Only concentric contractions occur with isokinetic exercise. The exerciser does not lift weight but pushes against a lever that moves at a fixed speed in both directions (e.g., flexion/extension). Thus, it allows the instructor to measure strength imbalances about a joint (e.g., knee flexors should be approximately 60% the strength of the knee extensors at slow velocities of contraction).

GENERAL GUIDELINES FOR ADAPTED WEIGHT TRAINING

When using resistive exercise, the weight training program can be divided into three phases (see Table 3-1). This same protocol can be followed whether using weight or manual resistance. The purpose of Phase I is to (1) develop neuromuscular coordination in the lifting pattern (mechanics of the lift); (2) practice the breathing pattern; and (3) prevent sudden injury to atrophied soft tissue. Individuals who have not exercised for an extended period of time are especially prone to sudden strains, soreness, or inflammations if they immediately begin a rigorous exercise regime. Phase I involves lifting on set of 15 repetitions at a relatively light poundage. This continues for approximately two weeks.

During Phase II, the poundage is increased while repetitions are decreased to between 8 and 12 per set (three set minimum). It is advisable to establish a 10-RM at this time and follow the PRE protocol (see PRE earlier in this chapter). ALWAYS HAVE YOUR STUDENTS PERFORM AT LEAST ONE WARM UP SET PRIOR TO A

10-RM! If the student can lift the weight more than twelve repetitions during the final set (i.e., exceeds the 10-RM), then increase the amount of weight on the next exercise day.

If muscular endurance is desired, the student can proceed to Phase III. Rather than increasing the amount of weight lifted, the repetitions are increased to between 12 and 20. This may be performed in sets of three. A poundage should be selected which allows only the desired number of repetitions to be completed. If manual resistance or PNF is used, one continuous set to fatigue may be used. For many persons who use manual wheelchairs, the development of muscular endurance may be more important than absolute strength..

TABLE 6-4. PHASES OF A STRENGTH/ENDURANCE PROGRAM			
	PHASE I	PHASE II	PHASE III
SETS	1-2	3	3
REPS	15	8-12	12-20
LOAD	light	moderate heavy	moderate
MINIMUM DURATION	2 weeks	6-8 weeks	indefinite
PURPOSE	practice	strength	endurance

Guidelines for Conducting a Safe and Beneficial Strength Program

1. Always keep accurate, daily records of your student's performance. This includes recording the date, poundage used, and the number of sets and repetitions performed.
2. Retest every few weeks to reestablish the 10-RM.
3. A spotter (assistant) should always be present when a student is lifting weights - no matter how light the poundage!
4. If possible, alternate the upper and lower body exercises so no two consecutive exercises involve the same prime mover.
5. When using weights, perform exercises which involve larger muscle groups first. Foe example, perform shoulder strengthening exercises before specific wrist

exercises.

6. Allow sufficient recovery time between sets (usually several minutes).
7. Do not lift more than every other day with the same strength training routine.
8. Each repetition should be performed rhythmically and without a pause at the beginning or end of the range of motion.
9. Always precede maximal lifts with a warm up.
10. FLEXIBILITY EXERCISES SHOULD FOLLOW A WEIGHT LIFTING SESSION TO PREVENT ADAPTIVE SHORTENING FROM OCCURRING. Muscles retain some residual tension or contraction after strenuous exercise.
11. Maintain good muscular balance by strengthening opposing muscle groups, unless an imbalance already exists.
12. Breathing pattern during weight lifting:
    a. inhale prior to lift.
    b. exhale during the effort.
13. Whenever possible, the student should watch himself/herself perform the movement. Vision is especially important when deficiencies in proprioception exist.
14. Begin an exercise from a position of "on stretch" and then move into a concentric contraction. This facilitates the intensity of the contraction.
15. Develop strength before endurance in a weight training or rehabilitation program.

THE EXERCISE PROGRAM CARD

Every student should have an individualized exercise program card designed BY THE INSTRUCTOR and based on the information obtained from the medical history, medical release, and the evaluation performed at the program site. The card should contain the following information: (1) name; (2) dates for every day the student exercised in the program; (3) names of exercises and prescription; (4) daily recording of exercise quantity performed (e.g., number of sets and repetitions performed, resting and exercising heart rate, time duration, etc); (5) description of disabilities; (6) contraindications; and (7) effects of any medications. The assistant should never change the exercise program card without approval from the instructor. The assistant should make sure the card is filled out completely and dated each year.

Consistent terminology should be used when describing exercises on the program card. This allows for interchanging of assistants without confusion. Exercises should be named according to the following system:

1. Anatomical movement: For single joint movements, write the name of the joint and its anatomical movement. The body position will also have to be indicated. For example: Knee flexion - prone. All anatomical movement and body

positions are described in the chapter entitled "Basics in Kinesiology".
2. Approved vernacular: If multi-joint movement is involved in performing the exercise,then use an approved vernacular. These types of exercises are described later in this chapter. For example: Lat Pull, Bench Press.
3. Abbreviated description: If the exercise has been modified for the student or there is no accepted name for it, a brief description should be written in.

A prescription should accompany the name of the exercise and the body position. Sets and repetitions may be prescribed in the following manner, respectively:

3 X 10

This is interpreted as three sets of 10 repetitions. The exercise program card should have boxes which allow for recording the number of sets, repetitions, and weight that were actually lifted on a given day.

SAMPLE PROGRAM EXERCISE CARD

	date	date	date	
MR 1 * 10 1. (R) knee flexion-prone				
3 * 10 2. Bench Press				

In addition, a card for "progress notes" should be attached to the exercise program card to allow for recording of qualitative information (e.g., pain occurring during a particular exercise; motivational level).

EXERCISES FOR DEVELOPING
MUSCULAR STRENGTH AND ENDURANCE

The exercises described in this section can be performed with the following strength training techniques: active-assistive, active, isometric, manual resistance, and isotonic (PRE). The photos provided here illustrate some active, manual resistive, and isotonic techniques (pulleys and free weights). The reader is referred to the chapter on Basics in Kinesiology for a listing of muscles which are strengthened in single joint, anatomical movements. For multi-joint exercises, the prime movers have been identified in this chapter.

This list is not meant to be inclusive of all possible strength exercises available to Adapted Physical Educators. Many of the manual resistive and free weight exercises in this section can be performed in body positions other than the ones presented. In addition, many of these exercises can be performed in the pool, using the water as the resistive medium. The use of a kickboard with the shoulder exercises adds additional resistance.

1. CERVICAL FLEXION

    Position: Sitting
    Action: Keep head in anatomical position.
                    Place palms on forehead.
                    Press forehead isometrically into palms, attempting to flex neck.
                    Hold each repetition (rep) for five seconds.

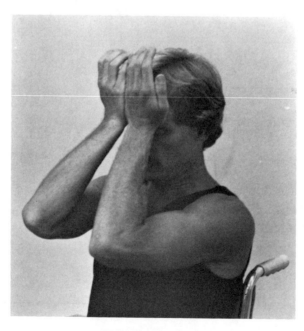

EXERCISE 6-1.

2. CERVICAL ROTATION

Position: Sitting
Action: Keep head in anatomical position.
Place left hand on lateral aspect of head.
Attempt to rotate head to left, creating an isometric contraction.
Hold each rep five seconds.
Repeat with right hand.

EXERCISE 6-2.

3. SCAPULAR ELEVATION

Position: Sitting (a), Standing (b)
Action: a. Assistant places hands on acromion process of student and attempts to keep shoulders depressed.
                 Student attempts to elevate shoulders up to ears.
             b. Student holds dumbbells in each hand and attempts to elevate shoulders up to ears.

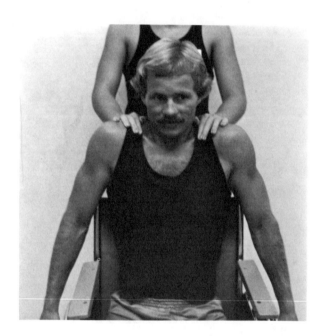

EXERCISE 6-3a.

4. SHOULDER FLEXION

Position: Sitting (a & b), Standing (c)

Action: a.   Student flexes elbow to 90 degrees.
Assistant places one hand on superior aspect of shoulder to stabilize and other hand on anterior aspect of upper arm. Student flexes shoulder against resistance provided by assistant.
Repeat to other side.

                 b.   Face sideways to pulley. Grasp lower pulley with one hand. Keeping the arm straight, pull up and across the front of the body, flexing and horizontally adducting at the shoulder.
Repeat to other side.

                 c.   Hold dumbbell in hand. Keeping arm straight, flex at shoulder, bringing weight out in front of body.
Repeat to other side.

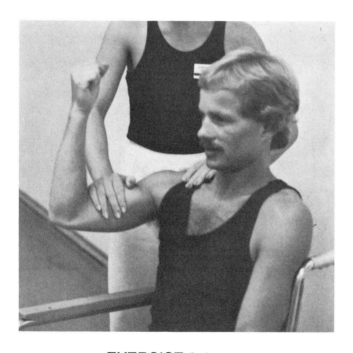

EXERCISE 6-4a.

EXERCISE 6-4b.

5. SHOULDER ABDUCTION

Position: Sitting (a & b), Standing (c)

Action: a. Student flexes elbows. Assistant places hand on lateral aspect arm, proximal to elbow.
Student abducts shoulder against assistant's resistance.

b. Student faces sideways to pulley. Keeping arm straight, lower pulley is brought up by abducting shoulder.
Repeat to other side.

c. Student holds dumbbell in each hand and abducts both shoulders, bringing weight above shoulders.

EXERCISE 6-5a.

EXERCISE 6-5b.

6. SHOULDER HYPEREXTENSION

Position: Sitting

Action:
a. Student flexes elbow to 90 degrees. Assistant places one hand on superior aspect on shoulder and other on posterior aspect of arm, proximal to elbow. Student attempts to hyperextend shoulder against resistance.
Repeat to other side.

b. Facing pulley and keeping the arm straight, student grasps upper pulley and hyperextends shoulder.
Repeat to other side.

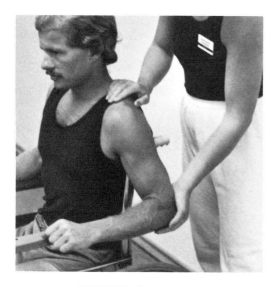

EXERCISE 6-6a.

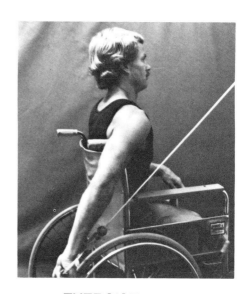

EXERCISE 6-6b.

7. UPRIGHT ROWS (elbow flexion & shoulder abduction)

   Muscles: Trapezium, Deltoids, Biceps
   Position: Sitting (a), Standing (b)
   Action: a. Face pulley and grasp lower handles. Pull and bring elbows up and behind body.
               b. Hold barbell in both hands. Bring bar up to chin. A cane with a sand weight attached may be substituted for the barbell.

8. SHOULDER HORIZONTAL ABDUCTION

   Position: Sitting (a & b), Prone (c)
   Action: a. Student flexes elbows and horizontally adducts shoulders. Assistant places hands on posterior aspect of arm, proximal to elbow. Student horizontally adducts shoulders against resistance.
               b. Face pulleys and grasp upper handles. Pull handles out to side with slightly flexed elbows. Attempt to bring hands behind back.
               c. Hold dumbbell in each hand and horizontally abduct shoulders, keeping elbow slightly flexed. Attempt to bring hands behind back.

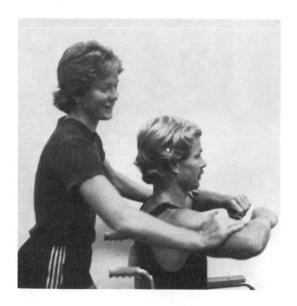

EXERCISE 6-8a.

EXERCISE 6-8b.

9. SHOULDER HORIZONTAL ADDUCTION

Position: Sitting (a & b), Supine (c)
Action: a. Student flexes elbows and abducts shoulders. Assistant places hands on anterior aspect of upper arms. Student horizontally adducts shoulders against resistance.
             b. Student faces sideways to pulleys, grasping the upper handles. Keeping the elbow slightly flexed, the handle is brought horizontally across the front of the body.
                 Repeat to other side.
             c. Holding a dumbbell in each hand, student keeps elbows slightly flexed and horizontally adducts shoulders, bringing the weight out in front of the body.

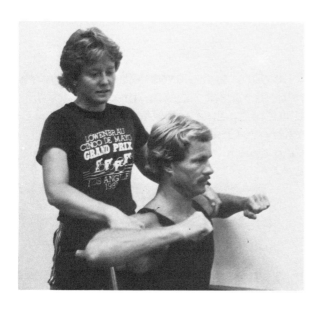

EXERCISE 6-9a.

EXERCISE 6-9b.

10. PULL-OVER
Muscles: Pectoralis Major, Triceps
Position: Supine hook-lying
Action: Student grasps one dumbbell with both hands at the midline. Keeping arms slightly flexed at the elbows, the dumbbell is brought up and behind the head.

11. BENCH PRESS
Muscles: Pectorals, Deltoids, Triceps
Position: Supine hook-lying on bench (a) or mat (b)
Action:
    a. Keep feet on bench. Grasp handles, keeping them as close as possible to the long axis of forearm. Press weight up and exhale simultaneously.
    b. Hold dumbbell in each hand, keeping forearms pronated. Shoulders are abducted. Press the weight upward and exhale until elbows are extended.

12. SHOULDER ADDUCTION
Position: Sitting
Action:
    a. Student abducts shoulders and flexes elbows. Assistant places hands on medial aspect of arm, proximal to elbow. Student adducts shoulders against resistance.
    b. Face sideways to pulleys. Grasp the upper handle and pull down to side, adducting shoulder. Keep arm straight.
       Repeat to other side.

EXERCISE 6-12a.

EXERCISE 6-12b.

13. LAT PULL DOWN

Muscles: Latissimus Dorsi, Trapezium, Teres Major, Rhomboids Minor, Deltoids, Biceps and Brachialis, Triceps, Pectorals

Position: Sitting or kneeling, facing apparatus

Action: Student should be positioned directly under bar.
Grasp bar with a wide grip and pull down to back of neck or down to sternum.

14. SHOULDER EXTERNAL ROTATION

Position: Supine hook-lying (a), Prone (b)

Action:
a. Student flexes elbow and abducts shoulder.
Assistant places one hand on dorsum of hand and with other stabilizes the elbow. Student externally rotates shoulder against resistance.
Repeat to other side.
b. Hold dumbbell in one hand with shoulder abducted and elbow flexed. Externally rotate shoulder slowly.
Repeat to other side.

EXERCISE 6-14a.

EXERCISE 6-14b.

15. SHOULDER INTERNAL ROTATION

Position: Supine hook-lying
Action: Student flexes elbow and abducts shoulder.
            Assistant places one hand on palmar surface and stabilizes the
            elbow with the other. Student internally rotates against resistance.
            Repeat to other side.

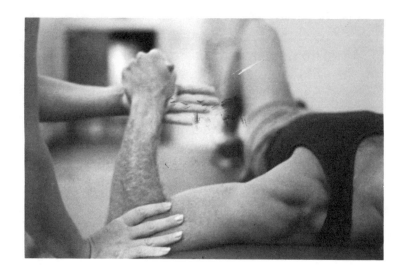

EXERCISE 6-15.

16. ELBOW FLEXION

Position: Sitting (a & b), Standing (c)

Action: a. Assistant places one hand against medial side of arm, proximal to wrist, while other hand stabilizes the elbow. Student flexes elbow against resistance. Repeat to other side.

             b. Facing pulley, student grasps lower handle and stabilizes elbow on armrest. Student then brings handle up, flexing at elbow. Repeat to other side.

EXERCISE 6-16a.

EXERCISE 6-16b.

17. ELBOW EXTENSION

Position: Supine hook-lying (a), Sitting (b & d), Long sitting (c)

Action:

a. Student flexes elbow. Assistant stabilizes elbow with one hand and places the other on lateral aspect of arm at wrist joint. Student extends elbow against resistance. Repeat to other side.

b. Face away from pulley. Grasping the upper handles, extend elbow (elbow should be stabilized on armrest). Repeat to other side.

c. Grasping push up blocks, student extends elbows, raising buttocks off the mat.

d. Use lat pull bar. Standing slightly behind bar, grasp handles and pull bar down until elbows are touching sides of trunk. Keep elbows into sides and extend at the elbows only.

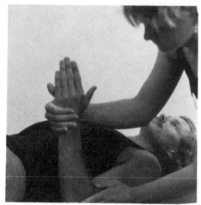

EXERCISE 6-17a.

EXERCISE 6-17b.

EXERCISE 6-17c.

18. FOREARM PRONATION

Position: Sitting
Action: Assistant shakes hands with student, keeping thumb off dorsum of student's hand. Forearm should be stabilized on a padded table. Student pronates forearm against resistance. Repeat to other side.

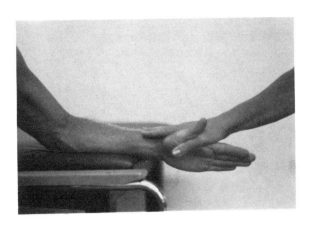

EXERCISE 6-18

19. FOREARM SUPINATION

Position: Sitting
Action: Assistant places one hand on dorsum of student's hand. Student's forearm should be stabilized on padded table. Student supinates forearm against resistance. Repeat to other side.

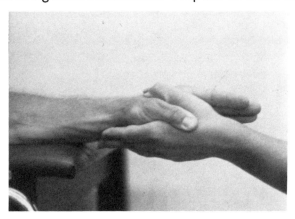

EXERCISE 6-19.

20. WRIST FLEXION

Position: Sitting

Action:
    a. Assistant places one hand in palm of student while stabilizing forearm with other hand. Student flexes wrist against resistance. Repeat to other side.
    b. Hold dumbbell in hand with wrist extended over edge of table. Flex wrist up. Repeat to other side.

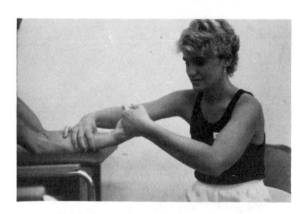

EXERCISE 6-20a

21. WRIST EXTENSION

Position: Sitting

Action:
    a. Assistant places one hand on dorsum of student's hand while stabilizing the forearm with the other. Student extends wrist against resistance. Repeat to other side.
    b. Hold dumbbell in hand, palm down, with wrist extended over side of table. Extend wrist up. Repeat to other side.

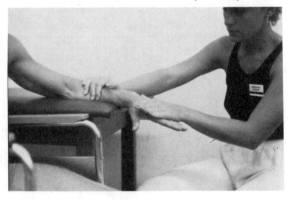

EXERCISE 6-21a

22. THUMB AND FINGER FLEXION, PINCH
Position: Sitting
Action: Use theraplast (silly putty) to squeeze with thumb and fingers simultaneously. Place a ball between thumb, index, and middle fingers - pinch.

23. SPINAL FLEXION (abdominal curls)
Position: Supine hook-lying (a, b, & c), Sitting (d)
Action:
  a. Flex hips and knees 90 degrees with the lower legs supported by a low bench. Place hands across chest. Slowly curl one-third of distance up (scapula should clear ground) and lower. May also slowly twist right and left.
  b. Reach left arm toward right knee. Contract abdominals, keeping low back pressed to floor.
  c. Place hands under hips. Bring knees to chest, lifting hips off mat.
  d. Face away from pulley, grasping upper handles. Flex spine forward.

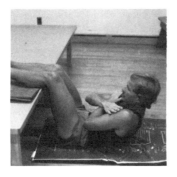

EXERCISE 6-23a.

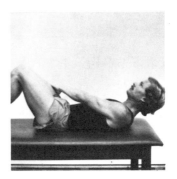

EXERCISE 6-23b.

EXERCISE 6-23c.

EXERCISE 6-23d.

24. SPINAL EXTENSION

Position: Sitting (a & b), Prone (c)

Action:
a. Assistant places hands on student's scapula. Student flexes forward as far as possible and then extends spine against resistance.
b. Face pulleys and grasp lower handles. Extend spine.
c. With shoulders abducted, rotate thumbs up toward the ceiling, raise upper trunk off mat, and pinch shoulder blades together. Hold for five seconds.

EXERCISE 6-24a.

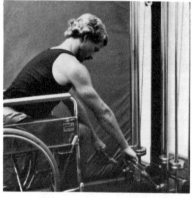

EXERCISE 6-24b.

EXERCISE 6-24c.

25. LATERAL FLEXION

Position: Sitting

Action: Face sideways to pulley. Grasping lower handles, laterally flex spine over armrest. Repeat to other side.

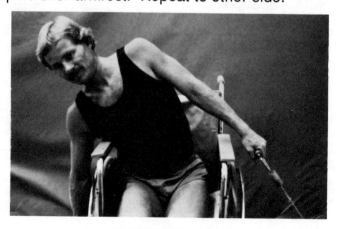

EXERCISE 6-25.

26. HIP HIKERS OR BRIDGES (lumbar extensors, hip extensors)

Position: Supine hook-lying
Action: Place feet and knees together. Elevate hip off mat. Hold five seconds.

EXERCISE 6-26.

27. HIP EXTENSION

Position: 4-point on elbows and knees
Action: Extend one leg out behind. Extend up and down at hip. Using an ankle weight will provide additional resistance. Repeat to other side.

28. HIP FLEXION

Position: Supine
Action: Assistant places one hand on anterior aspect of leg, proximal to knee. The other hand may need to stabilize the foot. Student flexes hip against resistance. Repeat to other side.

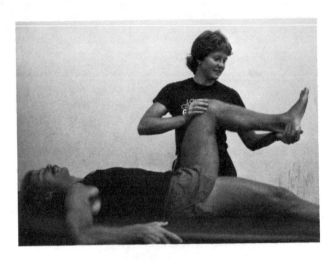

EXERCISE 6-28.

29. HIP ABDUCTION

Position: Supine (a), Side-lying (b), Standing (c)
Action: a. Assistant places one hand against lateral aspect of knee and the other against the lateral aspect of the ankle. Keeping the leg extended, student abducts hip against resistance. Repeat to other side.
            b. Using an ankle weight, student abducts hip, keeping leg rotated inward. Repeat to other side.
            c. Face sideways to pulleys and attach ankle to lower handles. Abduct hip. Repeat to other side.

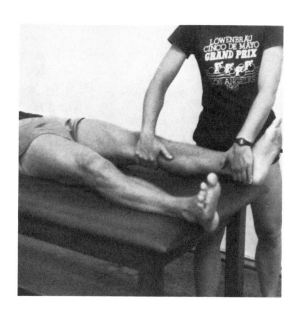

EXERCISE 6-29a.

30. HIP ADDUCTION

Position: Supine (a), Side-lying (b), Standing (c)

Action:
a. Assistant places one hand on medial aspect of knee and the other against the medial aspect of ankle. Keeping the leg extended, student adducts hip against resistance. Repeat to other side.
b. Prop up on elbow and place top leg in front, flexing at the knee. Using ankle weight, adduct hip of lower leg. Repeat to other side.
c. Face sideways to pulleys and attach ankle to lower handles. Adduct hip. Repeat to other side.

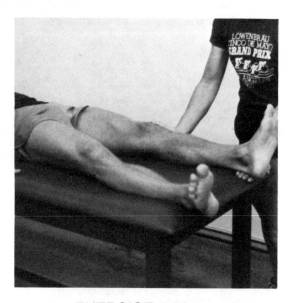

EXERCISE 6-30a.

31. HIP INTERNAL ROTATION
    Position: Supine
    Action: Assistant places one hand on lateral aspect of knee and the other on the medial aspect of foot. Student internally rotates leg against resistance. Repeat to other side.

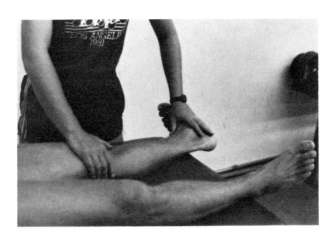

EXERCISE 6-31.

32. HIP EXTERNAL ROTATION
    Position: Supine
    Action: Assistant places one hand on lateral aspect of knee and the other on the lateral aspect of foot. The student externally rotates leg against resistance.

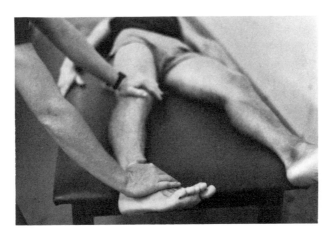

EXERCISE 6-32.

33. LEG PRESS

Muscles: Quadriceps, Gluteus Maximus
Position: Long sitting on Universal leg press
Action: Extend at the hip and knee. BE SURE <u>NOT</u> TO LOCK OR HYPEREXTEND THE KNEE DURING THIS EXERCISE!

34. KNEE EXTENSION

Position: Sitting (a & c), Long sitting on the elbows (b)
Action:
    a. Student sits on plinth with knees over edge. Assistant places one hand on dorsal surface of foot and the other on the medial side of heel. Student extends knee against resistance. Repeat to other side.
    b. Used in conjunction with a quad board and ankle weight. Dorsiflex ankle and extend knee, holding for five seconds. Emphasis should be on the bastus medialis. Quad board is adjusted to determine allowable range of motion.

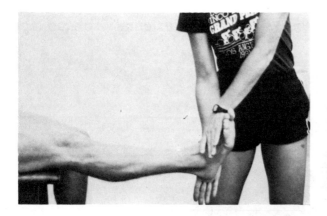

EXERCISE 6-34a.

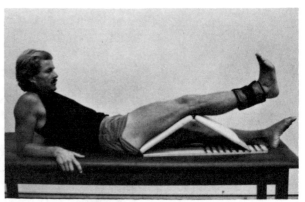

EXERCISE 6-34b.

116

35. KNEE FLEXION

Position: Prone
Action:
    a. Assistant places both hands on the posterior aspect of the knees, proximal to the ankle joint. Student flexes knees against resistance.
    b. Universal knee flexion machine. Flex knees, keeping pelvis flat on the bench.

EXERCISE 6-35a.

36. DORSIFLEXION

Position: Long sitting

Action: Assistant places one hand on dorsal aspect of foot, proximal to the metatarsophalangeal joints. Student dorsiflexes the foot against resistance, extending the toes as well. Repeat to other side.

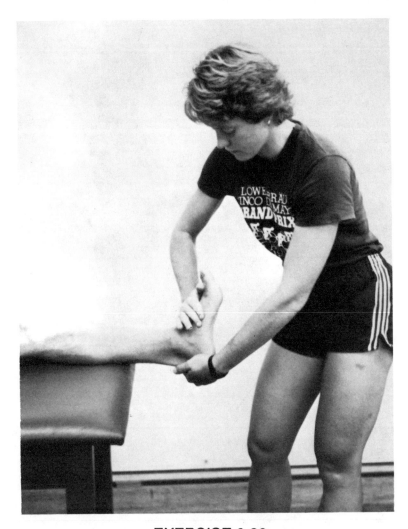

EXERCISE 6-36.

37. PLANTAR FLEXION

Position: Prone (a), Standing (b), Long sitting (c)
Action:
    a. Assistant places hands on the plantar surface of the foot. Student plantar flexes foot against resistance. Repeat to other side.
    b. Standing on stairs with the heels off, plantar flex the feet, raising them up and down.
    c. Universal machine (leg press). Keeping the knees extended (with slight flexion), plantar flex the ankles on the foot pedals.

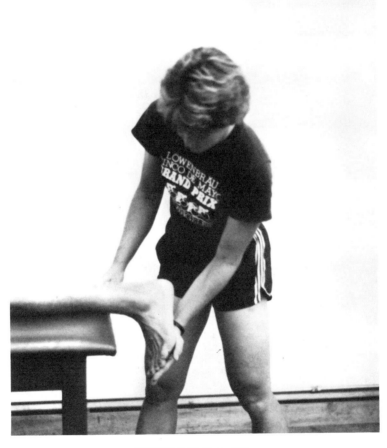

EXERCISE 6-37a.

38. INVERSION

Position: Long sitting (a), Sitting (b)

Action:
    a. Assistant places one hand against first metatarsal head. Student inverts foot against resistance. Repeat to other side.
    b. Place a towel underneath feet. Invert feet together, sweeping towel toward middle. Weights can be placed at the ends of the towel to increase resistance.

EXERCISE 6-38a.

39. EVERSION

Position: Long sitting (a), Sitting (b)

Action: a. Assistant places one hand against the fifth metatarsal head. Student everts foot against resistance. Repeat to other side.

b. Place a bunched towel underneath feet. Evert feet together, straightening towel out. Weights can be placed at ends of towel to increase resistance.

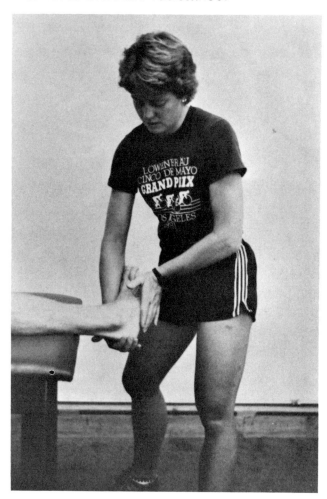

EXERCISE 6-39a.

STUDY QUESTIONS

1. Develop a strength program for T6 SCI student.

   a. Explain the rationale for each exercise.

2. When would PNF be best?

3. Discuss the procedures for increasing strength.

4. What are the key factors in developing an adapted weight training program.

REFERENCES

AAHPERD Health-Related Fitness Test. AAHPERD Publications, 1900 Association Drive, Reston, VA, 22091.

Crowe, W. C., Auxter, D., Pyfer, J. (1981). Principles and Methods of Adapted Physical Education (4th ed.). St. Louis: C. V. Mosby Co.

Daniels, L., & Worthingham, C. (1972). Muscle Testing. Philadelphia: W. B. Saunders Co.

Davis, G. M., Shephard, R. J., & Jackson, R. W. Cardio-respiratory fitness and muscular strength in the lower-limb disabled. Canadian Journal of Applied Sport Sciences, 6(4), 159-165.

Dreisinger, T. E., Whiting, R. V., & Hayden, C. R. (1982). Wheelchair exercise testing: comparison of continuous and discontinuous tests. Medicine and Science in Sports and Exercise, 14(2), 168.

Haskins, M. (1972). Evaluation in Physical Education. Dubuque: W. C. Brown Co.

Hoppenfeld, S. (1976). Physical Examination of the Spine and Extremities. New York: Appleton-Century Crofts.

Knutson, E. Lewnhaupt-Olsen, E., Thorsen, M. (1973). Physical capacity and physical conditioning in paraplegic patients. Paraplegia, 11, 205-216.

Nilsson, S., Staff, P. H., & Pruett, E. D. R. (1975). Physical work capacity and the effect of training on subjects with long-standing paraplegia. Scandinavian Journal of Rehabilitative Medicine, 7, 51-56.

Pyfer, J. & Johnson, R. Adapted Physical Education Manual. Evaluation and programming for students with handicapping conditions. Kansas State Department of Education, Topeka, Kansas.

Sharkey, B. J. (1979). Physiology of Fitness. Prescribing exercise for fitness, weight control, and health. Campaign, Illinois: Human Kinetic Publishers.

Sherrill, C. (1981). Adapted Physical Education and Recreation (2nd ed.). Dubuque: William C. Brown Co. Publishers.

CHAPTER 7

ASSESSMENT AND PROGRAMMING FOR FLEXIBILITY

ASSESSMENT OF FLEXIBILITY

Both active and passive range of motion tests should be utilized when determining limitations in flexibility. Active range of motion tests are performed under the students joint through the range. Passive testing is conducted when the student has difficulty completing the movement due to lack of strength and coordination. In general, if a student can move a limb through the normal range of motion actively, then a passive test is not required (Hoppenfeld, 1976).

The following section will present only active range of motion tests. Normal values are usually recorded on the evaluation sheet as "WNL" (Within Normal Limits). While limitations are recorded as Limitation of Motion (LOM). Always test bilaterally for comparison. The positions for passive range of motion testing can be found under Passive Range of Motion Exercises.

ACTIVE RANGE OF MOTION TESTS (Hoppenfeld, 1976)

1. <u>Finger Flexion and Extension</u> (metacarpophalangeal joint)

   Have the student make a tight fist, then extend the fingers. The fingers should completely close into the palm for flexion (90 degrees) and extend even with or beyond the dorsum of the hand for normal extension (45 degrees). Note whether the fingers work in unison.

   FIGURE 7-1.

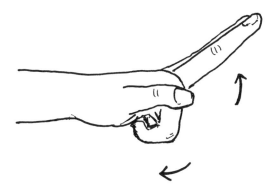

2. Wrist Flexion and Extension

With extended fingers, have the student flex and extend the wrist. Normal range of motion is approximately 80 degrees for wrist flexion and 70 degrees for wrist extension.

FIGURE 7-2.

3. Elbow Flexion and Extension

Beginning in anatomical position, have the student flex the elbow and touch the front of the shoulder with the hand. Normal range of motion is approximately 150 degrees for elbow flexion and 0 degrees for elbow extension.

FIGURE 7-3.

4. Forearm Supination and Pronation

Flex the elbows and hold them into the sides of the body. Hold a pencil, making a fist with the forearm pronated (palm facing down). Supinate the forearm as far as possible (palm facing up). Normal range of motion is approximately 90 degrees for both pronation and supination.

FIGURE 7-4.

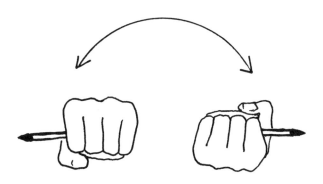

5. Shoulder Abduction

Abduct the arms to 90 degrees, keeping the arms straight. At 90 degrees turn palms up, and continue abduction until the palms come together overhead at 180 degrees.

FIGURE 7-5.

6. Shoulder External Rotation and Abduction
(Apley Scratch Test)

Reach with one hand and touch superior medial angle of the opposite scapula.

FIGURE 7-6.

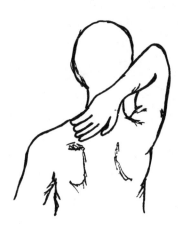

7. Shoulder Internal Rotation and Adduction

a. With one hand touch the inferior angle of the opposite scapula.
b. Touch one hand to the opposite shoulder.

FIGURE 7-7a.   FIGURE 7-7b.

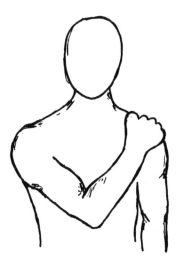   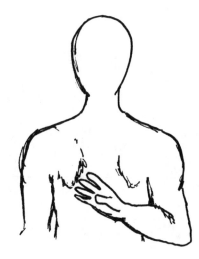

8. Spinal Flexion (sit and reach)

   Use the sit and reach box. Assume a long sitting position with the bare feet against the sit and reach box. Placing one hand on top of another (middle fingers even), reach forward as far as possible and hold for 10 seconds (allow one warm up trial). Using zero as point equivalent to reaching the toes, note the number of plus inches beyond the toes or minus inches below the toes. Few norm are available for adults. Flexibility declines with age.

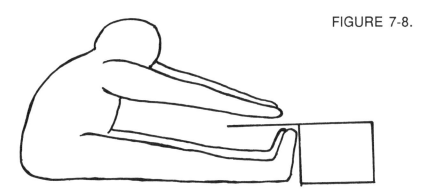

FIGURE 7-8.

9. Hip Flexion (Thomas Test)

   a. Assume a supine position on a table. Flex the hip, bringing one knee up to the chest. The anterior aspect of the thigh should make contact with the abdomen. Repeat to the other side.
   b. Hold one knee into the chest and attempt to extend the other leg. If the straight leg is not able to extend fully, a hip flexion contracture exists. Estimate the angle between the leg and the table at the point of greatest extension.

FIGURE 7-9a.   FIGURE 7-9b.

127

10. <u>Plantarflexion, Dorsiflexion, Inversion, Eversion</u>
From a standing or sitting position:

 a. Plantarflexion: bring the heels off the floor 50 degrees.
 b. Dorsiflexion: bring the toes off the floor 20 degrees.
 c. Eversion: bring the lateral borders of the feet off the floor 5 degrees.
 d. Inversion: bring the medial borders of the feet off the floor 5 degrees.

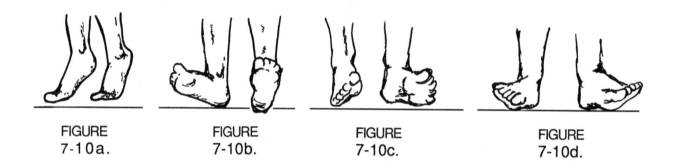

FIGURE
7-10a.

FIGURE
7-10b.

FIGURE
7-10c.

FIGURE
7-10d.

STRETCHING

OPTIMAL CONDITIONS FOR ELICITING A STRETCH

Connective tissue displays both elastic and plastic properties. To increase your flexibility, it is important to effect the plastic properties of connective tissue. The optimal conditions for achieving a more permanent increase in your flexibility includes the following:

1. **Engage in Warm Up Prior to Stretching**
Increasing your tissue temperature will facilitate the viscous properties of your connective tissue, resulting in a greater elongation or stretch. In other words, a warm muscle will stretch farther than a cold one! Warm up may include easy laps around the track until a sweat is broken (5-10 minutes). The same result may be achieved by performing calisthenics in place.

128

2. **Do Not Apply Too Much Force to the Stretch**

Lower amounts of force induce less injury and tearing than high amounts of force. Vigorous and/or ballistic stretching may cause bleeding in the joint, as well as tearing of tissue.

3. **Hold the Stretch for a Sufficient Duration (The Longer The Better)**

Although research has not demonstrated what the optimal duration for a stretch is, it has been agreed that longer durations will produce better results. For purposes of this workshop, it is suggested that each stretch be held for a duration of 30-60 seconds. If executed properly, discomfort felt due to stretching will diminish the longer the stretch is held.

4. **Stretching Should Always Be Performed Through the Pain-Free Range of Motion**

Do not perform stretching if pain, infection or edema is present.

5. **Incorporate Stretches at the End of Your Cool Down to Prevent Adaptive Shortening and Promote Relaxation of Muscle**

Muscle which has been subjected to a vigorous workout will generally be in a contracted state. Performing stretching at the end of the workout will return muscle to its resting length and promote additional elongation of connective tissue.

TECHNIQUES

There are two basic types of stretching techniques: active and passive. Active stretching is performed without assistance using a volitional muscle contraction to move the joint to the end of the range of motion. In contrast, passive stretching occurs without any muscle contraction and is performed by an assistant. The range of motion about joint is usually greater in a passive stretch than an active one. PNF Hold-Relax is a technique which utilizes both active and passive stretching.

ACTIVE STRETCHING (Slow Static)

This technique involves slowly stretching a muscle for 30-60 seconds (or longer) by contracting the opposite muscle group. If proper stretching is to be accomplished, the lengthened muscle must be held at a tension level that does not activate, to any marked extent, the stretch reflex mechanism. After holding the stretch for a period of time, the discomfort of tension should diminish to some degree. At this time, the individual may increase the stretch (i.e., establish a new point of limitation).

Over-stretching is recognized by discomfort that becomes greater the longer the stretch is held or when the lengthened muscle quivers or vibrates. Avoid bouncing or ballistic movements.

An active stretching routine for students in wheelchairs is presented below. Active stretches for ambulatory students are not provided in this section. The reader is referred to the comprehensive book by Anderson (1980) which is listed at the end of this chapter.

PASSIVE STRETCHING

This technique is applied when the individual cannot perform an active stretch. It is performed by the assistant and involves ranging every affected joint to keep it free and flexible. The assistant moves each joint slowly through the PERMISSIBLE range of motion. Hold at the end of each range for 30-60 seconds. Prolonged, moderate stretching is more effective than momentary, vigorous stretching. Two to five repetitions are usually sufficient for passive range of motion.

PNF Hold-Relax

PNF hold-relax is a relaxation/lengthening technique in which the individual isometrically and maximally contracts a muscle group prior to stretching it. When a maximal number of motor units are contracting simultaneously, the Golgi Tendon Organs within that muscle will fire, causing the muscle to relax. This is known as autogenic inhibition. During this post-contraction depression, the Golgi Tendon Organs override the relax activity of the muscle spindles. The individual or an assistant then moves the limb to a new point of limitation (establish a new end range). The maximal contraction lasts for six seconds, as well as the relaxation period which follows. This sequence is repeated until no new further range of motion is obtainable. This technique may be performed in single joint, single plane movements, or more ideally, in the spiral/diagonal PNF patterns.

Hold-Relax Sequence:

1. The assistant (passively) or the student (actively) moves the limb to the point of limitation. Active movement should be encouraged whenever possible. The student then isometrically and maximally contracts the muscle on stretch against a resistance provided by the assistant for SIX SECONDS. The limb should not be allowed to move during this period and the build up to maximal effort should be gradual, not sudden.
2. The student then relaxes the stretched muscle by contracting the opposing muscle while the assistant moves the limb further. This relaxation should last SIX SECONDS. Repeat the sequence of holds and relaxations until no further range is obtained.

CONTRADICTIONS FOR PERFORMING STRETCHING

1. Infections about a joint.
2. Exacerbations (attack) of inflammatory disease, especially when pain is present.
3. Edema (joint capsule is subject to tears)
4. Functional contractures (e.g., finger flexors, elbow flexors, and pronators may actually assist the disabled person to pull objects toward him/her).
5. VIGOROUS STRETCHING OF CONTRACTURES. This may cause bleeding in the joint. It is the role of the physical therapist, not the Adapted Physical Educator, to improve range of motion in severe contractures.

Performance Requirements for Performing Range of Motion

1. Know the motions that occur at each joint (see chapter 2).
2. Stabilize the extremities at the joint; for example, at the elbow or wrist. For someone with a painful joint, such as in arthritis, support the extremity in the muscular area. Try to avoid touching the muscle or tendons being stretched. Stretch in opposition to the line of pull of the muscle.
3. Use a firm but comfortable grip.
4. Perform motions slowly and smoothly.
5. Do not exceed the student's existing range of motion, especially in the case of paralyzed limbs. Movements should not be forceful.
6. Never force a stretch if spasticity occurs. Stop applying force and hold the limb or return to the starting position. When the spasticity has subsided, proceed again more slowly and smoothly.
7. Remember, two-jointed muscles need a two-jointed stretch
   (e.g., hamstrings).
8. To decrease upper extremity tone when stretching the shoulder and arm, spread the thumb and index finger apart.

PASSIVE FLEXIBILITY EXERCISES

SHOULDER AND ELBOW JOINTS

1. With student positioned prone, assistant places hands on either side of shoulder and lifts it off the mat, as if bringing the shoulder blades together.

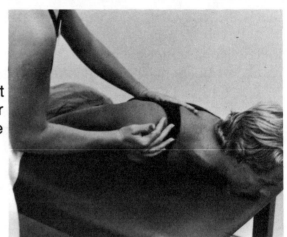

Passive Exercise 7-1.

2. With student supine, assistant places one hand in palm and the other hand on posterior aspect of upper arm. Flex shoulder to end range.

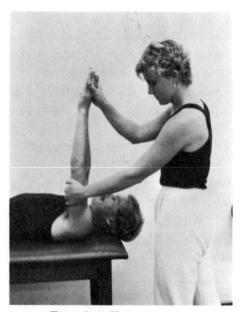

Passive Exercise 7-2.

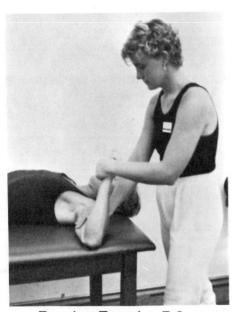

Passive Exercise 7-3.

3. With student supine, shoulder abducted, and elbow flexed, assistant places one hand in palm while the other hand stabilizes upper arm. Externally rotate arm to end range.

132

4. With student sitting, assistant abducts and externally rotates shoulder by placing one hand on posterior aspect of arm, proximal to elbow. The other hand stabilizes at shoulder.

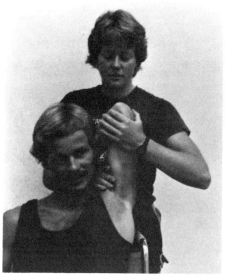

Passive Exercise 7-4.

Passive Exercise 7-5.

5. With student sitting, assistant places hands on palmar side of wrists and horizontally abducts arms. The student's palms should be facing forward.

Passive Exercise 7-6.

WRIST/FINGERS

6. With student sitting and elbows flexed, the assistant places hands on medial side of elbow and pulls elbows back.

7. With student supine and elbow flexed, assistant places one hand in palm while the other hand stabilizes upper arm. Assistant pronates and supinates forearm to each end range.

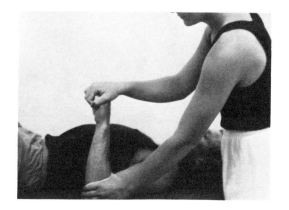

Passive Exercise 7-7.

8. With student supine and elbow flexed, assistant places one hand on dorsum of hand while the other hand stabilizes the elbow. Wrist is flexed to end range.

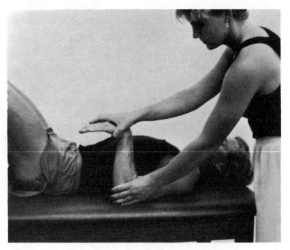

Passive Exercise 7-8.

9. With student supine and elbow flexed, assistant places one hand on palmar surface while the other hand stabilizes elbow. Wrist and fingers are hyperextended to end range.

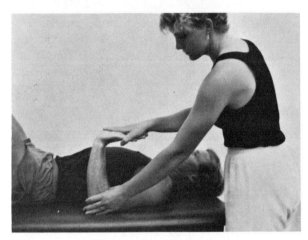

Passive Exercise 7-9.

10. With student supine and elbow flexed, assistant flexes (curls) fingers into a fist.

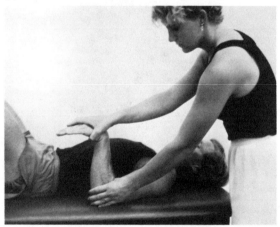

Passive Exercise 7-10.

11. Assistant holds student's fingers in extension while extending thumb.

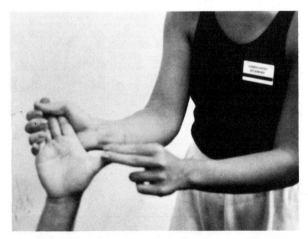

Passive Exercise 7-11.

12. Assistant holds student's fingers in extension while abducting thumb.

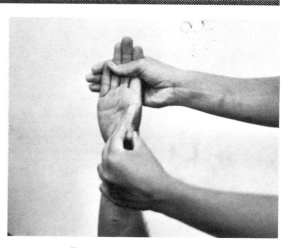

Passive Exercise 7-12.

13. With student supine, assistant places one hand on posterior aspect of thigh while the other hand stabilizes the foot. Assistant flexes hip and knee to end range.

Passive Exercise 7-13.

14. With student supine, assistant places hands on posterior aspect of thigh and lower leg, flexing the hip to end range.

Passive Exercise 7-15.

Passive Exercise 7-14.

15. With student prone, assistant places one hand under the anterior aspect of leg, proximal to knee, while stabilizing hip with the other hand. Hip is hyperextended to end range.

16. With student side-lying, assistant abducts leg by placing one hand under the medial aspect of the knee joint while the other hand stabilizes the hip.

Passive Exercise 7-16.

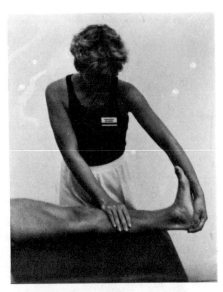

Passive Exercise 7-17.

17. With student supine, assist plantarflexes foot by placing one hand under heel (assistant's forearm rests on plantar surface) while the other hand stabilizes the lower leg.

Wheelchair Stretching Routines

1. Reach one arm across chest. Use other to stretch to end range.

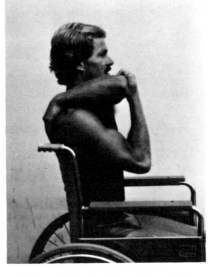

Wheelchair Exercise 7-1.

2. Reach arm behind head as if to touch opposite scapula. Use other to stretch arm further.

Wheelchair Exercise 7-3.

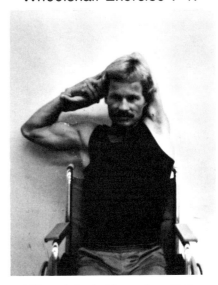

Wheelchair Exercise 7-2.

3. Interlock fingers, keep elbows extended, and flex shoulders, bringing arms above head.

4. Grasp hands behind back and flex forward, attempting to bring hands up as high as possible.

Wheelchair Exercise 7-4.

5. Abduct arm (elbow extended) so upper arm is near the ear. Laterally flex trunk. If necessary, hold on to wheelrim with opposite hand. Repeat to other side.

Wheelchair Exercise 7-5.

6. Flex forward, reaching hands out in front.

Wheelchair Exercise 7-6.

7. Hyperextend wrist and fingers by using other hand to pull back.

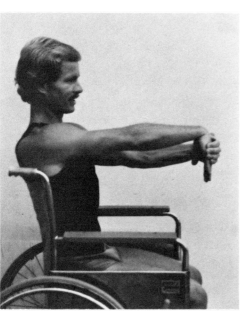

Wheelchair Exercise 7-8.

Wheelchair Exercise 7-7.

8. Flex wrist by using other hand to pull down.

STUDY QUESTIONS

1. Describe the technique of active stretching.

2. What are the advantages of active stretching vs. passive?

REFERENCES

Anderson, B. (1980). Stretching. Bolinas, CA: Shelter Publications

Sapega, A.A., Quenfeld, T.C., Moyer, R.A., and Butler, R.A. (1981) Biophysical factor in range-of-motion exercise. Physician and sports medicine, 9,(12), 57-65.

Talbot, D., Pearson, V., and Loeper, J. (1978). Disuse Syndrome:The Preventable Disability. Minneapolis: Sister Kennedy Institute

Toohey, P. & Larson, C.W. (1977). Range-of-Motion exercise: key to joint mobility. Minneapolis: Sister Kennedy Institute.1.   How you increase the hamstring flexibility in a student.

CHAPTER 8

ASSESSMENT OF AND PROGRAMMING FOR CARDIOVASCULAR ENDURANCE

ASSESSMENT OF CARDIOVASCULAR ENDURANCE

Testing for cardiovascular endurance includes a variety of methods and equipment, reflecting the wide difference in capabilities found among disabled adults. This section will provide protocol for submaximal tests in arm crank ergometry, leg cycle ergometry, and jogging.

ARM CRANK ERGOMETRY

Due to lower extremity paralysis found in quadriplegia and paraplegia, arm pedaling or wheelchair pushing have become standard methods for cardiovascular testing. The following is a partial list of ergometric equipment in use today for aerobic testing utilizing the arms (Figoni, 1982):

1. Wheelchair treadmills
   a. electric
   b. platform with rollers (free wheeling)
2. Arm crank ergometers
   a. friction
      i) Monark rehab trainers
      ii) Monark cycle ergometer (mounted on table)
   b. electromagnetically - braked
3. Wheelchair ergometers (interfaced with Monark cycle ergometer, Cybex, or electronic cycle ergometer)

Fitness testing for the physically disabled has included multi-stage progressive workloads of both continuous (load increased every one to six minutes until a maximal heart rate is achieved) and discontinuous (three to six minute bouts with load changes separated by one to five minute rest periods) protocols. Dreisinger (1982) has indicated that wheelchair ergometry yielded similar VO2MAX, heart rate, and systolic blood pressure, whether performed as a continuous or discontinuous test.

Several factors must be considered when determining heart rate response during testing. Stenberg and associates (1967) have demonstrated that the maximal heart rate averages approximately 11 beats per minute lower for arm than for leg exercise. Thus, when using Karvonen's predicted, age-adjusted maximal heart rate (220 - age) for determining work intensity, one must subtract about 10 beats per minute to correct for arm exercise.

In spinal cord injuries, especially cervical and high thoracic lesions, paralysis of the trunk and extremities limits significant heart rate increases. In addition, current research has indicated that responses in the sympathetic nervous system to exercise become increasingly deficient the higher the lesion in the spinal cord (Nillson et al., 1975; Wolf & Magora, 1976; Knutsson et al, 1973). In lesions above T-6, the inadequate regulation of the heart slows the development of exercise tachycardia. Increases in heart rate during exercise are generally restricted to between 100 and 130 beats per minute, even though a maximal effort is present.

Cadence during testing will vary depending upon the equipment used. Studies involving arm pedaling have used cadences between 50 and 70 rpm, while lower values were required for wheelchair ergometry. Although most researchers have found greater performances with arm crank ergometry than wheelchair ergometers, correlation data between the two has been high (Wicks et al., 1977).

Precautions During Testing

1. To facilitate the dissipation of body heat generated during aerobic exercise, have a fan blowing on the individual. Perspiring does not occur below the level of the lesion. Quadriplegics are especially prone to overheating.
2. Empty the bladder prior to exercise to minimize the effects on circulation of hyperactive distension reflexes or autonomic dysreflexia (Knutsson et al., 1973).
3. When testing untrained or elderly individuals, closely monitor the cardiovascular response (heart rate, heart rhythm, and blood pressure).
4. Orthostatic reactions (e.g., venous pooling, slugging blood pressure) resulting in faintness, require placement of placing the student in a horizontal position. The level of injury is not entirely accurate in determining orthostatic reactions.

Protocol for Submaximal Arm Ergometry Test (Monark Rehab Cycler)

1. The evaluation form used in conjunction with the test is provided following this listing (see "Arm and Leg Cycle Ergometer Work Test").
2. Adjust the height of the hand pedal crank so the fulcrum is at shoulder level.
3. Use a metronome to establish the cadence.
   Quadriplegics: 50-70 rpm

Paraplegics: 60-70 rpm
A pace of 65 rpm is considered to be the most mechanically efficient.
4. Take a resting heart rate and blood pressure.
5. Work stages are three to four minutes in duration.
6. Load: begin with zero load.
    Load increments with each stage will vary according to individual capabilities.
    Quadriplegics: 1/8 - 1/4 kp per stage (37.5 - 75 kpm) or 5 watts.
    Paraplegics: 1/4 -1/2 kp per stage (75 - 150 kpm) or 10 watts.
7. Following each stage, there is a five minute rest period between loads.
8. Take the heart rate and blood pressure at the beginning of the rest period.
9. The normal responses of blood pressure to exercise are the following: Systolic - progressive increase with incremental workloads. Diastolic - no change or slight decrease (less than 10 mm Hg during progressive workloads.
10. For individuals with lesions above T-6, the heart rate response will not correlate well with effort; thus, continue to test until fatigue is reached.
11. Do not test individuals with resting blood pressure exceeding 140/90 without prior medical approval.
12. If the student experiences pain or pressure in the chest, pain radiating into the left arm and/or jaw, nausea, faintness, or troublesome shortness of breath, the test must be discontinued. See "Contraindications for Exercise Testing" and "Indications for Terminating an Exercise Test". Exercise tests on persons over 40 years of age should be discontinued if the heart rate exceeds 140 beats per minute.
13. Take recovery heart rate and blood pressure two and five minutes after cessation of exercise.

ARM AND LEG CYCLE ERGOMETERS - SUBMAXIMAL EXERCISE TEST

NAME_____ DATE_____ AGE_____ SEX_____

HEIGHT_____in. WEIGHT_____lb. PREDICTED MAXIMUM HEART RATE_____bpm

#1 PRE-SEMESTER WORK TEST: DATE OF TEST_____ TIME OF DAY_____

RESTING HR_____bpm RESTING BP (mm Hg) #1_____ #2_____ #3_____ TARGET HR_____bpm

Time (min)	Load (kp)	Rate (rpm)	Work Rate (kpm/min)	Heart Rate (bpm)	Blood Pressure (mm Hg)	Mets	Comments/Symptons
0-2	Rec.						
4-5	Rec.						

#2 MID-SEMESTER WORK TEST: DATE OF TEST_____ TIME OF DAY_____

RESTING HR_____bpm RESTING BP (mm Hg) #1_____ #2_____ #3_____ TARGET HR_____bpm

Time (min)	Load (kp)	Rate (rpm)	Work Rate (kpm/min)	Heart Rate (bpm)	Blood Pressure (mm Hg)	Mets	Comments/Symptons
0-2	Rec.						
4-5	Rec.						

#3 POST-SEMESTER WORK TEST: DATE OF TEST_____ TIME OF DAY_____

RESTING HR_____bpm RESTING BP (mm Hg) #1_____ #2_____ #3_____ TARGET HR_____bpm

Time (min)	Load (kp)	Rate (rpm)	Work Rate (kpm/min)	Heart Rate (bpm)	Blood Pressure (mm Hg)	Mets	Comments/Symptons
0-2	Rec.						
4-5	Rec.						

TESTING PROTOCOL FOR SUBMAXIMAL LEG CYCLE ERGOMETRY
(Monark or Bodyguard Stationary Cycles)

1. Use the same evaluation form as for arm crank ergometry.
2. The seat height should be adjusted so that when the front part of the foot is on the pedal, there is approximately 15 degrees of flexion in the knee. This is the most effective position during heavy work.
3. Take a resting heart rate and blood pressure. Do not test a student with a blood pressure greater than 140/90 without medical consultation.
4. With the subject seat on the bicycle, but without touching the pedals, set the mark on the pendulum to "0" on the scale.
5. Use a metronome to establish the cadence.
    50 rpm   untrained, elderly, neurologic injury
    60-70 rpm   trained
6. Begin the test with the brake belt slack. When the correct cadence is achieved, set the desired workload and start the stopwatch.
    Suggest Beginning Loads
    300 kpm/min = 1 kp   untrained, elderly, neurologic injury
    600 kmp/min = 2 kp   trained males and females
7. Three minute work stages should be used.
8. Increase the load by 1/2 - 1 kp per stage (150 - 300 kpm).
9. Continue to test as long as the heart rate remains below 70% of the predicted maximum. Discontinue the test if the heart rate rises above 140 beats per minute for elderly students.
10. Take heart rate and blood pressure at the end of each work stage while the subject continues to pedal (last 15 seconds).
11. See normal blood pressure response during exercise under Testing Protocol for Arm Crank Ergometry.
12. See Contraindications to Exercise Testing and Indications for Terminating after cessation of exercise.
13. Take recovery heart rate and blood pressure two and five minutes after cessation of exercise.

ASSESSMENT OF CARDIOVASCULAR ENDURANCE IN AMBULATORY PERSONS

There are several methods to assess cardiovascular endurance in ambulatory student. The two most common methods are the 12 minute Run-Walk and the Step Test.

12 Minute Run-Walk

The goal of this test is to have the student cover as much distance as possible in 12 minutes. It is best to perform the test on track for ease of calculations. It is useful to place cones every 100 yards to facilitate measurement of the distance. For norms, see Cooper (1977) in the reference section at the end of this chapter. This test can be used to determine pre- and post-training levels of aerobic fitness.

Key Step Test

Another practical test that requires very little equipment is the Step Test. This test, along with the bicycle ergometer, is excellent for assessing visually impaired students. This test is also appropriate for all ages and both sexes. Since the test lasts only three minutes, only extremely unfit individuals would find this test too vigorous. Obviously, this test should only be performed if the student has been given a medical clearance by a physician.

The protocol of the test involves stepping up and down on a 12-inch high bench for three minutes at a pace of 24 steps per minute. After three minutes, immediately take the pulse. For further clarification of the test and listing of norms, see Kasch and Boyer (1968) in the reference section at the end of this chapter.

TECHNIQUES IN TRAINING FOR CARDIOVASCULAR ENDURANCE

Part of the disuse syndrome that occurs when an individual is immobilized in a chair is the loss of cardiovascular endurance. This reduction in aerobic capacity has many health implications in regards to obesity and heart disease. Regular, moderate physical activity may aid efforts to control cigarette smoking, hypertension, lipid abnormalities, diabetes, obesity, and emotional stress (American Heart Association, 1981). The following section provides some guidelines for instituting a cardiovascular training program for non-ambulatory students.

ARM CRANK ERGOMETRY

Duration of Exercise

Studies involving arm pedaling have primarily used interval training for improving fitness parameters of those with lower extremity disabilities. Significant improvements in physiological responses have occurred using three to four bouts of four minute durations with two to three minute rest intervals (Glasser et al., 1981). Pollock and associates (1974) alternated equal one minute intervals of high and low work bouts, progressing to 30 minutes of continuous high workload by the 19th week of training (see Table 3-2).

Frequency of Exercise

Researchers generally agree that frequency of training should occur between three to five times per week.

Intensity of Exercise - Target Heart Rate

The purpose of the target heart rate (THR) is to establish the intensity of exercise necessary to produce a training effect on the cardiovascular system. Several factors must be considered when determining THR for arm crank ergometry. The maximal heart rate averages about 10 beats lower for arm than for leg work. Thus, when using Karvonen's age-adjusted maximal heart rate (220-age) for determining work intensity, subtract 10 beats to correct for arm exercise (i.e., 210-age). Maximal heart rate decreases with age. Trained and untrained men and women of the same age have approximately the same maximal heart rates. Resting heart rates can be obtained by taking a 60 second count prior to the exercise bout.

Formula

Karvonen's Formula - Adjusted for Arm Crank Ergometry
(use for spinal cord lesions below T-6)

			Example:
	210		210
-	_____	(subtract age)	- 20
	_____	(age-adjusted, predicted maximum HR)	190
-	_____	(subtract resting heart rate)	- 70
	_____		120
x	_____	(multiply by exercise intensity, 60-80%)	x .70
	_____		84.00
+	_____	(add resting heart rate)	+ 70
	_____	(THR in beats per minute)	154 THR

The percentage entered into the formula for the intensity depends on how much training one has had in the past. The following percentages are recommended:

Over 30 years of age	beginning	60-70%
College age	beginning	70-80%
Trained	less than tow years	75-85%
Trained	more than two years	85-95%

Due to disturbances in the sympathetic nervous system and partial paralysis of the arm and shoulder musculature, persons with lesions above T-6 cannot use the Karvonen formula (deficient exercise tachycardia). The heart rate reaches a ceiling between approximately 100-130 beats/minute. Therefore, the individual at this level should attempt to achieve his/her ceiling heart rate.

Training Cadence (revolutions per minute)

Quadriplegics:	55-65rpm
Paraplegics:	65

TABLE 8-1. Interval Training for Adults with Quadriplegia and Paraplegia				
Level of Lesion	Pace	Duration	Intensity	Frequency
C-4 to C-8	50-70 rpm	30 sec. exercise 30 sec. rest until fatigue or 3 exercise bouts: 2-4 min. each 2-3 min. rest	Ceiling HR (100-130 beats per minute)	3-5 x/week
T-1 to T-6	60-70 rpm	3 exercise bouts: 4 min. each 2 min. rest or 1 min. high load 1 min. low load for 10-30 min.	Ceiling HR (unless over 140-150 beats per minute)	3-5 x/week
T-7 and below	60-70 rpm	same as for T-1 to T-6	70-80% of maximum (Karvonen's formula)	3-5 x/week

Note: The same precautions that apply to arm crank testing should be followed for arm crank training.

LEG CYCLE ERGOMETRY

The principles for leg cycle ergometry are very similar to those presented for arm crank ergometry. Precautions and contraindications for testing and training should be reviewed.

Duration
Interval training may be used for those initially beginning a program. The work and rest periods will vary depending upon the individual. Three bouts are recommended with approximately two minutes of rest between each. The duration of

each bout will depend upon the age, training level, and disability of the student. If a continuous training bout is used, 15 to 60 minutes is suggested.

Intensity

Use Karvonen's formula for determining the THR. A modified version of this formula was presented earlier. The same formula should be used but with the following change:

$$\frac{220 \\ -\underline{\qquad}}{\underline{\qquad}} \quad \text{(age)}$$

(age-adjusted, predicted maximum HR)

After this computation, the remainder of the formula can be used. The same guidelines for selection of intensity that were used for arm crank ergometry may be applied to leg work.

Frequency

Three to five days a week are recommended.

How to Take Pulse Rate

1. Take the pulse at the thumb side of the wrist on the palm or inner side of the forearm, as shown in Figure 3-1a. Place your fingers at the area marked "X" and you will feel a throb there. Do not use your thumb because it has its own pulse.
2. Look at the second hand of a clock and count how many beats you feel in 10 seconds. Multiply this by six to obtain the pulse rate for one minute. If the pulse is weak and irregular, count for a full minute.
3. If the pulse is difficult to feel or cannot be found at the wrist, use the temple or under the jaw at the carotid artery as shown in Figure 3-1b.

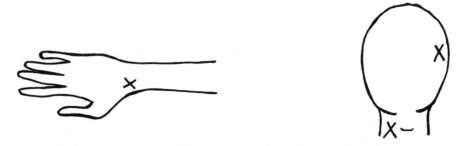

FIGURE 8-1. Locations for Taking Pulse.

150

<u>Determining Workload for Arm and Leg Cycle Ergometry</u> (Monark and Bodyguard)

The circumference of the ergometer wheel equals six meters on leg cycles and three meters on arm cycles. If the cadence is 50 rpm, the distance covered would be 300 and 150 meters per minute, respectively.

The wheel is mechanically braked by a belt strapped around the rim. This belt is adjusted by a handwheel, providing resistance which is measured in kiloponds. A kilopond is the force acting upon the mass of one kilogram at normal acceleration of gravity.

Computation for Work Rate:

$$\#kp \; * \; m/min \; = \; kpm/min$$

Where

#kp   = number of kiloponds set by adjustment of belt tension.
m/min = distance pedaled in meters per minute.
         (multiply circumference of wheel by cadence)

A kilopond meter (kpm) is defined as the work necessary to lift a one kilogram mass one meter against normal gravitational force. Expressed per minute, the work rate is written as kpm/min. A watt is a unit of power equal to 6.12 kpm/min.REFERENCES

STUDY QUESTIONS

1. What are the three components involved in a cardiovascular training program?

2. Use Karvonen's Formula to find your target heart rate.

REFERENCES

American College of Sportsmedicine (1983). Reference guide for workshop/certification programs in preventive/rehabilitative exercise.

Fox, S.M., Naughton, S.P., & Haskell, W.L. (1971). Physical activity and the prevention of coronary heart disease. Annuals of Clinical Research, 3, 404.

American Heart Association. Subcommittee on Exercise/Cardiac Rehabilitation (1981). Statement on Exercise. Circulation, 64, 1302A.

Pollock, M.L., Miller, H.S., Linnerud, A.C., Laughridge, E., Coleman, E. (1974)., & Alexander, E., Arm pedaling as an endurance training regimen for the disabled. Archives of Physical Medicine Rehabilitation, 55, 252-261.

Sherrington, C. (1947). The integrative action of the nervous system (2nd edition). New Haven: Yale University Press.

CHAPTER 9

ASSESSMENT AND PROGRAMMING FOR GAIT

ASSESSMENT OF GAIT

The assessment of gait may range from simple clinical observations to complex laboratory testing with video tape, digitization, force plate switches, and electromyography. This section will focus on utilizing clinical observations, as well as present a simple quantitative method, for performing gait evaluations.

NORMAL GAIT

Normal gait is typically evaluated by examining the gait or step cycle (heelstrike to heelstrike of the same foot). There are two phases in the gait cycle (see Figure 2-2):

1. Stance phase (60% of gait cycle).
   -period of partial or full weight bearing.
   -Begins with heelstrike and ends when same foot is plantarflexed in toe-off and weight is shifted to other extremity.
   -Divided into three stages known as heelstrike, midstance (weight shifted from heel to ball of foot), and toe-off.
2. Swing Phase 40% of gait cycle).
   -Begins as weight is shifted off extremity with accompanying hip and knee flexion. Ends when knee is in full extension prior to heelstrike.
   -Divided into three stages known as acceleration, midswing, and deceleration.

STANCE PHASE

a.   b.   c.

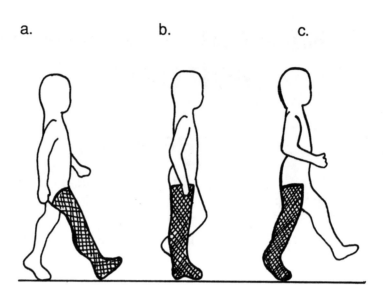

SWING PHASE

a.   b.   c.

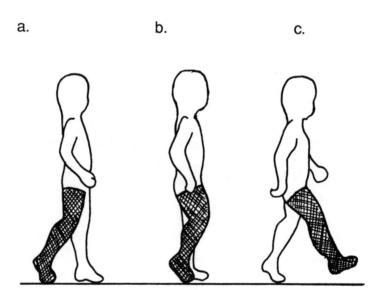

FIGURE 9-1. One Step Cycle.

154

Components of Normal Gait (Daniels & Worthingham, 1972; Hoppenfeld, 1976)

1. Head erect.
2. Shoulders level.
3. Trunk vertical.
4. Base of support: two to four inches from heel to heel.
5. Arms swing reciprocally and with equal amplitude.
6. Steps are the same length.
7. Vertical oscillations of the center of gravity (COG) are about two inches and even in tempo.
8. Knee flexes in stance (except at heelstrike) to prevent excessive vertical rise in the COG.
9. Pelvis slightly rotates in the transverse plane (four degrees).
10. Pelvis tilts in the frontal plane (five degrees downward).
11. Pelvis laterally tilts toward the supporting leg.
12. Pelvis and trunk shift laterally approximately one inch toward the supporting leg to center the body weight over the hip.
13. During swing the pelvis rotates 40 degrees forward and the opposite hip acts a fulcrum for rotation.
14. Average walking speed: three feet/second or 2-2.5 mph.
15. Average cadence: 90-120 steps/minute.
16. Average step length: 15 inches.

CLINICAL OBSERVATION

1. If possible, have the student walk barefoot in short pants or swimsuit.
2. If possible, observe the student walking both with and without supportive devices/ambulation aids.
3. Ask the student to walk about 25 feet away from the examiner. If possible, the student should make several excursions to allow observations from anterior, posterior, and lateral views, and to determine any consistent patterns.
4. If possible, observe the student walking at several speeds, ascending/descending stairs, and sitting/rising.
5. Note any dominant positions/posture of the arms, trunk, and legs.
6. Observe the stance phase first. Many problems become distinct during this phase since it accounts for 60% of the gait cycle and the affected extremity must assume full weight bearing.
7. Observe body segments separately (i.e., foot, knee, hip, trunk, and arms) in anterior, posterior, and lateral views.
8. Listen as well as look for disorders. Certain gait abnormalities will result in uneven step tempo, slapping or scraping sounds.

ABNORMAL GAIT PATTERNS (Dunn, 1982)

Gait	Characteristics
Gait	**Characteristics**
1. Antalgic	-pain on weightbearing -quick stance on affected lower extremity (LE) -short stride (swing) -less flexion of affected LE
2. Ataxic a. cerebellar	-wide-based, staggering gait -loss of stability with eyes open or closed -unilateral lesions result in sway toward side of lesion -may have foot stamping
b. spinal	-loss of position sense with eyes closed (involvement of proprioceptive pathways) -may evidence foot foot slap
3. Festinating	-short, accelerating shuffling steps
4. Dystrophic	-wide-based waddling gait with lateral lurch and trunk hyperextended.
5. Spastic/Scissors	-excessive hip flexion internal rotation and adduction -knee flexion or extension -ankles may be plantarflexed -knees cross in front of one another during gait due to spasticity -toes may drag
6. Steppage/Dropfoot	-excess hip and knee flexion during swing due to foot drop (flaccid dorsiflexors) -instead of heelstrike there is a plantigrade footplant (flat foot landing)
7. Trendelenburg	-gluteus medius lurch -exaggerated drop of the pelvis toward unaffected side during stance phase of the affected extremity
8. Circumducted	-during swing, circumduction of the hip so the lower leg and foot clear the ground -may also involve tilting the pelvis upward

QUANTITATIVE GAIT EVALUATION ("see Gait Analysis form")

A simple method has been developed by Robinson and Smidt (1981) which calculates the following temporal and distance factors of gait: velocity, cadence, stride length, and step length. This quantitative form of evaluation allows one to determine improvements which may not be readily observable to the eye. The method requires very little equipment (homemade grid floor pattern, stopwatch, tape measure, and portable tape recorder) and a minimum space and time. More specific details of the method can be found in Robinson and Smidt, "quantitative Gait Evaluation in the Clinic", Physical Therapy, March, 1981 (volume 61, number 3).

GAIT ANALYSIS

Name ———————————————————————— Date ——————————

Disability ——————————————————————————————————

Ambulatory Aids———————————————————————————————

GAIT PATTERN	RIGHT	LEFT
1. Antalgic		
2. Ataxic		
3. Festinating		
4. Dystrophic/Waddling		
5. Spastic/Scissors		
6. Steppage		
7. Trendelenburg		
8. Circumducted		
9. Foot		
10. Hip/Knee		
11. Trunk/Arms		
12. Other		

TEMPORAL AND DISTANCE FACTORS

1. Average Velocity

$$= \text{_____} \text{in/} \text{_____} \text{sec}$$

$$= \text{_____} \text{in/sec}$$

2. Average Cadence (90-120)

$$= \text{_____} \text{steps/sec} * 60$$

$$= \text{_____} \text{steps/min}$$

3. Average Stride Length   = R ————————in

4. Average Step Length   = R ————————in

L ————————in

158

TECHNIQUES IN GAIT TRAINING

Role of Adapted Physical Educator in Gait Training (Mason & Dando, 1979)

1. <u>Development of strength and endurance in muscles utilized in walking</u>. This includes muscles of the lower extremities, particularly the flexors and extensors of the hip, knee, and ankle. Strengthening muscles of the trunk and hip aids further stability during walking. Whenever possible, strength should be developed in whole patterns of movement (i.e., multi-joint movement) rather than single joint. This will allow more transfer to the desired skill.
2. <u>Development of even length and timing of steps</u>. The length of the step on the affected extremity will be shortened. The student should be encouraged to take larger steps on the affected side. A metronome may be utilized to aid with tempo of steps.
3. <u>Instruction in proper placement of feet, legs, trunk, and arms to facilitate stability and coordination</u>. Consistent cues and constant feedback should be provided to the student by the assistant. This requires careful observation by the assistant. Skill feedback is usually provided in the following areas:
   a. heel-strike (heel to toe progression of the foot).
   b. direction of forefoot (should point in line of travel).
   c. degree of flexion or hyperextension in the knee.
   d. lateral tilt of the pelvis.
   e. anterior tilt of the pelvis.
   f. relaxed, reciprocal movement of the arms.
4. <u>Development of dynamic balance and transfer of weight</u>. See the balance progression provided earlier in this chapter.
5. <u>Development of flexibility</u>. Contractures and spasticity may interfere the gait pattern.

Progression in Gait Training

1. Standing Frame
2. Kinetron
3. Parallel Bars
4. Walker
5. Crutches
6. Cane
7. Unsupported Gait

Kinetron Progression

1. Purpose - to increase or regain
   a. weight-bearing strength and endurance.
   b. range of motion in the hip, knee, and ankle.
   c. power (quickness) in extension and flexion;
      i.e., development of necessary forces quickly enough for efficient ambulation.
   d. coordination of weight transfer (reciprocate bilaterally).
2. Positioning
   a. adjust the length of kinetron arm so the foot pedals are at a comfortable distance from the seat.
   b. height of the actuator sets the degree of hip and knee flexion.
   c. height of seat determines the degree of hip and knee extension desired in the pattern of movement and the height of the arm rest.
   d. speed selector dials establishes the speed of movement on left and right sides.
3. Testing
   a. Warm-up: 10 submaximal efforts
   b. Have student perform a maximal thrust (hip and knee extension) on both affected and unaffected extremities at a selected speed. The highest reading on the gauge for the unaffected leg then becomes the goal for the affected leg.
4. Progression
   a. Retrain the ability to reciprocate bilaterally.
   b. Develop measured levels of weight-bearing. Achieve pressure gauge reading of 100-150 psi at all speeds. Begin at speeds of 1, 2, or 3 and progress to higher speeds. If necessary, the affected side may work at a slower speed to achieve 100-150 psi while the unaffected side continues to work submaximally at 3. When increasing the speed beyond 3, work both sides together. For strength, use a speed setting of 4. For functional strength, use a speed setting of 5.
   c. If necessary, use weights on rear tube of unaffected side to allow for passive extension of affected leg.
   d. Begin with 3 sets of 10 repetitions (strength) and progress to continuous 1-2 minute intervals (endurance).
   e. To achieve a more vertical position:
      -raise seat height
      -shorten arm length
      -bring seat back forward
   f. Have the individual strive to raise the foot (during knee and hip flexion) ahead of the rising footplate.

Gait Training with Crutches and Canes

There are approximately nine different types of crutch gaits. Selection depends upon the student's ability to take steps with either or both of the lower extremities (Sorenson & Ulrich, 1977).

FOUR-POINT ALTERNATE GAIT
1. right crutch
2. left foot
3. left crutch
4. right foot

TWO-POINT ALTERNATE GAIT
1. right crutch and left foot (simultaneously)
2. left crutch and right foot (simultaneously)

THREE-POINT GAIT
1. both crutches and the weak extremity
2. strong lower extremity

TRIPOD ALTERNATING GAIT
1. right crutch
2. left crutch
3. drag body

TRIPOD SIMULTANEOUS GAIT
1. both crutches (simultaneously)
2. drag body, both legs (simultaneously)

SWING-TO-GAIT
1. both crutches (simultaneously)
2. lift body and swing legs (simultaneously) to crutches

SWING-THROUGH GAIT
1. both crutches, simultaneously
2. lift both legs and swing beyond crutches (simultaneously)

ROCKING CHAIR GAIT
1. both crutches
2. one foot, alternating with
3. the other foot

TWO POINT AMPUTEE GAIT
1. right foot and right crutch (simultaneously)
2. left foot and left crutch (simultaneously)

Crutch Activities (Mason & Dando, 1978)
1. walking backward and sideward.
2. turning around.
3. opening and closing doors.
4. sitting down and standing up.
5. ascending and descending ramps, stairs, and curbs.
6. getting to and from floor from a standing position.
7. falling safely.
8. going over obstacles.
9. picking up objects from the floor.
10. carrying objects.

Ascending and Descending Stairs
When ascending stairs:
1. step up with the stronger leg
2. ambulatory aid is brought up (if being used)
3. bring up the weaker leg

When descending stairs:
1. ambulatory aid is brought down (if being used)
2. step down with weaker leg
3. bring down the stronger leg

Additional Ambulation Exercises (De Anza College, CA)
1. forward walking
2. backward walking
3. side walking
4. cross-over sideways - front and back
5. knee bends
6. high knee walking
7. bent knee walking
8. step over obstacles
9. treadmill - 1 mph, 3% grade
10. metronome walking
11. obstacle course
12. bicycle (stationary and three wheel)

Additional Teaching Tips

1. If a student has difficulty with coordinating a reciprocal arm swing, have him/her hold a cane in each hand. An assistant should stand behind the student, grasp the canes, and manually assist the student to achieve the proper coordination during walking.
2. A walking belt should be wore by the student during gait training. This provides the assistant with a grip to aid the student in stability.
3. If a student falls during gait training, the assistant should not attempt to hold the person up but break the fall by slowly lowering him/her to the ground with an eccentric contraction of the legs. This prevents injury to the assistant's back.
4. Sensory loss (proprioception) in the upper and lower extremities may affect balance and confidence during training. Use a mirror whenever possible and provide feedback regarding body positions.
5. If the student is using only one cane or crutch, make sure it is placed in the hand opposite the extremity.
6. Check to see that the height of the parallel bars, canes, or crutches allow for 15-30 degrees of flexion at the elbow.

STUDY QUESTIONS

1. What ideas do you have to help teach ambulation skills?

2. Someone who walks like they are drunk would be manifesting what type of gait?

REFERENCES

De Anza College. Adapted Physical Education Manual. Cupertino, CA 1984.

Mason, E., & Dando, H. Corrected Therapy and Adapted Physical Education.
(1975). Chillicothe, Ohio: American Corrective Therapy Association, Inc.

Moore, R. (1981). Handout for Therapeutic Exercise, San Diego State University,
    San Diego, CA.

Sorenson, L. & Ulrich, P.G. (1977). Ambulation Guide for Nurses (revised ed.).
    Minneapolis: Sister Kennedy Institute.

CHAPTER 10

ASSESSMENT AND PROGRAMMING OF PERCEPTUAL-MOTOR SKILLS

DEFINITION OF THE PERCEPTUAL-MOTOR PROCESS

The perceptual-motor process can be viewed as a continuous cycle of the following events:

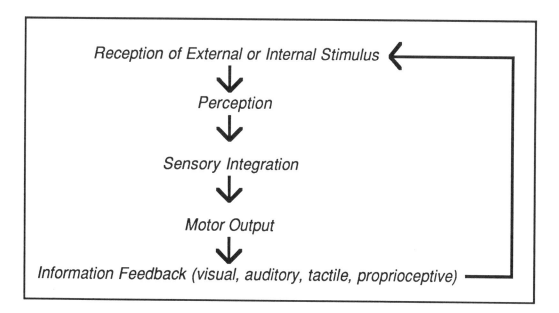

According to Harris (1983), the term perception refers to ". . . .the detection, recognition, discrimination, and interpretation of simple stimuli received through the individual sense modalities." The four regions of the brain which are responsible for perception are (1) cerebral cortex; (2) thalamus; (3) hypothalamus; and (4) cerebellum (Sherrill, 1981).

The following disabilities are typically associated with perceptual-motor deficiencies: learning disabilities, mental retardation, emotional disturbances, spinal bifida, cerebral palsy, multiply sclerosis, Freiderich's Ataxia, stroke, and aphasia. The natural course of aging can bring on perceptual-motor deficiencies, as well as the degeneration of the central and peripheral nervous systems. Perceptual-motor impairments may also be present with the following behavioral traits (Lerch et al., 1974): hyperactivity, emotional lability, short attention span, distractibility, and impulsivity.

Perceptual-motor tests which are standardized and include norms for the adult do not exist. This requires the Adapted Physical Educator at the post-secondary level to design a criterion-referenced test or survey. The instructor should select items which have "face validity" or borrow items from formal perceptual-motor tests for children. The survey should be comprehensive in scope since those with perceptual-motor deficiencies are a very heterogeneous group. The most frequently assessed areas in perceptual-motor functioning are listed below.

GROSS MOTOR
    Balance
        Static
        Dynamic
    Intersensory Coordination
        Eye-Hand
        Eye-Foot
    Kinesthesis
        Body Awareness
        Laterality
        Bilateral Coordination or Integration
    Motor planning (praxia)
FINE MOTOR
    Intersensory Coordination
        Eye-Hand (e.g., copying shapes, buttoning, cutting)
        Kinesthesis (e.g., finger opposition)
VISUAL PERCEPTION
    Spatial Awareness/Orientation
    Figure-Ground
    Memory
    Discrimination
    Ocular Tracking
AUDITORY PERCEPTION
    Figure-Ground
    Memory (e.g., remembering a series of directions)
    Discrimination
TACTILE PERCEPTION
    One-point Discrimination
    Two-point Discrimination

The following perceptual-motor checklist can be used to screen students suspected of having deficiencies in one or more areas. This will guide the instructor in determining which areas require more rigorous evaluation. For a more comprehensive listing of perceptual-motor test items, the reader is referred to excellent books by Lerch et al. (1974), Pyfer and Johnson (1983), Evans (1980), Williams (1983), Cratty (1970), and Sherrill (1981).

PERCEPTUAL-MOTOR CHECKLIST
(adapted from Sherrill, 1981)

1. Does not demonstrate opposition of limbs during walking/running.
2. Fails to shift weight from one foot to the other when throwing.
3. Fails to imitate various body positions of evaluator or identify body parts on command.
4. Evidences flaccid muscle tone.
5. Is unable to use one body part without "overflow" into another.
6. Is unable to keep rhythm by clapping hands or tapping feet.
7. Cannot jump rope.
8. Is unable to coordinate the hands at the midline or cross the midline with one hand during activities.
9. Has difficulty identifying the right and left sides of the body.
10. Has difficulty distinguishing between vertical, horizontal, up, down, and other directions in space.
11. Cannot hop.
12. Has difficulty maintaining balance on one foot.
13. Has difficulty tieing shoes, using scissors, manipulating small objects.
14. Has difficulty staying between lines.
15. Cannot discriminate tactually between different textures, shapes, and sizes.
16. Fails to maintain eye contact with moving objects.
17. Bumps into things; misjudges locations when moving to them. Is unable to move between or through objects.
18. Fails to match geometric shapes to one another (visually).
19. Cannot recognize letters and numbers.
20. Cannot distinguish between foreground and background in a picture.
21. Has difficulty catching balls.
22. Has difficulty walking on the balance beam.

PERCEPTUAL-MOTOR SKILL PROGRESSIONS

Perceptual-motor skills generally refer to a person's ability to receive, interpret, and respond appropriately to a sensory stimuli. A comprehensive program to enhance perceptual-motor skills should provide activities involving the visual, auditory, tactile, and proprioceptive (vestibular and kinesthetic) senses.

A perceptual-motor program may be useful for remediating many neurologic dysfunctions: brain trauma, learning disabilities, mental retardation, aphasia, cerebral palsy, multiply sclerosis, and Parkinson's disease. The following lists or exercises have proven successful with adults who evidence perceptual-motor deficiencies.

BALANCE PROGRESSIONS

Balance is a skill underlying nearly every static and dynamic posture which requires the body to be stabilized against the pull of gravity.

The physical management of the student with impaired balance should be progressive in design. Developmentally, balance proceeds in a "cephalo-caudal" pattern. Stability is acquired in the neck region first and then proceeds downward (i.e., neck before shoulders, trunk before lower extremities). More specifically, balance activities should progress in the following sequence:

1. Rolling side-to-side from a lying position.
2. Sitting with assistance.
3. Sitting without assistance.
4. Balancing with 4-point, 3-point, and 2-point stances.
5. Kneeling balance in a 2-point stance.
6. Standing balance with assistance (static).
7. Standing balance without assistance (static).
8. Standing balance with assistance (dynamic).
9. Standing balance without assistance (dynamic).
10. Ambulation training.
11. Training in ascending and descending stairs, ramps, and curbs.

Remember, when the student is relearning a psycho-motor activity, break the skill down into small components, give clear instructions, provide a proper demonstration, and provide corrective feedback. Watch for orthostatic hypotension when bringing an individual from a lying position to a seated one.

168

ACTIVITIES FOR DEVELOPING STATIC AND DYNAMIC BALANCE

SUPINE TO PRONE ROLL TO LEFT USING RIGHT ARM.
1. While supine, student reaches across body with right arm and grasps side of mat and swings right leg if possible.
2. While supine, student places right arm on mat at waist level, pushing and swing right leg to assist.

TO ROLL RIGHT USING RIGHT ARM.
1. While supine, student reaches for right edge of mat with right arm and grasps and pulls.
2. While supine, student grasps upper portion of mat with right arm and pulls hard.

TO ROLL LEFT WITH USE OF RIGHT LEG.
1. While supine, instruct student to flex and adduct leg at knee joint and place foot on mat at midline of body and thrust vigorously while extending at both hip and knee.
2. While supine, flex and adduct at knee, swinging leg across body with enough momentum to rotate trunk.

PRONE TO SUPINE USING RIGHT ARM TO TURN LEFT.
1. While prone, student places right hand on mat with arm flexed/abducted and extends arm forcefully.
2. While prone, student places right hand on mat with arm flexed/adducted and thrusts forcefully to a supine position.

USING RIGHT LEG TO TURN LEFT.
While prone, raise the right leg backwards, swinging it in such a fashion to pull the person to his back.

SUPINE ON MAT. (Or in bed.)
1. Roll form back to front, and reverse in one smooth, continuous movement.
2. Roll from right side to left, hold for 2 seconds, and reverse with proper momentum so as not to land on back or front side.

LONG-SITTING POSITION ON MAT. (Can be done in bed, chair, or on mat with support, as needed.)
1. Lean from side to side, using palms to retain balance.
2. Work up to leaning as far as possible with no arm support.
3. Resisted: Student attempts to maintain upright position while assistant slowly applies pressure forward, backward, to right and left sides, and in rotation right

and left. The assistant should hold each of these resistances for about 5 seconds each. Eventually, the assistant can give gentle pushes in the same directions while the student attempts to maintain balance.

4. Student attempts to bring right finger to nose. Repeat with left. Facing the assistant, the student attempts to touch the right fingers to the assistant's right shoulder. Repeat with left.

BRIDGES.
1. While in hook-lying position, student elevates buttocks off the mat. Assistant may need to straddle the student to keep the knees together and assist in elevating buttocks off mat.
2. If student can perform this maneuver independently, assistant can provide resistance at the anterior superior iliac spines (ASIS), attempting to push buttocks back down to mat or side to side. Student resists and attempts to maintain each position for about 5 seconds each.

4-POINT STANCE ON MAT. (On hands and knees.)
Increase holding time in this position. Assistant may need to straddle student and spot.

3-POINT STANCE ON MAT.
While on hands and knees, have student raise and hold requested extremities (e.g., right arm, left arm).

2-POINT STANCE ON MAT.
While on hands and knees, have student support body weight on two extremities while raising any combination of two (e.g., right arm with left leg).

CRAWLING FORWARD/BACKWARD.
Assistant kneels behind student and assists the student with crawling by moving arms and legs as needed. Once the student can maneuver forward and backward, teach student to go right and left.

** NOTE ** Many students with balance problems also have concomitant joint trauma; therefore, knee and shoulder pain or inflammation may preclude this activity.

KNEELING ON MAT.
Kneeling is more difficult because it raises the center of gravity and the base of support is smaller. The student should be taught to rise to the kneeling position from the prone position. Eventually the student is taught to rise from a kneeling position to a

standing position.

The assistant generally spots from the front of the student. As balance improves, the assistant can spot from behind. Once the student can master a skill independently, a mirror should be placed in front of the student. The student should practice leaning right and left, forward and backward, successfully recovering balance each time.

Assisted Kneeling.

The student is assisted to a kneeling position. The student then places the hands on the assistant's shoulders for support. The assistant may also need to stabilize at hips, trunk, or shoulders.

Resisted Kneeling.

1. Student should be able to balance on both knees, unassisted, for as long as possible.
2. Facing the student, the assistant places his/her hands on the ASIS and attempts to push the student backward. The student should resist for approximately 5 seconds.
3. The assistant gently eases up on the pressure and slides the right hand around posteriorly. From this position, the assistant attempts to rotate the trunk to the student's right. The student should resist for 5 seconds and maintain the face forward position.
4. The assistant eases up on the pressure and slowly slides the left hand around posteriorly. From this position, the assistant attempts to pull the student forward. The student should resist for about 5 seconds, maintaining the upright posture.
5. The assistant eases up on the pressure and slowly slides the right hand anteriorly to the ASIS. From this position, the assistant attempts to rotate the trunk to the student's left. The student should resist for 5 seconds and maintain the face forward position.
6. Placing both hands on the ASIS, the assistant should attempt to push the student to the side or at a diagonal. The student should resist for 5 seconds, maintaining an upright posture.

Knee Walking.

1. Have the student walk forward, to each side, and backwards on knees with or without assistance.
2. Gradually increase distance.
3. Rock side-to-side in a rhythmic fashion.
4. Balance on one knee only.

Kneeling to Standing.

1. Student faces stall bars in supported kneeling position. Standing behind the student, the assistant will place one hand on the shoulder and the other on the hip of student. Ask the student to position strong leg (flexed and slightly abducted) under body and extend with leg while pulling with strong arm.
2. Eventually the student should be taught to come to standing position without use of stall bars.

STANDING IN PARALLEL BARS.

1. Increase time for standing stationary (both supported and unsupported).
2. Add swaying by shifting weight from side to side, gradually widening the base of support.
3. Place one foot forward and one foot back to sway forward and back. Switch positions of the feet. If one foot is more disabled, keep that one in front first.
4. All of the above can be performed with the eyes closed.
5. Resisted Balancing: See resisted balance activities under Resisted Kneeling. Perform same sequence in a standing position. Use both foot positions (i.e., side-by-side and forward-back).

STANDING STATIC BALANCE IN PARALLEL BARS.

1. With arms abducted out to sides, student attempts to balance on one leg. The other leg should be flexed at the knee and adducted at hip. This is called a stork stand. As balance improves, hands can be moved to hips and then placed across the chest. The stork stand should be performed with the eyes closed as well.
2. Have student perform these static positions on a balance beam.

TILT BOARDS

1. Have student begin with a wide base of support and progress to a narrow base.
2. Increase time on the tilt board.

DYNAMIC BALANCE.

1. Have student step over low objects placed on the floor. Use a mirror to allow student to observe. Other variations include crossing leg over the midline while walking sideways.
2. Have student walk a straight line marked on the floor with a spotter.
3. Have student walk heel-to-toe on the balance beam. Practice forward, back, sideways. Always have a spotter present. Vary the width of the balance beam.
4. Have student walk heel-to-toe on a circle marked on the floor with a spotter.
5. Have student ascend and descend ramps and stairs. Step up stairs with the

strongest leg first. Step down the stairs with the weakest leg first.

6. Have student practice vertical jumps.
7. Have student practice horizontal jumps (standing broad jump). Progress to taking successive jumps.
8. Have student practice hopping on both right and left feet. Progress to hopping across room.

ACTIVITIES FOR DEVELOPING KINESTHETIC AWARENESS.
(body awareness, laterality, bilateral coordination)

A prerequisite to the development of gross motor coordination is the kinesthetic awareness of one's body in space. A simple test for up, down, right, left, forward, backward, and sideways may be given to determine the starting level for the individual. The following activities are designed to increase the individual's body awareness, laterality, and bilateral coordination.

IDENTIFICATION OF BODY PARTS.
1. Have student touch body parts one by one in response to one-word commands. For example: elbow, wrist, chin.
2. Upon command, touch two body parts simultaneously.
3. Touch five body parts in the same sequence as they are called by the assistant.
4. Repeat all of the above with eyes closed.

RIGHT-LEFT DISCRIMINATION.
1. Use the right hand to touch parts named on the right side.
2. Use the right hand to touch parts named on the left side. (This involves crossing the midline and should be more difficult than the previous task.)
3. Use the left hand to touch parts named on the left side.
4. Use the left hand to touch parts named on the right side.
5. Given opportunities to touch body parts of a partner who is facing the student:
   a. Use right hand to touch body parts on the right side of the partner.
   b. Use right hand to touch body parts on the left side of the partner.

IMITATION OF POSTURES/MOVEMENTS.
Have the student imitate the arm and leg movements of the assistant in the sequence outlined below:

1. Imitate bilateral movements.
   a. Move both arms apart and together while legs remain stationary.
   b. Move both legs apart and together while arms remain stationary.

    c. Move all four limbs apart and together simultaneously.
    d. Move any three limbs apart and together while the fourth limb remains stationary.

2. <u>Imitate unilateral movements</u>.
    a. Move the right arm and right leg apart and together simultaneously while the left limbs remain stationary.
    b. Move the left arm and leg apart and together simultaneously while the right limbs remain stationary.

3. <u>Cross-lateral movements</u>.
    a. Move the right arm and left leg apart and together simultaneously while the other limbs remain stationary.
    b. Move the left arm and right leg apart and together simultaneously while the other limbs remain stationary.

4. Given opportunities to imitate the arm movements of the assistant, as described on the following page, have the student start and stop both arms simultaneously WITHOUT verbal instruction or mirroring.

OTHER MAT EXERCISES (SUPINE).
1. Lift right knee and intercept it with the right palm. Repeat to the left side.
2. Lift right knee and intercept it with the left palm. Repeat for the left knee and right palm.
3. With one leg raised, have the student "write" numbers, letters, and names in the air with the foot.

4-POINT STANCE. (On hands and knees.)
1. Bring the right knee to touch right wrist. Repeat to the left side.
2. Bring the right knee to touch left wrist. Repeat with the left knee and right wrist.

SITTING. (Work up to standing.)
These activities are to be mirrored. Start with the fingertips of both hands touching the shoulders.

1. Extend arms overhead, then bring back to shoulders.
2. Reach both arms forward, then bring back to shoulders.
3. Stretch both arms out to side, then back to shoulders.
4. Repeat entire sequence 5-10 times, gradually increasing the speed. Eventually, have student perform without mirroring the teacher.
5. Starting with arms down by the side, move the right hand to the right shoulder.

Repeat to the left side.

PERCEPTUAL-MOTOR GAMES

Activity	Objective	Description
Move It	Directionality	Hop to right; skip to left, etc.
Bean Bag Toss and Catch	Laterality Flexibility	Toss back up and catch over shoulder, under leg, etc.
Stone Walk	Motor Planning Laterality Directionality Balance	Place #'s on sheets of paper on ground. Give verbal or written directions of how to go through sequence.
Bean Bag Toss	Hand-Eye Coordination Laterality	Throw bags at target with assigned point value; stress proper throwing techniques.
Step and Walk	Visual-Motor Coordination Dynamic Balance	Step over objects of various heights and widths.
Name Body Parts	Body Awareness	Touch specific body parts.
Crisscross Walk	Bilateral Coordination	Step across line with each leg.
Ball Bounce in Hoops	Eye-Hand Coordination	Bounce ball once in hoop #1. Bounce twice in hoop #2.
Jump and Turn	Directionality Body Awareness Dynamic balance	Jump and turn to specific angle or direction requested.
Walk and Dribble	Eye-Hand Coordination Spatial Awareness	Walk around course of cones while maintaining ball control.
Walk and Toss	Dynamic Balance Eye-Hand Coordination Tactile Awareness	While walking a straight line on balance beam, throw nerf ball at target.

Roll It	Laterality Body Awareness	Roll ball up and down leg, around body, through legs. Emphasis on concepts of up and down, in, out.
Bounce It	Gross Motor	Bounce ball to assistant using one arm and two arms. Bounce ball to designated heights.
Throw It	Gross Motor	See above.
Cross It	Tactile Awareness Kinesthetic Awareness	Have various objects of different sizes, weights, and textures. Have student find similar object from inside of surprise box.
Pick It	Fine Motor Eye-Hand	Fill pan with small objects. Use a tweezer to pick objects up.
Listen and Do	Following Directions	Student imitates the actions of assistant who puts hands on head, etc. Have client follow spoken word while assistant touches unrelated body parts.
Cats in the Sand	Crossing Midline	Student responds to directions for movements. Example: Move right arm and left leg while lying supine.

FINE MOTOR TASKS

Fine motor tasks usually refer to those involving use of the hands and fingers. Prehension and opposition are two commonly used terms when referring to tasks of this nature. Prehension refers to the ability to grasp an object with the fingers, while opposition refers to the ability to oppose any of the fingers with the thumb.

The following exercises emphasize this fine motor coordination. Fine motor activities are generally harder to perform than gross motor.

1. Make a fist and then extend the fingers completely. Keep moving as fast as

possible. Try to perform with one palm facing up and the other palm facing down. Reverse directions of palms for each hand. Try to perform with one fist open and one closed simultaneously.

2. With fingers extended, abduct and adduct them together simultaneously. Try abducting and adducting them one at a time. Do one and then both hands at the same time.

3. Make a circle with each individual finger.

4. With the dominant hand, touch the thumb to each finger of that hand individually. Proceed from the index finger to the little finger, and reverse the direction back up to the index finger again. Work up to using both hands at the same time. Eventually, increase the speed and perform with the eyes closed.

5. With arm stretched out in front, touch the index finger to nose, and to a real (dot on board) or imaginary point straight ahead. Repeat as fast and accurately as possible within 30 seconds. Later, try the same with the eyes closed. Use the dominant arm before the non-dominant arm.

6. Try to touch the right index finger to the nose while extending the left arm out to the side. Alternate by touching the nose with the left index finger while simultaneously extending the right arm out to the side.

STUDY QUESTIONS:

1. Design a perceptual-motor lesson plan for a mild CVA student.

2. Make up a perceptual-motor game and explain its purpose.

CHAPTER 11

ASSESSMENT AND PROGRAMMING FOR POSTURE

ASSESSMENT OF POSTURE

Before assessing postural deviations, it is necessary to have an understanding of the possible underlying causes of a deviation and in which instances medical referral or exercise prescription is the more appropriate intervention. The following glossary provides some simple definitions of common postural deviations. A more thorough discussion of each deviation may be found in Sherrill (1981).

The posture evaluation requires a posture screen or plumb line used in conjunction with observations. A plumb line is a thick piece of rope suspended from the ceiling with a weighted end (weight should not touch the floor).

If pictures are used, the student should be photographed in anterior, posterior, and lateral views. The student should be barefoot, wearing a swimsuit, and have the hair pulled back behind the ears. If a large group has to be screened at the same time, stations should be set up with individuals rotating to each station. When reading the description of the posture evaluation, refer to the corresponding items on the "Posture Evaluation Form".

DESCRIPTION OF POSTURE EVALUATION

A. <u>STRENGTH</u>
   <u>Abdominals</u>. Weak abdominal musculature has been implicated in the occurrence of low back pain. No test exists which purely measures abdominal strength without including the hip flexors. A modified sit-up test with norms for those between the ages of 5 to 17 years can be found in the AAHPERD Health Related Physical Fitness Test Manual (see references at end of this chapter). This exercise partially eliminates the action of the hip flexors during movement. The score is recorded as the number of sit-ups performed in one minute.

B. <u>FLEXIBILITY</u>
   1. <u>Chest and Shoulders</u>. Student assumes hook-lying position. Keeping the low back pressed to the floor ((assistant should check by placing a hand between

the lumbar area and floor), the student extends the arms overhead and presses the back of the arms and hands to the floor. Elbows must remain locked at all times.

Scoring: Within Normal Limits (WNL) -- contact of the dorsum of the hands with the floor.

Limitation of Motion (LOM) -- contact of fingers only or cannot make contact with floor without arching the low back.

2. Spine and Hip Extensors. See Sit and Reach test under Evaluation of Flexibility earlier in this chapter.

Scoring: Record the number of inches or centimeters reached by the fingertips.

3. Hip Flexors. See Thomas test under Evaluation of Flexibility in this chapter.

Scoring: WNL -- if thigh remains flat on the table.

LOM -- if thigh lifts upward. Estimate angle between leg and table.

Note: If thigh rotates outward or inward, rotators are tight. Indicate on evaluation form.

C. ORTHOPEDIC EVALUATION.

1. Foot Examination. Note pes planus, pes cavus, Achilles flare, hallux valgus, overlapping toes, hammer toes, corns, and calluses.

Flexible pes planus. Involves measurement of the navicular. According to Crowe, Auxter, and Pyfer (1980), ". . . .the instructor first marks the farthest medial projection of the navicular with a dot or short line parallel to the floor. The (student) is then asked to place the foot on a flat surface without bearing weight on it, and the instructor measures the distance from the supporting surface to the mark on the navicular bone. The (student) then stands on the foot and the height of the mark is again measured."

Scoring: Record the degree of fluctuation of the navicular between weight-bearing and non-weight bearing. If greater than 1/4 inch, pes planus is indicated.

2. Scoliosis Check. See "Procedures for Spinal Screening." Scoliosis screening is usually performed on children in elementary and secondary grades since treatment is very difficult after bone growth is complete. However, older students experiencing low back paid may benefit from this type of screening to determine the nature of their pain.

180

3. Anterior View. Draw a plumb line from a point equidistant between the medial malleoli and extending perpendicular to the floor, bisecting the body (see Figure 11-1). Note any of the following:
   a. Head Twist (torticollis) or Head Tilt -- Check the evenness of the earlobes and indicate left or right drop.
   b. Shoulder Level -- Note evenness of acromion processes and indicate left or right drop.
   c. Linea Alba -- Indicate a left or right shift.
   d. Anterior Spines (hip) -- Note evenness and indicate a left or right drop.
   e. Leg Alignment -- Beginning at the center of the knee, draw a line perpendicular to the floor.
      1) Internal or external rotation at the hip. The knee and foot both point outward or inward.
      2) Internal tibial torsion. The patella faces inward when the feet are together.
      3) Genu Valgum (knock knees). Note the space between the medial malleoli (knees are touching).
      4) Pronation. The big toe (first metatarsal) falls lateral to the plumb line drawn from the center of the knee.

4. Lateral View. Draw a plumb line beginning with a point one and 1/2 inches anterior to the lateral malleolus and proceed upward, perpendicular to the floor. In ideal posture the plumb line should pass through the following fixed check points: center of the knee (behind the patella), center of the hip (greater trochanter), center of the shoulder (acromion process), and through the earlobe (tragus). Postural abnormalities are based upon the deviation (forward or backward) from this line (see Figure 11-2).
   a. Body Lean -- Indicate whether forward or backward.
   b. Head -- Considered forward if the earlobe is in front of the plumb line.
   c. Shoulders -- Considered forward if acromion is in front of the plumb line.
   d. Kyphosis -- Excessive flexion in the thoracic spine. Check for structural kyphosis in Adam's position.
   e. Lordosis -- Excessive hyperextension in lumbar spine
   f. Ptosis -- Abdominal protrusion. Abdominals should not extend beyond a line drawn down from the sternum.
   g. Genu Recurvatum (hyperextended knees) -- Patella falls behind plumb line.

5. Posterior View.
   Winged Scapula -- Indicate whether right or left.

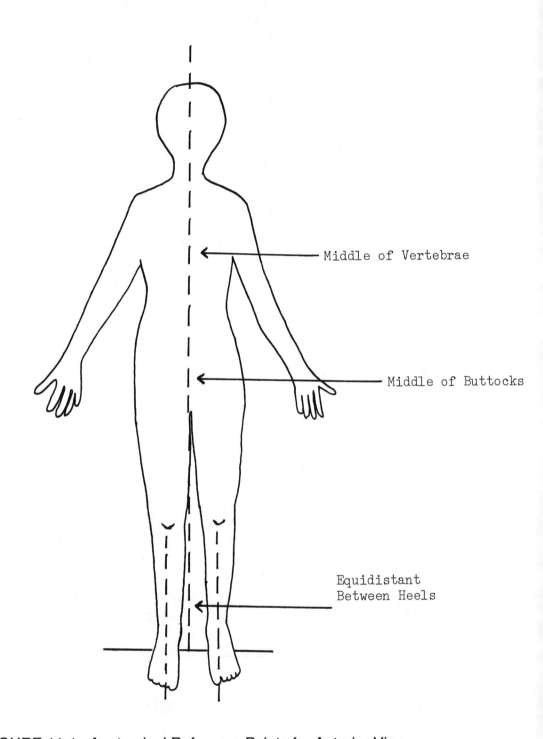

FIGURE 11-1. Anatomical Reference Points for Anterior View.

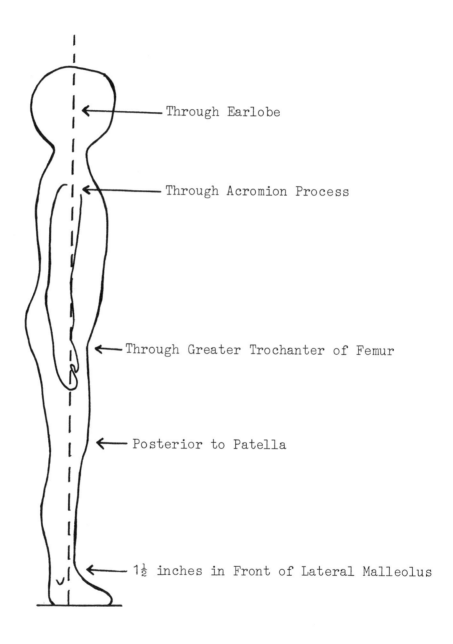

FIGURE 11-2. Anatomical References for Lateral View.

Through Earlobe

Through Acromion Process

Through Greater Trochanter of Femur

Posterior to Patella

$1\frac{1}{2}$ inches in Front of Lateral Malleolus

PROCEDURES FOR SPINAL SCREENING
(adapted from Children's Hospital, San Diego, California)

FIRST Ask if there is a history of scoliosis in the family.

SECOND Look at the students' backs while they are standing. Ask yourself:
1. Are the shoulders the same level?
2. Are the tips of the scapulae the same level?
3. Are the arms the same distance from the body?
4. Are the trunk contours the same?
5. Are the hips level?
6. Are the poplitial creases level?
7. Are both knees straight?

The above are pieces of a puzzle. A positive finding in any of the above may be a normal variant or may indicate scoliosis. The next check is perhaps the most important.

THIRD The student bends forward about 90 degrees with hands together, head down as if diving into a pool. View the student from the back. Ask yourself:

Is one side of the thoracic or lumbar spine higher than the other?

FOURTH The student bends forward as above, but you view the student from the front. Ask yourself:

Is one side of the thoracic or lumbar spine higher than the other?

FIFTH Take a quick look at the side view of the student as a check for kyphosis. Ask yourself:

Is the curve even of does it peak?

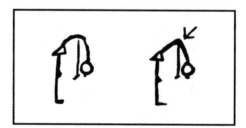

Now you make the decision for referral. The primary reason for referring a student is a rib hump which is usually accompanied by asymmetry of some type in the back.

184

POSTURE EXERCISES

A. <u>FORWARD HEAD</u>

STARTING POSITION	MOVEMENT	PURPOSE
1. <u>Neck Flattener</u>	1. Press back of neck firmly to floor (feel contraction in both neck extensors and flexors.) 2. Hold 5 seconds. 3. REPS:_____ SETS:_____	1. To strengthen neck flexors and extensors.
2. <u>Revolving Neck Flattener</u>	1. Press back of neck firmly to floor. 2. Slowly turn the head from side to side. 3. REPS:_____ SETS:_____	1. To strengthen neck flexors, extensors, and rotators.
3. <u>Side Head Lift</u>	1. Turn head to right side, right ear to floor. 2. Keeping head in this position, lift toward ceiling. 3. Hold 5 seconds. 4. REPS:_____ SETS:_____	1. To strengthen neck rotators.
4. <u>Military Tuck</u>	1. Pull chin and head backward as far as possible (keep eye on a horizontal plane). Do not tilt head. 2. Hold 5 seconds. 3. REPS:_____ SETS:_____	1. To strengthen neck flexors and extensors.

185

STARTING POSITION	MOVEMENT	PURPOSE

B. FORWARD SHOULDERS/KYPHOSIS

STARTING POSITION	MOVEMENT	PURPOSE
1. Butterfly 	1. Clasp Hands over low back. 2. Attempt to draw elbows together. 3. Hold 10 seconds. 4. REPS:____ SETS:____	1. To strengthen muscles which retract the shoulders and adduct the scapula. (rhomboids, trapezius)
2. Prone Lift -- Arms Overhead 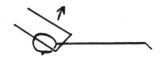	1. Lift arms only from floor (elbows extended). 2. When capable, lift arms and head only. 3. When capable, lift arms, head, and shoulders only (do not arch low back). May be performed with upper back over table. 4. Hold 5 seconds. 5. REPS:____ SETS:____	1. To strengthen muscles which retract the shoulders and adduct the scapula. 2. To strengthen upper back extensors.

STARTING POSITION	MOVEMENT	PURPOSE
3. <u>Wall Lean</u>	1. Face corner of room, one hand on either wall at shoulder height. 2. Incline body toward the corner, bending elbows (heels on floor). 3. Hold 10 seconds. 4. REPS:____ SETS:____	1. To stretch anterior chest muscles (pectorals).
4. <u>Prone Lift --</u> <u>Arms Extended Sideward</u> 	1. Pinch shoulder blades together. 2. Raise arms slightly from mat. 3. Raise head from mat (<u>chin in</u>). 4. Hold for 5 seconds. 5. REPS:____ SETS:____	1. To strengthen muscles which retract the shoulders and adduct the scapula. 2. To improve alignment of upper back and head.
5. <u>Sitting Hand Slide</u>	1. Hands placed on low back. 2. Slowly slide hands up back attempting to bring elbows together. 3. REPS:____ SETS:____	1. To stretch anterior chest muscles. 2. To strengthen muscles which retract the shoulders and adduct the scapula
6. <u>Towel Stretch</u>	1. Raise towel overhead. Hold for 10 seconds. 2. Lower towel obliquely across back. Hold for 10 seconds. 3. Reverse position. 4. REPS:____ SETS:____	1. To strengthen muscles which retract the shoulders and adduct the scapula. 2. To strengthen outward rotators of shoulders. 3. To stretch anterior chest muscles.

STARTING POSITION	MOVEMENT	PURPOSE
7. <u>Shoulder Stretch</u> 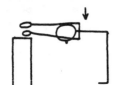	1. Allow gravity to hyperflex the shoulder joint. 2. It may be necessary to flex the knees slightly if the hamstrings are tight. 3. Hold 10 to 30 seconds. 4. REPS:_____	1. To stretch the anterior chest muscles and inward rotators of shoulders.
8. <u>Bent Arm Press -- Supine</u> 	1. Elbows flexed, arms in outward rotation. 2. Press back with the back of the hand against a hard surface, keeping low back on floor. 3. Hold for 10 seconds. 4. REPS:____ SETS:____	1. To strengthen outward rotators of the shoulders.
9. <u>Push Up</u> 	1. Tighten abdominal and gluteal muscles. 2. Bend elbows, lowering body to floor. 3. Raise the body. Do not bend at the waist. 4. REPS:____ SETS:____	1. To strengthen the shoulder girdle muscles, especially the serratus anterior. 2. To assist in correcting winged scapula. 3. To activate the abdominals and gluteals.
10. <u>Prone Flies</u> 	1. Slowly raise dumbbells out to side and above level of body. 2. Arms may be slightly bent. 3. Repeat 10 times. 4. REPS:____ SETS:____	1. To strengthen the muscles which retract shoulders and adduct the scapula.

STARTING POSITION	MOVEMENT	PURPOSE
11. <u>Shoulder Flexion with Pulleys</u>	1. Keeping arms straight, slowly lift pulleys overhead. 2. Do not arch lower back. 3. Repeat 10 times. 4. REPS:____ SETS:____	1. To strengthen upper back extensors (trapezius).
12. <u>Backward Shoulder Rolls</u>	1. Rotate both shoulders <u>slowly</u> in circles up (to ears) and backward. 2. REPS:____ SETS:____	1. To strengthen muscles which retract the shoulders and adduct the scapula.
13. <u>Horizontal Ladder</u>	1. Travel along one side of ladder. 2. Travel with one hand on each side of ladder. 3. Travel across ladder, one rung at a time. 4. Travel across ladder, skipping one rung each time. 5. REPS:____ SETS:____	1. To stretch the muscles of the shoulder and spine.

C. LOWER EXTREMITIES

STARTING POSITION	MOVEMENT	PURPOSE
1. Heel Cord Stretch -- Standing at arms length from wall, body inclined slightly forward, back flat, feet toed in slightly.	1. Hands on the wall shoulder high and shoulder width apart, elbows slightly bent. Bend arms until chest nearly touches the wall. Keep body in straight line, keep heels on the floor. 2. Progression: From starting position, move backward an inch or so at a time keeping the heels on the floor. 3. Heel cord stretch board with back flattened against the wall may be used as an advanced exercise. 4. Hold for 30 seconds. 5. REPS:____	1. To stretch heel cord and back of leg. Beneficial in pes planus, pronation.
2. Ankle Stretch -- Standing on lower rung of stall bar, feet slightly pigeon-toed and weight on balls of feet. Grasp an upper rung for support to aid in balancing.	1. Raise on toes as high as possible. 2. Lower body to stretch heel cord as heels are slowly below the level of the support. Be sure weight is on the outer margin of feet at all times and stand tall throughout the exercise. 3. Hold stretch for 30 seconds. 4. REPS:____	1. To stretch anterior tibial and calf muscles. 2. Beneficial in pes planus and pronation, fractures of the ankles, post-operative repair, and following the use of a cast on the limb.

STARTING POSITION	MOVEMENT	PURPOSE
3. <u>Foot Supinator</u> -- Sitting Tall	1. Cross leg so the ankle of right foot rests across left knee, keeping the foot at right angles to the right leg and turning the sole of the foot upward. 2. Place left palm on medial border of right foot. Attempt to push the right foot down-ward (pronation). Resist and hold the right foot in supination. 3. Hold for 10 seconds. 4. REPS:____ SETS:____	1. Strengthens invertors, supinators of foot. 2. Beneficial in pes planus and pronation.
4. <u>Frog Kick</u> -- Sitting on floor with legs extended. Place hands on mat behind buttocks with fingers pointed forward.	1. Fully flex the knees and place the soles of the feet together. 2. Then with the heels on the floor and the feet perpen-dicular (toes pointing upward) to the floor, extend the legs keeping the soles of the feet together. 3. Hold and stretch for 10 seconds. 4. Return slowly. 5. REPS:____ SETS:____	1. Strengthens invertors of the foot. 2. Beneficial in pes planus, pronation, and tibial torsion.
5. <u>Knee Flexion</u> (with boot) -- Lying face down with a boot strapped on the foot, leg and ankle extended.	1. Raise lower leg to vertical position, hold, slowly return. 2. Do not bend knee more than 90 degrees.	1. Strengthens hamstrings (knee flexors). 2. Beneficial in genu recurvatum.

STUDY QUESTIONS

1. Assess your posture with a partner or use a mirror.

2. Develop an exercise program to correct any deviations you might have.

CHAPTER 12

ASSESSMENT AND PROGRAMMING FOR ADAPTED AQUATICS

ADAPTED AQUATICS -- HYDROGYMNASTICS

Hydrogymnastics is an individualized exercise program performed in the water. The purpose of Hydrogymnastics is to utilize the water as a therapeutic modality to habilitate the disabled individual.

The adapted aquatic setting provides the student with the opportunity to do activities that may not be possible on land. Hydrogymnastics can be enjoyed by persons with most disabilities, but it is especially well-suited to people with orthopedic/joint limitations, obesity, ambulation difficulties, and low-back syndrome. There are a few conditions, however, where an adapted aquatics program would be contraindicated, such as severe hypertension or hypotension, cardiac conditions, infective skin disorders, and incontinence.

Within an adapted aquatic session, the student can experience both success and mobility. This is due in part to the buoyancy of the water. Buoyancy neutralizes the effects of gravity. In the pool, the water will support the individual and he/she will notice a sensation of weightlessness. This allows the student to move more freely and with less energy expenditure than when on land.

The goal of most swimmers is to decrease resistance, and this may be the goal of some students within your Hydrogymnastics program. However, one advantage of performing exercises in the pool is the ability to modify resistance easily. As the student's strength increases, simple changes in the speed of movement or in the placement of the extremities against the line of movement will increase the resistance. If further resistance is desired, the incorporation of hand paddles, kickboards, or swim fins while performing the exercises will generate significant resistance.

Many people prefer Hydrogymnastics because it occurs in a warm pool (92-93 degrees F). It is believed that warm water decreases pain and induces relaxation. With this decreased pain, many students can see noticeable improvements in their range of motion. It is a well established fact that warm water is a vasodilator which increases peripheral blood flow. An important physiological point to remember is that as one enters the water, cutaneous vessels constrict momentarily causing a rise in blood pressure. However, during immersion, the arterioles will dilate, possibly causing the student to feel light-headed.

The benefits of Hydrogymnastics are many and can be categorized into three areas: physiological, social, and psychological. The following listings were adapted from the American Red Cross Instructor's Manual.

PHYSIOLOGICAL BENEFITS

1. Increases muscular strength and endurance.
2. Facilitates improvement in flexibility.
3. Enhances peripheral circulation and provides opportunities to address cardiovascular endurance.
4. Provides an exercise setting where respiration and metabolic rates are elevated.
5. Allows the student an opportunity to develop gross motor coordination skills.
6. Will induce relaxation in a warm water environment.

PSYCHOLOGICAL BENEFITS

Student's self-image and self-confidence may be boosted. Within the water, the disability is less noticeable. The student is less handicapped in the water. Therefore, the water environment provides an opportunity where the physically limited student is more like his/her able-bodied peers.

SOCIAL BENEFITS

1. Provides an enjoyable activity. The time spent in the pool may be the only time when joints and muscles don't hurt.
2. Offers an opportunity to socialize. The pool is a place where able-bodied and disabled can share and compete equally.
3. Provides a recreational opportunity. Within an aquatic session, the disabled can participate in vigorous physical activities not possible on land.
4. Sets up healthy recreational opportunities. From learning to swim, the student can branch out to other water activities, such as sailing, water skiing, or snorkling.

In order to have your student derive the aforementioned benefits, your comprehensive adapted aquatics program should include:

1. Therapeutic exercises to develop muscular strength and endurance, flexibility, and cardiovascular fitness.
2. Water safety skills.

3. Instruction of swimming skills, modified to the capabilities of the student.
4. Gait training, employing the use of weighted canes, walkers, etc. Students with paralysis of the lower extremities should wear socks to prevent scrapes.
5. Lap swimming to provide opportunity for cardiovascular training.
6. Instruction in games and sports to enhance psycho-motor skills, as well as fostering greater interaction and sportsmanship.

Entrance and exit into the pool can present a potentially difficult situation for the more impaired student. It is essential that assistants be present both on the deck and in the pool as lifeguards, assistants, and spotters.

For students who will be entering and exiting the pool with the use of the ladder, it is important to teach them to always face the ladder. This method allows for greater control and safety.

If your program includes students who have incurred a CVA, it is recommended that you pad the rungs of the ladder. This prevents bruising of the shins. Students with hemiparesis should lead with the weak leg with going down the ladder as they enter the pool. When exiting from the pool, the student should lead with the strong leg up the ladder (remember the adage: up with the good; down with the bad).

If the student is unable to maneuver down the ladder, the decision of using a Hoyer lift or a two-man transfer must be made. it is important to ask the student which method is preferred, because many disabled do not like the Hoyer lift. This method tends to attract attention to the student, and it is uncomfortable to sit in a wet, cold lift while waiting to be placed in the water. Before deciding which method will be used, it is essential to take into consideration the weight of the student and the strength of the assistants.

Generally, the two-man transfers are easily and safely accomplished when the assistants work as a team. Each assistant takes a position on either side of the student. The assistants should employ the same techniques used in a typical two-man transfer (see Chapter 2). Once the student is on the deck, one assistant will stand behind the student and grasp the forearms from under the axillas. The second assistant should be in the water guiding the student into the pool. The second assistant should position his/her hands around the student's waist.

When assisting the student out of the pool with the two-man lift, utilize the buoyancy of the water by bouncing the student several times before lifting. Extreme care should be taken so that the student will not hit his/her tailbone on the deck after being pulled out of the water.

In addition, flotation devices should be placed in position prior to entering the water. In exiting the pool, this procedure should be reversed.

TEACHING SUGGESTIONS

The following techniques have proven useful when working with students in a hydrogymnastic setting. These tips are categorized into two groups: (1) tips related to swim instruction; and (2) tips related to ambulation training and therapeutic exercise.

<u>Swim Instruction Tips</u>:
1. Set up the situation so that the student will succeed.
2. Teach the appropriate sequence of skills, dependent upon disability, motivational level, and interests.
3. For students with hemiparesis, teach symmetric, bilateral, underwater recovery strokes first (e.g., elementary backstroke, breast-stroke).
4. Use flotation and swim aids as necessary. Try not to develop over-dependency on such equipment.

<u>Hydrotherapy Tips</u>:
1. When teaching ambulation skills, make sure that the student is sufficiently buoyant.
2. During gait training, do not allow student to drag the feet on the bottom of the pool. This can be avoided by having the student wear socks or shoes.
3. It is recommended when teaching ambulation skills to have the assistant wear a face mask in order to observe leg movements.
4. "Draft" the weaker students when practicing walking. This is accomplished when the assistant walks backwards to decrease the resistance of the water. Later, if additional resistance is desired, have the student push a kickboard while walking.
5. The water is an excellent medium to teach the student the techniques of self-range of motion.

THERAPEUTIC AQUATIC EXERCISES

EXERCISES FOR THE LOWER EXTREMITIES

POSITION: STANDING WITH BACK OR SIDE TO POOL WALL. STUDENT HOLDS ON TO POOL GUTTER.

1. Raise heels off the ground. Lower. Repeat 15 times.
2. With arms at side, stretch by slowly bending to the left. Repeat to the other side. Repeat 10 times each side.
3. Raise left knee to chest. Extend left leg straight out. Drop leg to starting position. Repeat with the left leg. Repeat 10 times each leg.
4. Raise left foot as high as possible with leg straight. Swing foot and leg to left side. Recover to starting position by pulling left leg

vigorously to right. Reverse to right leg. Repeat 10 times.

5. Raise left leg and clasp calf with both arms pulling to chest. Return to starting position. Repeat exercise with the right leg. Repeat 10 times.

6. With pool edge on right, stretch left arm out in front at shoulder height. Standing on tiptoes, swing left leg forwards and then backward.s Repeat for right leg. Repeat 10 times.

7. With pool edge on right, stretch left arm out to side. Circle the left leg. Repeat for right leg. Repeat 10 times.

8. With back to edge, bend left knee. Extend foot, then return to bent-knee position. Repeat for the right leg. Repeat 10 times.

POSITION: HOLDING ON TO GUTTER WITH BACK TOWARDS EDGE. FEET NOT TOUCHING THE BOTTOM OF POOL.

1. Bring knees to chest. Extend legs without the feet touching the bottom. Return to the starting position. Repeat 10 times.

2. With the legs extended, swing legs far apart. Bring legs together crossing left leg over right. Swing legs far apart. Bring legs together crossing right over left. Repeat 10 times.

EXERCISES FOR THE UPPER EXTREMITIES

POSITION: STANDING FACING THE POOL EDGE.

1. Standing approximately 12 inches from the wall with the shoulders under water, twist left and try to touch wall with both hands. Twist right and try to touch wall with both hands. Repeat 10 times.

2. With shoulders under water, stretch arms out in front at shoulder height. Swing them down together past the sides of the body and out behind. Swing back again the same way to starting positions. Repeat 15 times.

3. With shoulders under water, raise arms to shoulder height and flex elbows so hands touch each other, palms down in front of chest. Flap elbows up and down quickly. Repeat 20 times.

4. Stretch arms out in front and swing them around and as far behind as possible, keeping them at shoulder height. Return to the starting position. Repeat 20 times.

5. With shoulders under water, circle arms. Make small and large circles. Repeat 20 times.

6. With shoulders under water, bring arms towards ears in lateral direction, palms facing up. In returning, turn palms down. Repeat 20

times.
7. With shoulders under water, circle wrists in one direction, then switch to the other direction.
8. Make a fist, then extend fingers.

ADAPTED AQUATICS EVALUATION SHEET
TEST A: PRE-SWIMMING SKILLS

STUDENT'S NAME:_____

ADMISSION DATE:_____

Evaluator:_____Date:_____
Evaluator:_____Date:_____
Evaluator:_____Date:_____

		Date Achieved
1. Enters water:	with assistance	_____
	without assistance	_____
2. Stands in waist/chest deep water:	supported	_____
	unsupported	_____
3. Walks forward in waist/chest deep water:	supported	_____
	unsupported	_____
4. Walks side-stepping in waist/chest deep water:	supported	_____
	unsupported	_____
5. Walks backward in waist/chest deep water.	supported	_____
	unsupported	_____
6. Holds onto wall:	with assistance	_____
	without assistance	_____
7. Holds onto wall and traverses perimeter of pool		_____
8. Jumps up and down in chest deep water:	with assistance	_____
	without assistance	_____

Comments:_____
_____
_____
_____

199

ADAPTED AQUATICS EVALUATION SHEET
TEST A: PRE-SWIMMING SKILLS

STUDENT'S NAME:_____

ADMISSION DATE:_____

Evaluator:_____Date:_____

Evaluator:_____Date:_____

Evaluator:_____Date:_____

		Date Achieved
1. Enters water:	with assistance	_____
	without assistance	_____
2. Stands in waist/chest deep water:	supported	_____
	unsupported	_____
3. Walks forward in waist/chest deep water:	supported	_____
	unsupported	_____
4. Walks side-stepping in waist/chest deep water:	supported	_____
	unsupported	_____
5. Walks backward in waist/chest deep water.	supported	_____
	unsupported	_____
6. Holds onto wall:	with assistance	_____
	without assistance	_____
7. Holds onto wall and traverses perimeter of pool		_____
8. Jumps up and down in chest deep water:	with assistance	_____
	without assistance	_____

Comments:_____

_____

_____

_____

ADAPTED AQUATICS EVALUATION SHEET
TEST B: BEGINNER SWIM SKILLS

Test B: continued

Date Achieved

18. Retrieves object from bottom:
with assistance (2' depth) _____
without assistance (2' depth) _____
with assistance (3' depth) _____
without assistance (3 ' depth) _____

19. Surface dives to bottom:
assisted (5' depth) _____
unassisted (5' depth) _____

20. Jumps into deep water:
assisted and is caught _____
unassisted and is caught _____

21. Jumps into deep water:
assisted and swims to side _____
unassisted and swims to side _____

22. Changes direction:
to left _____
to right _____

23. Changes position:
horizontal plane, front to back _____
back to front _____
vertical plane, front to back _____
back to front _____

24. Uses kickboard:
with assistance _____
without assistance _____

Comments:_____
_____
_____
_____

ADAPTED AQUATICS EVALUATION SHEET
TEST C: ADVANCED SWIM SKILLS

STUDENT'S NAME:_____

ADMISSION DATE:_____

Evaluator:_____Date:_____

Evaluator:_____Date:_____

Evaluator:_____Date:_____

TEST A Skills passed on (date):_____

TEST B Skills passed on (date):_____

		Date Achieved
1.	Bobs without pushing off bottom (6' depth)	_____
2.	Crawl (C) stroke with out of water arm recovery:	
	20'	_____
	40'	_____
3.	Crawl stroke with breathing to the side:	
	20'	_____
	40'	_____
4.	Basic Backstroke (40')	_____
5.	Racing Backstroke (RBS): 20'	_____
	40'	_____
6.	Breast-stroke (BS): 20'	_____
	40'	_____
7.	Side-stroke (SS): 20'	_____
	40'	_____
8.	Head first dive: with assistance	_____
	without assistance	_____
9.	Surface dive: 7' depth	_____
	9' depth	_____
10.	Distance swim (30 minutes) with any stroke	_____

Comments:_____

_____

_____

_____

HYDROGYMNASTICS ASSESSMENT TOOL

STUDENT'S NAME:_____

PRE-TEST DATE:_____ POST-TEST DATE:_____

ABILITY TO SWIM ACROSS POOL?   Yes _____ No _____

Stroke Used_____

Crawl Stroke	+	o	-
Elementary Back	+	o	-
Side Stroke, lt.	+	o	-
Side Stroke, rt.	+	o	-
Breast Stroke	+	o	-
Butterfly	+	o	-
_____	+	o	-
_____	+	o	-

FLEXIBILITY:

Apley Scratch Test	rt.	up	yes	close	no
	lt.	up	yes	close	no
Straight Leg Raises	rt.	up	yes	close	no
	lt.	up	yes	close	no

MUSCULAR ENDURANCE:

Kickboard push #30 _____

Arm Circle #30 _____

Leg Flutters #30 _____

Knees to chest #30 _____

Jog across pool rate _____ # of sec. & heart

Body composition _____% _____%

ALTERNATES

_____   _____

_____   _____

Evaluator's Name_____ Date_____

Name_____ Date_____

Subjective, did the student show improvement:?_____

_____

_____

_____

DEFINITION OF TEST ITEMS ON HYDROGYMNASTIC ASSESSMENT TOOL

APLEY SCRATCH TEST
  See Apley Scratch Test under Active Range of Motion Tests earlier in this chapter.

STRAIGHT LEG RAISES
  Stand in the pool with the back to the wall. Raise the leg up as close to the surface of the water as possible.

KICKBOARD PUSH #30
  Stand in the water with the kickboard held lengthwise. Push and pull kickboard as fast as possible for 30 seconds.

ARM CIRCLE #30
  Stand in the water with the arms abducted. Make large circles backwards for 30 seconds.

LEG FLUTTERS #30
  Holding onto the wall in a prone position, kick as fast as possible for 30 seconds.

KNEES TO CHEST #30
  Holding the edge of the pool with the back against the wall, bring the knees to the chest repeatedly for 30 seconds.

JOG ACROSS POOL
  In chest deep water, jog across pool as fast as possible. Measure the time it takes to cross the pool and note the heart rate.

STUDY QUESTIONS

1. Which disabilities would benefit the most from the gentle water environment found in Adapted Aquatics?

2. Make up three new water exercises and explain their purpose.

CHAPTER 13

SPECIFIC DISABILITIES

ACQUIRED BRAIN INJURY (ABI)

In the last ten decades, it has been reported that injuries to the brain have increased largely as the result of automobile accidents, stroke, hang glider accidents, and to a lesser extent gunshot wounds. The etiology of a person with an acquired brain injury may be the result of one of the following:

1. Traumatic Head Injury
   a. Closed Head Trauma
   b. Penetrating Tissue Wound
2. Cerebral Vascular Accident (CVA or stroke)
3. Ingestion of Toxic Substances
4. Brain Tumors
5. Hypoxia
6. Infections of the Brain

As you can see, there are many causes of ABI, the impairment itself does not depend on the cause of the lesion, but rather the location affected within the brain.

DEFINITION OF ACQUIRED BRAIN INJURY

An acquired impairment of brain functioning resulting in the loss of cognitive motor, linguistic, psycho-social, sensory perceptual abilities that may display dysfunctions in the following domains:

Cognitive	Impairment of memory function, attention and concentration, judgment, organizational thinking skills, spatial orientation, information processing.
Psycho-Motor	Involvement of neuromotor system. Impairment of motor tone, balance, coordination, and strength.
Linguistic	Impairment of speech, language, and related communication skills.
Psycho-Social	Impulsivity, disinhibition, denial, poor social judgment,

emotional disability, initiation, untoward social behavior.

<u>Sensory-Perceptual</u>   Primary perceptual deficits, visual, auditory, tactile modalities.

In order to understand a student with a brain injury, it is critical to understand the basic functional components of the brain. The brain is the control board for all of the body's functions, including thinking, moving and breathing. It receives messages, interprets them, and then responds to them by enabling the person to speak, move or show emotion.

The brain is protected by a thick layer of bone (the skull) and is surrounded by cerebrospinal fluid which allows the brain to "float" slightly within the skull. This fluid also fills the open areas within the brain (the VENTRICLES). The brain is comprised of the

CORTEX	where most thinking functions occur
CEREBELLUM	which coordinates movement
BRAIN STEM	which controls consciousness, alertness and basic bodily functions such as breathing, respiration and pulse.

The cortex is the largest part of the brain and is divided into four "lobes", each of which specializes in particular functions and skills.

FRONTAL LOBE: emotional control, motivation, social functioning, expressive language, inhibition of impulses, motor integration, voluntary movement.
TEMPORAL LOBE: memory, receptive, language, sequencing, musical awareness.
PARIETAL LOBE: sensation, academic skills such as reading, awareness of spatial relationships.
OCCIPITAL LOBE: visual perception.

The cortex is divided into two hemispheres. The dominant hemisphere (usually the left hemisphere) controls verbal functions (speaking, writing, reading, calculating), while the right hemisphere generally controls functions that are more visual-spatial in nature (visual memory, copying, drawing, rhythm). Figure 13-1 provides more specific information regarding the capacities of the right and left brain.

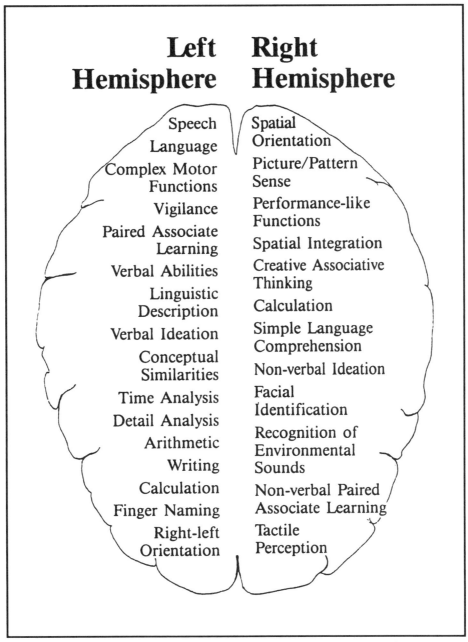

Left Hemisphere

Speech
Language
Complex Motor Functions
Vigilance
Paired Associate Learning
Verbal Abilities
Linguistic Description
Verbal Ideation
Conceptual Similarities
Time Analysis
Detail Analysis
Arithmetic
Writing
Calculation
Finger Naming
Right-left Orientation

Right Hemisphere

Spatial Orientation
Picture/Pattern Sense
Performance-like Functions
Spatial Integration
Creative Associative Thinking
Calculation
Simple Language Comprehension
Non-verbal Ideation
Facial Identification
Recognition of Environmental Sounds
Non-verbal Paired Associate Learning
Tactile Perception

FIGURE 13-1. Left and Right Hemispheres of the Brain

Many characteristics are common among persons with injuries on the same side of the head. Damage to the right side of the brain often results in impaired perceptions and paralysis on the left side of the body (i.e., left hemiplegia). Persons with injury to the left side of the brain manifests problems in communication related to speech, comprehension, reading, and writing, along with paralysis of the right side of the body.

Head injured persons often show changes in personality and emotional control no matter which side the injury occurred.

Other disorders that are secondary to head injury are:

1. Spasticity (flexion and extension synergies)
2. Joint Contractures
3. Bowel and Bladder Dysfunctions
4. Pneumonia
5. Seizures
6. Depression
7. Loss of Judgment
8. Headaches
9. Memory Loss
10. Impulsive Behavior

Most of the students seen in Adapted Physical Education Programs at the post-secondary level have incurred either a CVA or a head trauma. The following chart will shows the major differences between a person who had a CVA vs. a head trauma.

DIFFERENCES BETWEEN PERSONS WITH
CVA AND ACQUIRED BRAIN INJURY

	CVA	ABI
AGE AT ONSET	50 years +	16-25 years (most common age)
INJURIES	Brain tissue and secondary dysfunctions	Brain, secondary dysfunctions orthopedic
BRAIN DAMAGE	Local, specific	General, nonspecific
FAMILY	Head of household	Dependent or new head
VOCATION	Retirement or approaching	Unestablished, student
BEHAVIOR	Somewhat predictable	Unpredictable
SEXUALITY	Mature, adjusted	Immature, confused

TEACHING TIPS

LEFT BRAIN DAMAGE RIGHT HEMIPLEGIA	TEACHING TIPS
* Speech & Language Problems	* Speak slowly, use short sentences.
* Slow, Cautious & Disorganized Behavioral Styles	* Give frequent and accurate feedback.
* Memory Deficit Relating to Speech	* Be helpful but not a nag.

TEACHING TIPS

RIGHT BRAIN DAMAGE LEFT HEMIPLEGIA	TEACHING TIPS
* Spatial-Perceptual Problems; i.e., decreased ability to judge distances, sizes, etc.	* Have person demonstate skills rather than taking their word for it.
* Impulsive & Too Fast Behavioral Style	* Have person talk self through tasks.
* Over-Estimate Abilities	* Use caution. Assess abilities. Progress from easy to difficult tasks.
* One-Sided Neglect	* Arrange environment to maximum sensory input.

INDICATED EXERCISE PROGRAM

Often, persons with ABI are resistant to physical activity on the basis that it will aggravate headaches, cause dizziness, or fatigue them. Generally, exercise will not aggravate any conditions. It is recommended that the individual spend at least 30 to 60 minutes daily participating in activities that will develop muscular strength and endurance, cardiovascular endurance, balance, and coordination. Small group activities teaching balance and range of motion have been found to be successful and beneficial, provided that progress is monitored regularly. The time spent partaking in exercise, swimming and/or sports activities is not only valuable physically, but is also psychologically stimulating.

A suggested program for the ABI student should consist of:

1. MUSCULAR STRENGTH

    Initially, strength exercises are usually best performed using PNF or manual resistance. A weight training program can be gradually introduced to facilitate independence. Flexibility exercises should be performed before and after strength exercises to promote relaxation and range of motion. If a student with ABI demonstrates a significant amount of spasticity, flexibility and coordination exercises should be emphasized as weight training may exaggerate muscle tonus and synergy.

2. FLEXIBILITY

    Range of motion should be performed on all major joints (i.e., ankle, knee, hip, shoulder, elbow, and wrist). Hold-relax techniques are preferable to active or passive ROM.

3. BALANCE AND COORDINATION

    For some head injured, a significant portion of the exercise program should be devoted to balance activities and coordination.

4. CARDIOVASCULAR TRAINING

    This activity is not only useful to increase aerobic capacity, but it encourages reciprocal movements of the arm and leg. Obtain medical clearance prior to allowing student with a stroke to participate in a cardiovascular program.

5. PERCEPTUAL MOTOR

    Many head injuries display deficiencies with spatial awareness (ability to judge time, distance, sizes, etc.), right/left discrimination, atopographic memory loss, etc.

APHASIA

Many times the head injured person will suffer from aphasia. This handicap is the inability to comprehend spoken language (receptive aphasia) and/or execute speech (expressive aphasia). These are due to a lesion in the auditory cortex of the brain.

The following list contains suggestions for communicating with aphasic individuals.

1. Allow the person to make mistakes while speaking. Occasional corrections are appropriate. If corrected too often, the aphesic student may not want to speak.
2. Do not interrupt the aphasic student or supply words unless help is requested.
3. Some responses may be unrelated to what the aphesic student actually wants to say. Casually restating what was said may help the student in correcting errors.
4. Don't force the aphesic student to speak to people when he/she doesn't want to.
5. Don't speak for the person unless asked or absolutely necessary.
6. An aphasic student often has to stop after a few words to think of the next word. Don't supply the word at this point.
7. Don't be overly optimistic with the aphasic student in regard to regaining speech (i.e., do not suggest that speech will return soon).
8. Build up the person's self-confidence by emphasizing the activities he/she can do.
9. Encourage the aphasic student in all of his/her efforts. Praise even the smallest gain.
10. Don't take it for granted that the aphasic student understands what you are saying. Occasionally have the student repeat what is expected of him/her.
11. Keep material short, simple and concrete. Give directions in short phrases, rather than long sentences.
12. Reword what you've said in various ways if the aphasic student doesn't understand the first time.
13. The person with aphasia is an adult. Treat him/her like one.

Lastly, it is of paramount importance to keep in mind that many ABI students will have concomitant disabilities which make it imperative that each student be treated individually. It is then critical to relate to each student as an individual and to react to their personality rather than their disability. Also, not every right hemiplegic will manifest the same dysfunctions.

The hope of an Adaptive Physical Education Program for the ABI is to allow the student the opportunity to attain the highest level of functional ability possible, and in doing so, enhance their feelings of self-worth.

STUDY QUESTIONS

1. Name three causes of ABI.

2. Develop an exercise program to address sensory perceptual and motor deficits for an ABI student.

3. The motor strip inside the brain is responsible for what?

AMPUTATIONS

DEFINITION

Amputation refers to the loss of an upper or lower extremity. The term includes both acquired and congenital limb losses.

ETIOLOGY

1. Trauma (reconstructive surgery not feasible)
2. Peripheral Vascular Disease
3. Diabetes
4. Frostbite
5. Chronic Infection of Bone (e.g., osteomyelitis)
6. Tumor
7. Congenital Deformity where existing limb is not capable of functioning properly.

The "phantom limb" syndrome is a frequent complaint of the amputee. This refers to the persistent awareness of the removed limb. This pain may occur shortly after surgery or later. Generally, these sensations are temporary, becoming less common when the prosthesis is applied.

TYPES (named according to the site and level of loss)

CONGENITAL ABSENCES (birth defects)	AMPUTATION LEVEL
Amelia (terminal transverse).	Shoulder Disarticulation.
Hemimelia (terminal transverse).	Above the Elbow (AE).
Partial Hemimelia	Below the Elbow (BE).
Acheiria.	Wrist Disarticulation; Trans-metacarpal Amputation.
Amelia (terminal transverse).	Hip Disarticulation.
Hemimelia (terminal transverse).	Above the Knee (AK).
Partial Hemimelia.	Below the Knee (BK).
Apodia.	Syme Amputation.
Adactylia.	Trans-metatarsal Amputation.

Hemimelia denotes a half of a limb. Amelia refers to total absence of a limb.

INDICATED EXERCISE PROGRAM

The initial rehabilitation program for an amputee consists of training in the use of the prosthesis. For the lower extremity amputee this includes:

1. Balance Activities
2. Ambulation
3. Pivoting
4. Stair Climbing
5. How to Fall To and Rise From the Ground

After this stage, the exercise treatment should develop strength and endurance in both the impaired and normal extremities. Manual resistance would be employed for strengthening the stump.

The aerobic capacity of the amputee should be maintained as much as possible. Swimming is an excellent aerobic choice for even the bilateral BK amputee. Swim fins may be attached to the stumps by special prosthesis. Arm crank ergometry may be another choice for those with limited weight-bearing capabilities.

STUDY QUESTIONS

1. How would you teach swimming to a bilateral amputee?

2. Do you think it would be appropriate for a person with AK amputation to be mainstreamed into regular physical education? If so, why? If not, why not?

ARTHRITIS

More than 36 million people in the United States have arthritis, making it America's number one crippler. Although arthritis literally means "inflammation of a joint", a more accurate description would be "problems with a joint". There are over 100 types of arthritis, all of which have something to do with one or more joints of the body. Children are affected as well as adults.

Joint disease can take two forms: inflammatory or non-inflammatory. Rheumatoid arthritis (RA) is an example of inflammatory joint disease. The site of inflammation is the synovial membrane. Normally, the synovial membrane contributes to the production of synovial fluid (which nourishes joint cartilage and keeps the joint lubricated) and provides for removal of synovial fluid from the joint. Inflammation of the synovial lining results in impairment of both functions. An excess of joint fluid is produced, the drainage mechanism becomes inadequate, and fluid becomes trapped

214

within the capsule. This process damages the capsule, ligaments, cartilage and bone. This mechanical stress makes the joint vulnerable to overstretching during functional use. Pain results due to the increased intra-articular pressure on the innervated capsule. Symptoms of inflammation include pain, swelling, warmth and decreased range of motion. In rheumatoid arthritis, inflammation usually symmetrically affects the smaller joints (i.e., hands, elbows, feet). It is systemic, causing generalized fatigue, decreased appetite, and weight loss. RA can affect people of any age, including children (juvenile rheumatoid arthritis) and there is a greater incidence in women.

Non-inflammatory joint disease primarily refers to degenerative joint disease (DJD)/osteoarthritis (OA) and traumatic arthritis. OA is localized usually affecting the weight-bearing joints (i.e., hips, knees, spine). Degenerative wear and tear of the articulating surface of a joint is characteristic of this condition. Inflammation can be, but is usually not, present. Most people over 65 years of age are affected by OA to some degree. Injury or consistent strain can also lead to OA.

Individually tailored programs should be supervised by a physician and involve a combination of rest, medication, nutrition, exercise, joint protection, application of heat/cold, splinting or surgery if needed. Collectively, these forms of treatment are designed to relieve pain, decrease inflammation, minimize damage to joints and to maintain or increase function.

Unfortunately, many people with arthritis think exercise is harmful. Others become discouraged because progress is slow or their exercises are painful. Participation in specially designed exercise programs can significantly contribute to decreased pain and increased functional level. Range of motion exercises will increase joint mobility, strengthening exercises will increase stability of vulnerable joints, and endurance exercises will promote cardiovascular fitness. Programs must be designed to meet the needs for each person. It is critically important that individuals with arthritis increase their understanding of the disease so that they may use good judgment regarding necessary exercise modifications.

Research to determine appropriate exercise programs has been difficult due to the spontaneous course of exacerbations and remissions arthritis exhibits. Arthritis also affects people in different parts of their bodies and to varying degrees -- everyone is unique. Continued research is needed in this area so that we can best utilize exercise techniques to maximize the quality of life of individuals affected by arthritis.

DEFINITION

Arthritis literally means inflammation of a joint. The definition is a little misleading as many types of arthritis do not evidence joint inflammation. Arthritis is used to describe nearly 100 different conditions which cause aches and pain in the joint or surrounding connective tissue. Several of the most common forms are osteoarthritis, rheumatoid arthritis, anklyosing spondylitis, and gout.

Osteoarthritis is a degenerative condition usually associated with aging, although it can occur in young people. It affects the cartilage of the joints, particularly in the weight-bearing areas (i.e., hips, knees, and ankles). The diagnosis of osteoarthritis is usually based upon an x-ray coupled with blood tests. The prognosis is usually good as the condition progresses slowly, even in severe cases. Profound crippling is relatively rare.

Unlike osteoarthritis, rheumatoid arthritis often begins before the age of 40 years. Symptoms include inflammation, pain, swelling, and tenderness of the joint. It is typical to see periods of inflammation (i.e., exacerbations) followed by remissions. The time interval of exacerbations and remissions will vary among individuals. Symptoms of an exacerbation include loss of appetite, fatigue, fever, and the development of rheumatoid nodules which form under the skin. Various blood tests help the physician recognize rheumatoid arthritis. X-rays are not very useful in diagnosis because it takes several months before the changes in the bones and cartilage appear. It is estimated that only one in six people with rheumatoid arthritis develop any deformities.

Ankylosing spondylitis is a chronic form of arthritis which occurs primarily in individuals under 35 years. The etiology of the disease is unknown. However, many individuals have a genetic marker known as B-27. Generally, ankylosing spondylitis begins with pain and stiffness in the lower back and progresses up the spine. It may eventually involve the hips, shoulders, and occasionally the knees. The symptoms may disappear spontaneously, the extent of rigidity that has occurred thus far will remain.

Gouty arthritis is caused by an inherited metabolic disorder which allows uric acid to accumulate in the blood. Crystals of uric acid are then deposited in the joints, promoting inflammation. The most common site of deposition is the big toe, but other joints may be affected. Gout is an extremely painful condition as the joint becomes hot, red and swollen.

INDICATED EXERCISE PROGRAM

Along with drug therapy, surgery, and good health habits, regular range of motion is the indicated treatment for most forms of arthritis. Joints should be gently placed through their range of motion several times daily. Active stretching of joints is preferable to passive because it aids in maintaining the strength of muscle groups opposing a contracture. Flexibility exercises should always be performed through the pain-free range of motion.

It is paramount to keep the body weight under control. Obesity accelerates the damage to diseased weight-bearing joints. This suggest aerobic exercises such as swimming and bicycling at low resistances. Many hospitals have instituted "arthroswim" programs for their arthritic outpatients.

For the client with rheumatoid arthritis, careful consideration must be given to the proper combination of rest and exercise. Rest is necessary to reduce inflammation; yet, disuse also allows the joints to become stiff and the muscles to atrophy. As a general rule, the intensity and duration of exercise should be determined by pain.

Strength exercises are indicated if they are performed actively, isometrically, or with gentle resistance. PNF is especially beneficial as it strengthens all muscles about a joint. Traction and approximation should not be performed when utilizing PNF techniques.

CONTRAINDICATIONS

1. Exercising with the presence of pain other than discomfort from normal exercise exertion.
2. Use of isotonic weight equipment for strength training causes excessive compression of joints or traction-loading.

IMPORTANCE OF EXERCISE

1. Increases student's strength and flexibility.
2. Helps maintain or increase bone strength.
3. Provides nourishment and lubrication to joints.
4. Prevents disuse syndrome.
5. Provides feelings of control and self-worth.

WHEN SHOULD EXERCISE BE PERFORMED?
1. On a daily basis.
2. When there is the least amount of pain and stiffness during the day.
3. When the individual is least tired.
4. When the individual receives the maximum benefit from medications during the day (generally 10-11 am).
5. After preparation with massage, heating pad, warm shower, or gentle rhythmic movements.

PRECAUTIONS
1. Find out what type of arthritis the student has.
2. Minimize stress to joints. Teach about selection of appropriate activities such as swimming.
3. Avoid vigorously exercising an inflamed joint, but gently put joint through range of motion.
4. Discourage increasing medications without physician's approval.
5. Wear warm clothes.
6. Modify the exercise routine with how the person feels. The arthritic condition will

fluctuate from worse to better on a daily basis.

7. Use the two-hour rule: If exercise-induced pain lasts longer than two hours, then cut back on intensity, but do not stop exercising altogether (e.g., decrease repetitions or force).
8. Individualize the exercise program to address problem areas.
9. Do not perform neck hyperextensions or pushups with the hands.

DESCRIPTION OF ARTHROSWIM PROGRAM
("Arthroswim" -- Arthritis Foundation, San Diego Area Chapter)

The Arthroswim Program deals with a diverse group of participants whose expression of disease is wide and varied. Therefore, the program must also be wide and varied to meet their needs.

EXPLANATION TO INSTRUCTORS
This exercise program has essentially been divided into five parts:

1. Warm Up Exercise
2. Stretching Exercise
3. Aerobic Cardiopulmonary Exercise
4. Strengthening Exercise
5. Cool Down Exercise

A new swimmer (a student not now actively swimming at least twice a week for approximately 20 minutes) may find it to be less painful and most beneficial to do the warm up and stretching portions on the first visit to class. Then, as the student continues to attend, the aerobic exercise and then lastly (approximately the third visit to class) the strengthening exercises and cool down activities may be added slowly. This approach allows some program flexibility to be applied individually to each student as per the student's needs.

The previous paragraph may also be applied to students returning from vacation/hospital stay/illness/arthritis flare up.

Students should be encouraged to always consult their physician about changes in anything having to do with their arthritis (i.e., medications, pain, endurance, strength, complications from a fall, accident, fever, etc.).

Class Variables:

1. Repetitions
2. Speed of pulling an arm/leg through the water
3. Walk-Jog-Run
4. Time spent in water
5. Duration of each exercise
6. Rest periods
7. Water depth-buoyancy

8. Fun
9. Type of arthritis
10. Stationary exercise (standing still for each exercise -- walking forward and backward with water resistance -- not a variable)

ARTHROSWIM PROGRAM

INTRODUCTION
   Every person in the class must be considered individually. All exercises are not for everyone. The best rule is: If it hurts, STOP!

A. WARM UP

B. STRENGTHENING EXERCISES
   1. Pelvic Tilt: Place back against the wall with knees slightly bent, push the small of your back and shoulders flat against the wall, hold this position and do some breathing exercise like counting or singing.
   2. Shoulder Girdle Rolling: With arms at side, roll shoulders in a circle (forwards and backwards).
   3. Single Knee to Chest: Take three steps and pull one bent knee to your chest, alternating knees.
   4. Shoulder External Rotation: Elbows bent with fingertips toward shoulders, squeeze elbows to touching in front of your jaw, stretch elbows out to the side and breathe deeply.
   5. Isometric Knee Exercise: With low back flat against the wall, tighten ankles to lift toes and tighten knees very straight, hold and relax toes and knees.
   6. Shoulder Internal Rotation: With hands behind your back, bend elbows to reach towards shoulder blades, breathe in deeply, relax and exhale as you lower hands.
   7. Neck Exercise: Pull head back keeping chin level as if at attention, lower shoulders and inhale deeply, relax neck and shoulders as you exhale.
   8. Heel Cord Stretching: Face wall placing forearms against the wall standing with one foot in front of the other, keeping heels on floor, bend front knee and slowly lean toward wall until a pull is felt at heel of back leg. Push out with arms to standing position.
   9. Pronation and Supination: With elbows at rib cage and palms facing down, push palms down through the water until elbows are straight, now turn palms up and pull up through the water keeping elbows at rib cage.
   10. Finger Curls : Squeeze hands into a fist, uncurl so that fingertips touch the base of fingers, then stretch fingers and thumbs out very straight. Repeat, curl, fist,

uncurl and stretch.

C. RUNNING, CARDIOPULMONARY ACTIVITY, SWIMMING LAPS, WALKING, HOPPING

D. WORK OUT
1. Hula: Rotate hips around in a large circle.
2. Around the World: With side to the wall, bend outside knee to chest, stretch leg out to side, touch foot to floor, then stretch leg behind you.
3. Sweep and Pull: Sweep one hand to opposite shoulder and pull away to straighten elbow, alternate.
4. Pendulum: With low back flat against wall, raise one leg out to the side, drop leg to touch floor and stretch across body to opposite side, swing leg down to touch floor and raise leg out to the side again. Repeat, then swing other leg.
5. Squeeze and Stretch: Squeeze hands reaching out in front of body, stretch hands open and press straight arms close to body and back behind body, bring arms forward without turning hands.
6. Can-Can: Pull one knee to chest, kick foot and lower leg in and out.
7. Breast-stroke Arms: While walking across pool, do breast-stroke with palms down.
8. Leg Circles: With side to wall, raise outside leg and circle leg forwards and backwards.
9. Pull and Leap: Starting position -- arms out to side walking sideways, pull hands and arms up and out to chest height.
10. Ankle Exercise: Pull one knee to chest, point foot up and down several times, then circle foot in both directions.
11. Radial Strengthening: With elbows touching rib cage and palms facing each other, tilt hands to thumb side, pointing thumb and fingers towards ceiling, hold and then relax hands back to beginning position.
12. Heel and Toe: Walk up on toes for three steps, then walk on heels for three steps.

E. COOL DOWN

STUDY QUESTIONS

1. Develop a sample exercise program appropriate for a 65-year old man who has osteoarthritis of the shoulder.

2. What activities do you participate in that may contribute to the development of osteoarthritis.

ASTHMA

DEFINITION

Asthma is classified as a reversible (spontaneous or therapeutically) obstructive airway disease, resulting in the sudden onset of muscle spasms, swelling, and the presence of mucous in the tracheobronchial tree. It is caused by a hyperirritability to a variety of stimuli (inhalants, ingestants, environment, exercise). Exercise-induced asthma (EIA) is brought on by sustained exercise such as running or bicycling for longer than six minutes.

SYMPTOMS

1. Cough or hack (due to increased mucous)
2. Wheezing and dyspnea, leading to difficult exhalation
3. Severe bronchial obstruction where individual becomes cyanotic, constituting an extreme medical emergency

EMERGENCY PROCEDURES

1. Have individual sit and attempt to relax.
2. Provide glass of warm water to break-down mucous.
3. Administer medication.

   The following information should be in the student's medical file:
   1. Type and frequency of medication.
   2. Possible side effects of drugs.
   3. Procedures to follow during an attack.
   4. Substances which trigger the attack (allergies).
   5. Anecdotal record of all attacks.

PHYSICAL CHARACTERISTICS OF INDIVIDUALS WITH ASTHMA

1. Weak abdominals.
2. Loss of flexibility in the shoulder, low back, and hamstrings.
3. Weak upper back muscles (rhomboids).
4. Reduced FEV_1 during and after cessation of exercise. FEV_1 refers to the forced expiratory volume of air in one second. It is a flow rate measuring the amount of air (liters) expired in one second from a maximal exhalation. It is usually expressed as a percentage of the total amount of exhaled air (Forced Vital Capacity or FVC). In unaffected subjects, 80% of the FVC should be expired within the first second.

During exercises, this value falls below 60% in asthmatics. A drop in FEV_1 is one parameter signaling the onset of asthma. EIA becomes increasingly severe as the duration of exercise is increased. The response appears to be greatest after six to eight minutes of aerobic activity.

INDICATED EXERCISE PROGRAM

The following outline provides recommended activities to help prevent the onset of EIA:

A. WARM UP (Sufficient duration to break a sweat.)
   It appears that bronchoconstrictors are slowly depleted during warm up.
   1. Walking alternated with slow jog (equal periods of walk and jog).
   2. Strengthening activities for the abdominals and upper back.
   3. Rhythmic and gentle calisthenics.
   4. Interval or anaerobic activity.

B. MAIN ACTIVITY
   1. Swimming. Found to be one aerobic activity which is not asthmogenic (asthma-provoking).
   2. Team sports/anaerobic activities: Volleyball, softball, tennis, etc.
   3. If jogging or cycling program is instituted, begin with intervals (three bouts of three minutes with rest periods). Increase duration as tolerated.

C. WARM DOWN
   1. Flexibility exercises for shoulders, low back, hamstrings, hip flexors, and ankles.
   2. Should be a low level activity for five minutes or until heart rate returns to within 20 beats per minute of resting level.

CEREBRAL PALSY

DEFINITION

Cerebral palsy is a non-progressive neuromuscular dysfunction occurring from destruction or congenital absence of upper motor neurons and the pyramidal tract during the period of early brain growth. The lesion is permanent but presents no further degeneration. There exist several distinct types, depending upon the site of the lesion.

ETIOLOGY

1. Birth Trauma (cerebral hemorrhage) -- insufficient oxygen
2. Prematurity
3. Rubella
4. Rh factor
5. Child Abuse

TYPES

1. Spastic

   a. Hyperactive tonic and phasic stretch reflexes.
   b. Clonus (reverberating jerky movements).
   c. Lesion to motor cortex.
   d. Muscle appears hypertonic.
   e. Postural deformities secondary to spasticity and contractures (e.g., spastic crouch, scoliosis).
   f. Scissors gait -- excessive hip flexion-adduction-internal rotation, knee flexion, plantarflexion.
2. Athetoid
   a. Rotary and dystonic movements (distorted positions).
   b. Range of motion is normal.
   c. Lesion to basal ganglia.
3. Ataxia
   a. Disturbance of balance.
   b. Hypotonic muscle tone.
   c. Lesion to cerebellum.

ASSOCIATED CHARACTERISTICS (not present in all individuals)

1. Seizures
2. Mental Retardation
3. Impairment of Sight, Hearing, and Speech
4. Perceptual Problems and Learning Disabilities
5. Motor Deficits
6. Strabismus

INDICATED EXERCISE PROGRAM FOR SPASTIC CEREBRAL PALSY

Restore muscular balance at all affected joints.
1. Resistive exercises for atrophied and lengthened muscle. This typically includes the hip extensors, hip abductors, hip external rotators, knee extensors, and dorsiflexors.
2. Provide range of motion for hip flexors, hip adductors, knee flexors, plantarflexors, wrist flexors, elbow flexors, shoulders. Use hold-relax or active stretching techniques if possible. Passive stretching often has to be instituted for the more severely involved (see Chapter 3).

INDICATED EXERCISE PROGRAM FOR ALL TYPES OF CEREBRAL PALSY

1. Increase cardiovascular endurance through arm or leg cycling, swimming, running, or wheelchair pushing.
2. Balance activities for lying, kneeling, sitting, and standing position (see Chapter 3).
3. Perceptual motor activities, especially manipulative activities involving grasp and release.
4. Activities promoting control of reciprocal movement: Climbing, skipping, marching, cycling, stepping in and out of tires, and swimming.
5. Practice walking, concentrating on heelstrike.
6. Kinetron for strength and endurance.

DIABETES

Diabetes is a disease in which the body is unable to use food properly. It is caused by an insufficient supply of insulin. Insulin is produced in the pancreas. The function of insulin is to regulate the rate at which the body uses or stores sugar. Much of the food we eat is converted into a form of sugar called glucose or stored as glycogen. Glycogen is stored in the liver and muscles and may be broken down into glucose when needed. Insulin is needed by the body to burn glucose which provides energy for the muscles. If the pancreas fails to produce enough insulin, glucose cannot be used by the muscles or stored and glucose accumulates in the bloodstream and causes blood sugar levels to rise above normal.

Two signs of diabetes are:
1. Excessive amounts of sugar in the blood (hyperglycemia).
2. Excretion of sugar in the urine (glycosuria).

The symptoms of diabetes are related to the increased amount of sugar in the blood. Diabetes may be without symptoms; such may be the case with elderly weakness. Other symptoms include pain, numbness, tingling in the hands and feet, disturbances in vision, irritability and nervousness. In children, the classic symptoms manifest themselves, such as weight loss, polyuria, polydipsia and fatigue.

There are two types of diabetes:

> Type 1, also known as Juvenile Diabetes, Insulin Dependent.
> Type 2, Adult on-set Diabetes, Non-Insulin Dependent.

Juvenile diabetes generally occurs in childhood or adolescence and can develop rapidly with acute symptoms. Adult diabetes is less abrupt in on-set and results in resistance to the individual's own insulin. However, both types may occur at any age.

Diabetes can lead to:

1. Cardiovascular Disorders. A person with diabetes is two times more likely to develop Coronary Artery Disease.
2. Macrovascular Disease. Diabetes contributes to the development of vascular problems; i.e., amputation.
3. Microvascular Disease. Diabetic retinopathy results when tiny blood vessels in the retina break and cause little hemorrhages on or near the retina. This can lead to permanent visual loss (blindness) over time. Cataracts also seem to be more prevalent in persons with diabetes. Because of the relationship between diabetes and eye disorders, the diabetic should always inform an ophthalmologist about his/her condition.
4. Neuropathy Destruction of nerves caused by excessive blood glucose and poor blood supply.

TREATMENT

Diabetes cannot be cured, but can be controlled. Treatment may include medication (insulin), daily exercise and diet therapy. Exercise in consistent amounts is very important in managing Type 2 diabetes. Blood glucose levels should be checked prior to exercise to determine any adjustments in food intake. If blood sugar levels are 300 mg or greater, do not begin exercise. Table 13-1 provides guidelines for adjusting food intake according to blood sugar levels.

DIABETIC REACTIONS

The most frequent complications of diabetes are the insulin reaction and diabetic coma. The former will most likely occur during an exercise session since the effects of exercise and insulin are similar except where blood sugar levels exceed 300 mg. If the levels of blood glucose are insufficient to fuel the brain, then symptoms appear, such as confusion, nausea and blurred vision. Administering fruit juices, non-dietetic carbonated beverages, or hard candies usually will terminate the insulin reaction in two to three minutes. If the diabetic does not respond promptly to sugar, medical help should be sought immediately. (Bleck, 1975).

THE EFFECTS OF TOO MUCH OR TOO LITTLE INSULIN

	Insulin Reaction	Diabetic Coma
Onset:	Rapid (minutes)	Gradual (hours)
Symptoms:	Headache Nausea Vomiting Tremulousness Irritability	Fatigue Thirst Hunger Frequent Urination
Skin:	Cold and Moist	Warm and Dry
Breathing:	Normal and Shallow	Deep
Urine:	Negative Glucose Negative Acetone	4+ Glucose Positive Acetone
Treatment:	Sugar	Insulin Medical Attention

TABLE 13-1. Guidelines for Adjusting Food Intake
According to Blood Sugar Levels

GENERAL GUIDELINES FOR MAKING FOOD ADJUSTMENTS FOR EXE

Type of Exercise and Examples	If Blood Sugar Is	Increase Food Intake By	Suggested Foods
Exercise of short duration and of low to moderate intensity Examples: Walking a 1/2 mile or leisurely bicycling for 30 minutes.	Less than 100 mg 100 mg or above	10-15 gms of carbohydrate per hour Not necessary to increase food	1 fruit or 1 bread exchange
Exercise of moderate intensity Examples: Tennis, swimming, jogging, leisurely bicycling, gardening, golfing, or vacuuming for one hour	Less than 100 mg 100-200 mg 200-300 mg 300 mg or greater	25-50 gms of carbohydrate before exercise, then 10-15 gms per hour of exercise 10-15 gms of carbohydrate per hour of exercise Not necessary to increase food Don't begin exercise until blood glucose is under control	1/2 meat sandwich with a milk or fruit exchange 1 fruit or 1 bread exchange
Strenuous activity or exercise Examples: Football, hockey, racquetball or basketball games; strenuous biking or swimming, and shoveling heavy snow for one hour	Less than 100 mg 100-170 mg 200-300 mg	50 gms of carbohydrate, monitor blood glucose carefully 25-50 mg of carbohydrate, depending on intensity and duration 10-15 gms of carbohydrate per hour of exercise	1 meat sandwich (2 slices of bread) with a milk and fruit exchange 1/2 meat sandwich with a mik or fruit exchange 1 fruit or 1 bread exchange

EPILEPSY

DEFINITION

According to the Epilepsy Foundation of America (1974), epilepsy is symptomatic of a central nervous system disorder due to excessive electrical discharges in the cerebrum (i.e., seizure). Epilepsy is a syndrome in which seizures occur repeatedly and is classified according to the severity of electrical discharge and the brain region where the epilepsy originates.

DIAGNOSIS

Diagnosis of epilepsy involves a complete physical and neurological examination (including x-rays) and occasionally a spinal tap. The electroencephalogram (EEG) is useful, not only in identifying epilepsy, but determining the most effective treatment. This method records the brain's electrical patterns on a graph.

ETIOLOGY

1. Idiopathic (cause unknown)
2. Genetic Disposition (possible metabolic disorder)
3. Acquired (tumors, anoxic brain, hemorrhage)
4. Prenatal (infections, rubella)
5. Postnatal (infections such as meningitis)

FACTORS WHICH PROVOKE ONSET OF A SEIZURE

1. Increased alkalinity of blood (dietary fat and exercise will increase acidity of blood)
2. Flashing strobe lights
3. Emotional stress
4. Edema
5. Hyperventilation at rest
6. Excessive fatigue

TYPES OF SEIZURES

1. PETIT MAL (ABSENCE). This type is more common in children than adults and frequently disappears in adolescence. It is a very mild form of seizure. Although the individual is unconscious during the seizure (5-20 seconds), the posture is maintained and convulsions do not occur. The only signs may be staring with a rapid blinking or rolling of the eyes upward. Petit mal seizures may occur up to 100

times per day.

2. GRAND MAL (TONIC-CLONIC). The Grand Mal seizure has two phases which last a total of approximately five minutes. In the tonic phase, the individual becomes unconscious and rigid, falling to the ground. The clonic phase follows, characterized by rhythmic, muscular convulsions. After the seizure has ceased, the individual is very tired and may need to rest or sleep. These seizures often occur during sleep.

3. PSYCHOMOTOR (COMPLEX-PARTIAL). This type of seizure involves only a portion of the brain and will present varying symptoms between individuals, depending upon the portion of the brain affected. The duration of the seizure is usually between two to five minutes. The person often will perform purposeless, repetitive movements such as picking at clothing or rubbing of the hands. It is not unusual for the individual to walk around and he/she should be steered clear of any danger.

Any type of seizure may be preceded by an aura. This is an unusual feeling or sensation such as disturbed vision or a peculiar taste in the mouth.

Seizures are characteristic and prevalent in persons with suspected neurological damage such as cerebral palsy, mental retardation, learning disabilities, autism, and head injuries.

INDICATED EXERCISE PROGRAM

Historically, vigorous physical education and competitive/contact sports were contraindicated for epileptics by physicians. It was assumed that additional head trauma contact from sports might increase the incidence or intensity of seizures. However, research studies have never substantiated this notion. Furthermore, since aerobic exercise actually increases the acidity of the blood (due to metabolic acidosis), moderate physical activity may actually create a "buffer" against tonic-clonic seizures. The Adapted Physical Educator should be cautioned, however, that over-fatigue may be a factor in all types of seizures.

When selecting physical activities, consider the individual's desire to participate and weight it against the medical management. Well-controlled seizures usually indicate unrestricted participation in contact sports, swimming, and tumbling. ALWAYS OBTAIN A MEDICAL CLEARANCE FROM A PHYSICIAN BEFORE ALLOWING THE INDIVIDUAL TO PARTICIPATE IN AN EXERCISE PROGRAM. Close supervision is always a must, especially in any activity involving heights or a pool.

FIRST AID FOR A GRAND MAL (TONIC-CLONIC) EPILEPTIC SEIZURE

1. Keep calm. The person is usually not suffering or in danger.
2. Help client to a safe place, but DO NOT restrain convulsions.
3. Loosen tight clothing and protect his/her head from injury by placing something soft underneath it.
4. As soon as possible, turn the person on his/her side. This will prevent the tongue from falling to the back of the throat and blocking the air passage. Choking from vomit or saliva will also be prevented by having the person on his/her side.
5. DO NOT PUT ANYTHING BETWEEN THE TEETH.
6. DO NOT give him/her anything to drink.
7. Stand by until the person has fully recovered consciousness and from the confusion which sometimes follows a seizure.
8. Let him/her rest if tired.
9. It is rarely necessary to call public authorities, a doctor, or an ambulance. However, in cases of repeated or prolonged seizures (over 10 minutes of stiffening or jerking), it is suggested that medical help be secured.
10. Fill out an anecdotal record provided by the instructor. It is important to observe the progression of the seizure, especially if it is a first-time occurrence. The diagnosis of the type of seizure can be greatly aided by your observations.
11. If injured, it may be necessary to call the paramedics. Fill out an injury report form.

REFERENCES

Bleck, E. E. & Nagel, D. A. (1975). Physically Handicapped Children - A Medical Atlas for Teachers. New York: Grune & Stratton.

Epilepsy Society (1981). Epilepsy Handbook for Teachers and Nurses. 1612 30th Street. San Diego, CA, 92102.

GERONTOLOGY

Aging and death have intrigued man since the beginning of time. Particularly frightening is the loss of physical and mental abilities associated with aging. Aging is a progressive, irreversible, and cumulative series of structural and functional changes which occur throughout one's life. Studies show that cells are lost from many tissues during the process of aging. Organs gradually change their structure and function less efficiently in older individuals.

Many older people believe that their health is at the mercy of their doctor. Physical fitness may be the key to both mental and physical health. The purpose of exercise is not to add years to one's life, but rather add life to one's years!

Degeneration associated with aging should be distinguished from disease and disuse. Aging is often associated with weight gain, an accumulation of body fat, loss of lean body tissue and a decrease in aerobic capacity.

Since much of the decline in bodily function seen in aging is analogous to that which accompanies a sedentary life style, one might hypothesize that this decline might be reversed with proper exercise which is now under investigation.

There are many physiological parameters that change with age. There are:

MUSCULOSKELETAL CHANGES
1. Muscle atrophy (not irreversible until 60's)
2. Decreased connective tissue elasticity; dehydration of connective tissue and intervertebral disks
3. Bone demineralization resulting in postural deviations such as kyphosis and increased likelihood of fractures
4. Postural deviations which result from narrowing of the intervertebral disks, osteoporosis and adaptive shortening of connective tissue

CARDIO-RESPIRATORY CHANGES
1. Decreased Max HR
2. Decreased Max O2 consumption
3. Decreased vital capacity and expiratory volumes
4. Decreased minimum ventilation

ADDITIONAL CHANGES
1. Loss of balance due to degeneration within the nerves

Many community colleges provide Adaptive Physical Education programs in retirement facilities. The primary role of the Adaptive Physical Education program in these facilities is to provide exercise programs that satisfy the physiological, social, and psychological needs of the senior adult. Although aging is not a disability, many physical limitations are associated with old age such as heart disease, arthritis, hypertension, and visual impairments. Thus, this population is more susceptible to injury during exercise and requires close supervision by assistants. Seniors are also more likely to be using medication than younger individuals.

CONTRAINDICATED EXERCISES

1. Isometric contractions of the arms, trunk, or legs.
2. Rapid twisting movements.
3. Ballistic stretching.
4. Standing toe touches.
5. Strenuous weight training.

TEACHING SUGGESTIONS

1. Exercise programs for seniors should be progressive in design.
2. Do not overwork any joint or muscle group.
3. Do not stress activities that require vision or static balance without support.
4. Teach the whys of exercise.
5. Do not force people to participate.
6. Do not exacerbate existing conditions.
7. Routine needs to be adaptable to the needs of students.
8. Treat students as adults; validate their experience.
9. Present material slowly and in small steps.
10. Speak slowly and give good demonstrations.

STUDY QUESTIONS

1. What is the definition of Gerontology ? (See reference materials.)

2. What factors should be considered when developing an exercise program for older adults?

3. What are the current thoughts on weight training for seniors? Can they develop muscle mass, etc.? (See reference materials.)

HEARING DISORDERS

Hearing disorders may result in both loss of amplitude (decibels) and pitch (hertz). The term "deaf" signifies that speech can not be heard even through amplification. Total deafness if rare. Hearing disorders are one of the most common chronic physical impairments in the United States.

The real handicap of a hearing disorder is the inability to communicate in the mainstream. New methods of standardized sign language, finger-spelling techniques, and even lip reading provide the hearing impaired with greater opportunities for interacting with others. Remember that lip reading is a developed skill and that most hearing impaired persons do not read lips.

TYPES OF HEARING IMPAIRMENTS

Congenitally deaf refers to those individuals who have been deaf since birth. Adventitiously deaf refers to someone who became deaf later on in life.

Conductive deafness occurs when sound waves cannot be transmitted through

232

either the outer or middle ear. The causes of this type of deafness could be the result of:

1. Congenital atresia
2. Middle ear infection due to
   a. Upper respiratory infection
   b. Diseased tonsils
   c. Adenoids
   d. Childhood diseases
   e. Otitis media
   f. Osteosclerosis

Sensorineural deafness occurs when sensory nerves of the inner ear are irreversibly damaged. A partial loss of equilibrium responses is frequently associated with sensorineural hearing losses.

INDICATED EXERCISE PROGRAM

For those with sensorineural hearing loss, balance is important. This is understandable due to the fact that the auditory organ has dual function of hearing and equilibrium. Many hearing impaired are withdrawn socially from games, dances and group activities.

SUGGESTED PROGRAM FOR HEARING IMPAIRED

1. Group activities and sports to foster social development.
2. Balance and coordination exercises.
3. Body mechanic exercises.
4. Comprehensive physical fitness program that addresses muscular strength and endurance and cardiovascular fitness.

Although it is true the hearing impaired frequently have special needs that could be met in an Adaptive Physical Education program, many times the hearing impaired do very well in mainstreamed physical education classes.

SPECTRUM OF HEARING IMPAIRMENTS

Mild	Marginal	Moderate	Severe	Profound
20-30 db. loss	30-40 db. loss	40-60 db. loss	60-75 db. loss	75+ db. loss
	Hearing Aid	Special	"Educationally	Respond reflexively
	Language	Education	Deaf"	to loud sounds.
	Deficiencies			

HEARING IMPAIRMENT CHARACTERISTICS

1. Balance (static or dynamic): When there exists a sensorineural (inner ear) loss. However, may compensate through the use of visual and kinesthetic cues.
2. Hyperactivity: In order to maintain visual contact with all action occurring in the environment; boredom due to incomprehension.
3. Socially Immature: Due to delay in acquisition of speech and language; has difficulties grasping intricacies of team strategy.

TEACHING STRATEGIES

1. Do not have child face sun.
2. Do not talk while facing away from child. Circle formations are ideal.
3. Remove hearing aid during contact sports. Harness for hearing aid during PE.
4. Keep spare battery (obtain from parents).
5. Keep hearing aid away from excessive moisture.
6. Use pictures and charts to reinforce demonstrations.
7. If balance dysfunction exists, supervise climbing and apparatus work
8. Do not exaggerate or raise voice when speaking to someone with a hearing aid. (Causes tension headaches.)
9. Assign teammate to act as a partner and inform deaf student of changes in the environment.
10. Use visual cues (red flag, turn off lights) to get attention during activities.
11. Teach principles of equilibrium:
    a. Broad base of support.
    b. Lower center of gravity.
    c. Use of arms out to side.
    d. How to fall properly.
    e. Use of kneeling and sitting positions.
    f. Falling outside base of support.

COMMUNICATING WITH A PERSON WHO IS DEAF

Get the deaf person's attention before speaking. A tap on the shoulder, a wave, or another visual signal usually does the trick.

Key the deaf person into the topic of discussion. Deaf people need to know what subject matter is to be discussed in order to pick up words which help them follow the conversation. This is especially important for deaf people who depend on oral communication.

Speak slowly and clearly, but do not yell, exaggerate, or over-pronounce. It's estimated that only 3 out of 10 spoken words are visible on the lips. Exaggeration and over-emphasis of words distort lip movements, making speech-reading more difficult. Try to enunciate each word, without force or tension. Short sentences are easier to understand than long one.

Look directly at the deaf person when speaking. Even a slight turn of your head can obscure their speech-reading view.

Do not place anything in your mouth when speaking. Mustaches that obscure the lips, smoking, pencil chewing, and putting your hands in front of your face all make it difficult for deaf persons to follow what is being said.

Maintain eye contact with the deaf person. Eye contact conveys the feeling of direct communication. Even if an interpreter is present, continue to speak directly to the deaf person. He/she will turn to the interpreter as needed.

Avoid standing in front of a light source, such as a window or bright light. The bright background and shadows created on the face make it almost impossible to speech-read.

First repeat, then try to rephrase a thought rather than again repeating the same words. If the person only missed one or two words the first time, one repetition usually will help. Particular combinations of lip movements sometimes are difficult for deaf persons to speech-read. Don't be embarrassed to communicate by paper and pencil if necessary. Getting the message across is more important than the medium used.

Use pantomime, body language, and facial expression to help communicate. A lively speaker always is more interesting to watch.

Be courteous to the deaf person during conversation. If the telephone rings or someone knocks at the door, excuse yourself and tell the deaf person that you are answering the phone or responding to the knock. Do not ignore the deaf person and carry on a conversation with someone else while the deaf person waits.

Use open-ended question which must be answered by more than "yes" or "no". Do not assume that deaf persons have understood your message if they nod their head in acknowledgment. Open-ended questions ensure that your information has been communicated.

1. A certain amount of planning is necessary to ensure successful integration of hard-of-hearing students into a regular physical education program. Make a list of things that will create the best possible teaching environment for a class that has mainstreamed hearing impaired students.

2. Teaching the totally deaf person requires the use of special techniques. Select any sport skill and indicate how you would teach it to a student who is totally deaf. Specify the techniques you would use to teach the various components of the skill.

   Sport Skill:

   Method of Teaching:

   Techniques:

3. According to Public Law 94-142, what are the definitions of deaf and hard-of-hearing?

LEARNING DISABILITIES

The term "Learning Disabilities" has been used to describe a variety of problems in processing, retrieving and storing information. Students with a learning disability receive inaccurate information through their senses and/or have trouble processing that information.

The term learning disability has been used to describe a variety of problems in processing visual, auditory, tactile, vestibular, and kinesthetic information. Educationally, it results in a discrepancy between estimated IQ (average or above average) and academic performance (below average). It affects the ability to effectively use written or spoken language (dyslexia and aphasia, respectively).

The most commonly used definition is taken from The Education for All Handicapped Children Act of 1975. Public Law 94-142 states:

The term "children with specific learning disabilities" means those children who have a disorder in one or more of the basic psychological processes involved in understanding or in using language, spoken or written, which may manifest itself in imperfect ability to listen, speak, read, write, spell or do mathematical calculations. Such disorders include such conditions as perceptual handicaps, brain injury, minimal brain dysfunction, dyslexia and developmental aphasia. Such terms do not include children who have learning problems which are primarily the result of visual, hearing or motor handicaps, of mental retardation, of emotional disturbances, or environmental, cultural or economic disadvantage.

Some learning disabled people have social skills problems because their perceptual problems make it difficult for them to understand others. A person who is unable to discriminate visually between the letters V and U might also be unable to see the differences between a friendly smile and a sarcastic smile. A person unable to discriminate between two different musical notes might be unable to hear the difference between a joking and a questioning voice. People with auditory handicaps work so hard to understand the words of a statement that they might ignore the nonverbal meaning. This confusion can cause learning disabled people to have difficulty fitting in with others. They might have trouble meeting people, working with others, talking to authority figures, and making friends.

However, other learning disabled adults have superior social skills, which they have developed in order to compensate for their handicaps.

Many people confuse mental retardation and learning disabilities. The basic difference is that a learning disabled person has an average or above average IQ. Many famous people had a learning disability -- Leonardo da Vinci, Hans Christian Anderson, Albert Einstein. Can you name any current famous people who are learning disabled?

THEORETICAL CAUSES OF LEARNING DISABILITIES

The following list of theories attempts to provide explanations of learning deficits. No theory completely explains learning disabilities; each theory offers only a partial explanation. One study suggests that there was a genetic factor in about 20% of 500 case histories reviewed. The genetic link seems to be more common from male to male family members. There are a myriad of non-inherited dysfunction theories, and more still coming through recent and future research. Some of the present major theories include brain injury, biochemical imbalances, maturational or developmental delay of the central nervous system, neurological disorganization of the brain, and sensorimotor dysfunctions.

1. **Minimal Brain Dysfunction** -- Caused by damage to the brain at birth or during prenatal and post-natal periods. Lesions or scar tissue may be present.
2. **Neural Transmission Defects** -- Caused by improper transmission of nerve impulses from one neuron to another across the synapse. Depending on the ratio of the chemicals, acetycholine and cholinesterase, which are present at the synapse, the nerve impulse may be transmitted either too slowly or too quickly.

3. **Maturational or Developmental Lag** -- Relates mainly to the delay of the myelin sheath that encases the nerve fibers.
4. **Neurological Organization of the Brain** -- According to the Delacato and Doman Theory, the right and left hemispheres of the brain have not developed properly. The left hemisphere has not become dominant over the right. Remedial treatment consists of retraining at the early stages of motor development, such as creeping or crawling, during which proper development naturally occurs.
5. **Perceptual-Motor Match** -- According to Kephard and Barsch, poor perceptual-motor-spatial abilities are related to learning deficits. Therefore, the ability to relate the self to time and space (balancing, laterality, directionality) should be remediated if learning deficits are to be overcome.

ETIOLOGY

1. Breakdown in chemical neurotransmitters.
2. Artificial food additives.
3. Genetic predisposition.
4. Malnutrition.
5. Infections (e.g., meningitis).
6. Toxins (e.g., lead).
7. Prematurity.
8. Other suggested causes are: lack of oxygen at birth, premature birth, low birth weight, Caesarean birth, as well as food allergies.

CHARACTERISTICS OF LEARNING DISABLED

Learning disabilities can manifest itself in many forms. The following are but a few of the common areas of deficiencies.

1. Visual Perception
   a. Figure-ground: Difficulty in seeing a specific image within a competing background.
   b. Sequencing: Difficulty seeing figures in correct order; for example, seeing letters reversed.
   c. Discrimination: Difficulty seeing the differences between two similar objects, such as the letters "c" and "e".
   d. Spatial Awareness: Difficulty in judging distance, depth, and direction.
   e. Ocular Tracking: Difficulty in tracking a moving object with the eyes.
   f. Other Characteristics -- Hyperactivity, disorders of attention, poor self-concept, and impulsivity.

INDICATED EXERCISE PROGRAM

Activities found to be useful for the LD student are: jogging, relaxation, perceptual-motor activities, highly structured teacher-directed routines and noncompetitive games -- all of which must be taught in a sequential fashion. In general, an exercise program for the LD person should follow guidelines established for a total fitness program. Perceptual-motor training programs which are progressive in design have been developed by Jack Capon, Marianne Frostig and Newell Kephart.

Although traditional perceptual-motor training has not been shown to conclusively remediate academic deficiencies, it can improve the perceptual-motor skills of the clumsy student in physical education. Active learning games, developed by Dr. Bryant Cratty of UCLA, do help to reinforce the teaching of academic concepts.

STUDY QUESTIONS

1. Relationship of Motor and Academic Skill Improvement. A learning disability is frequently defined as a disorder in understanding or using language, written or spoken, in the decades of the fifties and sixties. Many authors of articles assumed that improvement of motor skills through perceptual-motor programs improved language skills. How can perceptual-motor programs be utilized to improve language skills?

2. Motor Activities have been found to improve perceptual-motor ability. Activities ,that provide specific experiences in perceiving and responding to stimuli with motor movement, may be helpful in alleviating perceptual deficiencies that often hinder effective motor movement. Develop one motor activity that might help decrease the perceptual motor problem for each of the following deficiencies listed below.
   a. Visual Discrimination
   b. Figure-Ground (background) Discrimination
   c. Depth Perception
   d. Object Consistency
   e. Visual Agnosia

4. Activities to Develop Body Awareness. Body awareness is often defined as the ability to know where the body is in space, and how it moves. Learning disabled children often have poor body awareness. Design three different activities that will be useful in helping children to:
   a. Identify parts of the body.
   b. Move the body to achieve and maintain good balance.
   c. Move the body through space.

MULTIPLE SCLEROSIS

DEFINITION

Multiple Sclerosis (M.S.) is a demyelinating disease of the brain and spinal cord. Myelin is the protective covering around nerve fibers which preserves the speed and intensity of the electrical nerve impulse. When M.S. is present, myelin is destroyed and replaced by scar tissue; consequently, nerve signals to and from the brain are distorted or blocked. The scarring plaques are usually present in the pyramidal and extrapyramidal tracts, cerebellum, brain stem, cerebral hemispheres, and optical pathways (Calliet, 1984). The lesions may occur in one or any combination of these sites. The damage to the upper motoneurons causes reflexes which are normally inhibited by these centers to become hyperactive. It strikes young adults, usually those between 20 and 40 years of age.

CLINICAL PICTURE

Symptoms include diplopia, nystagmus, ataxia, dysarthria, ipsilateral and bilateral paresis, and spasticity in the upper and lower extremities (Mankey, 1984). Demyelination also leads to early onset of fatigue. Optimal energy periods appear to be early mornings and evenings, and times of depressed metabolic rates. Heat, either external or internal, increases fatigue and worsens the symptoms. Shauf and Davis (1974) attributed the increased fatigue to a blockage of conducting fibers in the spinal cord.

The prognosis for M.S. varies, but mortality statistics favor longevity.

TYPES

1. Chronic Relapsing M.S.
   This is the most common form. It begins with symptoms of numbness, vertigo, and blindness. Episodes of symptoms lasting for several weeks tend to recur with increasing frequency. After 5 to 8 years, neurologic defects in the form of tremor, spasticity, speech or cerebellar incoordination persist. These abnormalities progress to the point that disabilities become irreversible.
2. Chronic Progressive M.S.
   This form occurs most often in older persons and is characterized by gradual development and slow progression of spasticity and motor incapacity after 5 to 10 years. Death is usually caused by respiratory infection or some unrelated condition.

240

3. Acute M.S.

   This is characterized by the rapid development and steady progression of paralytic symptoms, mainly affecting the function of the brain stem and often leading to death in several months. Curiously, patients, who recover from an attack of acute M.S., are often free from subsequent attacks.

INDICATED EXERCISE PROGRAM

1. Techniques of PNF should be employed as a primary means of restoration or maintenance of function. Hold-relax or contract-relax can be used to decrease spasticity and improve range of motion. Contractures are typically present in the plantarflexors, hamstrings, hip flexors, and hip adductors. If PNF relation techniques are not possible, then active or passive range of motion should be utilized. For strengthening, PNF slow-reversals should be employed to strengthen muscles (arms, trunk and legs) and facilitate reciprocal movement.

2. Swimming is recommended since active exercise may be performed more easily and with less fatigue than on land. The individual can sit in the shallow end and perform such movements as hip flexion, hip adduction, knee extension, knee flexion, dorsiflexion, ankle eversion, trunk flexion, and trunk extension.

3. Balance activities are usually the common component for all M.S. students, although each person's ability will vary.

4. Due to balance deficits and muscular weakness (e.g., drop foot), gait training is usually instituted. This may be initiated on the Kinetron and progress to the parallel bars. The M.S. student typically focuses on lifting one extremity through swing phase (dorsiflexion, knee flexion, and hip flexion). Characteristics of the M.S. (ataxic) gait include a wide base of support, drop foot, and circumducted hip during swing. Stationary bicycling promotes reciprocal movement and strengthens the leg extensors. Interval training should be used so fatigue is minimized.

5. Cardiovascular endurance is difficult to develop in M.S. students due to fatigue factors. Since excessive fatigue may induce some numbness or loss of function, M.S. students should be cautious in over-exerting themselves. Interval training is recommended.

6. Frenkel exercises were developed for conditions involving ataxia. They may be used with the M.S. student and are described below:

   a. Lying position: Flexion and extension of each leg at the knee and hip joints. Abduction and adduction with the knee flexed; later, abduction and adduction with the knee extended.
   b. Flexion and extension of one knee at a time with the heel lifted off the mat.
   c. Knee flexed and heel paced upon some definite part of the other leg (e.g., patella). These exercises may be given by changing the heel from one position to another or else by calling for extension between different placings.

SPINAL CORD INJURY

DEFINITION

Spinal cord injury involves damage to the soft neural tissue of the spinal cord. Once destroyed, nerve cells cannot be replaced. Spinal nerve fibers are unable to cross the site of injury and reestablish communication (unlike the peripheral nervous system). In contrast to some portions of the brain, the spinal cord has no alternate pathways or spare nerve cells that can take over the function of the damaged portion.

Damage to the spinal cord results in motor, sensory, and autonomic impairments. Sensory tracts (afferent) ascend through the cord and carry information from the sensory organs. If these tracts are injured, sensation (e.g., pain, temperature, touch) is lost below the level of injury. When motor tracts (efferent) are damaged, voluntary muscle control is lost below the level of injury. Autonomic deficits refer to damage to tracts which innervate smooth muscles of the body. Depending on the location and extent of damage, function of the viscera, heart, vasomotor responses, sweat glands, temperature control, bladder, and bowel may be impaired below the level of injury.

ETIOLOGY

Most traumatic injuries are associated with trauma to the boney structure of the vertebral column (e.g., contusion, crushing/compression, dislocation, fracture), while many non-traumatic injuries how little or no boney involvement. Non-traumatic injuries are generally associated with pathology such as infection, vascular disease, or degenerative disorders.

TYPES

The degree of impairment as a result of spinal cord injury varies according to the level and extent of damage. Injuries are designated as complete or incomplete. Complete compression or transection of the spinal cord results in the complete loss of any sensory, motor, and autonomic function below the level of injury. An incomplete injury results in a partial preservation of neurologic tracts, with any combination of motor, sensory, and autonomic function being retained. The prognosis will vary with incomplete injuries.

The level of the spinal cord injury is designated as the lowest nerve root segment with preserved function. For example, a person with a C-7 injury will have preserved function in the nerve root that exists below the seventh cervical vertebrae.

1. **Lower Motor Neuron Lesion (LMN)** -- Injury occurs below the first lumbar vertebrae (L-1). It is characterized by a loss of voluntary motor/sensory function and the presence of flaccid paralysis below the level of injury. Reflex arcs are destroyed, preventing involuntary spasms.

2. **Upper Motor Neuron Lesion (UMN)** -- Injury occurs at or above the 12th thoracic vertebrae (T-12). It is characterized by the loss of voluntary control and the occurrence of spastic paralysis below the level of the injury. Spastic paralysis occurs when the reflex arc is intact below the level of injury; therefore, uninhibited stretch reflexes cause persistent involuntary muscular contractions. In flaccid paralysis, both voluntary control and reflex arcs are absent.

Medical Complications (Upper Motoneuron Lesions)
1. Spasticity
2. Contractures (hip flexors and adductors, hamstrings, plantarflexors)
3. Orthopedic deformities (e.g., scoliosis)
4. Inability to perspire below the level of lesion
5. Bladder infections
6. Bladder stones
7. Gastrointestinal disorders
8. Infections from catheterizations
9. Respiratory disorders
10. Autonomic dysreflexia (lesions above T-6)
11. Decubiti ulcers (pressure sores)

243

Predicted Functional Potential According to Level of Lesion

C-5	Partial strength of all shoulder motions
	Electric chair
	Attendant for help with ADL
	Elbow flexion
C-6	Normal shoulder, elbow flexion
	Wrist extension
	Minimal assistance with transfer
C-7	Independent transfers
	Manual wheelchair
	Elbow extension
	Finger extension
T-1	Normal arms and hands
	Totally independent in most activities
T-6	Upper trunk muscles
	Inadequate bronchial hygiene
	Weak cough
	Limited chest expansion
T-6 to T-12	Potential for community ambulation with braces
T-12	Thorax, abdomen, and low back muscles
L-2 to L-5	Ambulation with the use of braces
L-4	Hip flexion
	Knee extension
L-5	Partial strength of hip motions with normal flexion
	Partial strength of ankle and foot motion

INDICATED EXERCISE PROGRAM

1. Provide passive range of motion for paralyzed muscle groups (e.g., plantarflexors, hamstrings, hip flexors and adductors) and active range of motion for innervated muscle groups.
2. Strengthen and hypertrophy those muscles that are suitable substitutes for others

that are permanently weakened or paralyzed (e.g., shoulder internal rotators for forearm pronators). A combination of techniques can be utilized, including PNF, manual resistance, and PRE.

3. Provide training for cardiovascular endurance (see protocol and precautions for arm crank ergometry in the chapter on Assessment and Programming for Cardiovascular Endurance).

4. Wheelchair dips (if elbow extension present) prevent decubiti ulcers by allowing circulation. Lift buttocks off chair by extending at elbow and hold 60 seconds.

5. If possible, use standing frame or parallel bars to help prevent contractures, disuse osteoporosis, and maintain any residual strength in legs. It may be possible to use one of the crutch gait patterns (see chapter on Assessment and Programming for Gait).

6. Encourage sitting balance activities.

7. Development of the triceps (elbow extension) is extremely important in facilitating transfers, gait training, and wheelchair propulsion. In addition, strengthening of the latissimus dorsi is highly indicated (shoulder adduction) for spinal cord injured students. This muscle bridges the paralyzed parts of the body with the nonparalyzed muscles and assists in sitting balance and postural awareness.

SPINAL CORD INJURY TERMINOLOGY

Autonomic Function
The functions of the body (such as breathing or heart beats) which do not require conscious thought in order to function.

Complete Lesion
A complete compression or transection of the spinal cord resulting in complete loss of sensory, motor, and autonomic function below the level of injury.

Flaccid Paralysis
Paralysis of an extremity characterized by no residual muscle tone. In this case the reflex arc has been broken.

Incomplete Lesion
An incomplete transection or compression of the spinal cord resulting in partial preservation of neurological function. Any combination of motor, sensory, and autonomic function may be retained.

Motor Function
Muscle control through nerve impulses that originate in the Central Nervous System (CNS) and travel to a target muscle. Within the spinal cord itself, these nerves can be referred to as descending or efferent tracts.

Sensory Function

Information received by the sensor organ of the body (such as pain, heat, pressure, etc.) and transmitted back to the CNS via the Peripheral Nervous System (PNS). Within the spinal cord, these nerves can be referred to as ascending or afferent tracts.

Spastic Paralysis

Paralysis of an extremity characterized by muscle tone and spasms. The reflex arc remains intact, but there is some impairment of the inhibitory control from the brain.

CATHETERS

In many instances of spinal cord injury, the bladder becomes neurogenic (paralyzed). This may necessitate the use of a catheter, a device used for draining the urine from the bladder.

Types   The types of catheters worn by individuals include:
1. Indwelling Urethral
2. Suprapubic
3. External (condom)

Occasionally, exercise positions will have to be modified so as not to interfere with the functioning of these devices. It is suggested that the instructor obtain this information during the initial evaluation with the student.

AUTONOMIC DYSREFLEXIA

Autonomic dysreflexia occurs in individuals with spinal cord lesions above T-6. It is considered an acute emergency requiring immediate medical attention. Early recognition of dysreflexia symptoms is essential in order to prevent bleeding in or near the brain (cerebrovascular accident). The symptoms include the following (Larson & Snobl, 1978):

1. Pounding headache (due to severe rise in blood pressure)
2. Profuse sweating above the level of injury
3. Goose bumps
4. Splotching of the skin
5. Nasal obstruction

The causes for dysreflexia vary, the most common being over-distention of the bladder (blocked catheter), severe spasms, infection, kidney stones, distention of the bowel, or pressure sores.

If the person is in a horizontal position when the dysreflexia occurs, elevate the head or bring the body to a sitting position as quickly as possible to induce a drop in blood pressure. The catheter for the bladder should be immediately checked for blockages (e.g., kinks in the tubing, overfull bag, clamps which have not been removed, blocked inlets to the leg bag)). Do not forget to call the paramedics immediately.

WHEELCHAIR ATHLETIC INJURIES -- COMMON PATTERNS & PREVENTION

Soft Tissue Injuries
Causes
1. Tearing and overstretching of ligaments (falls, physical contact)
2. Chronic overuse of muscles and tendons
3. Overexertion without proper warm-up
Prevention
1. Routine stretching, warm-up and cool-down for each workout
2. Slowly progress strengthening/conditioning program -- don't jump into it at once
3. Preventive taping, splinting for better stabilization/protection of old injuries

Blisters
Causes
1. Traction or irritation of skin in contact with wheelchair rim
2. Irritation of skin at top of seat post or back of wheelchair upholstery
Prevention
1. Encourage callous formation as initial protection
2. Taping of fingers
3. Wearing gloves
4. Padding over seat post area
5. Wear shirt between skin and wheelchair back

Abrasions/Lacerations/Cuts
Causes
1. Fingers, thumbs in contact with brakes or metal edge of arm rest socket or push rim
2. Inner arms in contact with larger tires of track chair on downstroke
3. Chair contact (basketball) trapping fingers between wheels
Prevention
1. Remove brakes
2. Use arm rests or file off sockets for arm rests
3. Wear clothing or protective covering for upper arms
4. Camber wheels for wheelchair basketball chairs

Decubitus/Pressure Areas   (mainly a problem for those without sensation)

Causes
1. Shear forces and pressure over sacrum and buttocks with friction on chair
2. Track wheelchair design with knees higher than buttocks may contribute
3. Sweat, moisture in combination with shear forces

Prevention
1. Adequate cushioning and padding for buttocks
2. Frequent skin checks over buttocks and sacrum
3. Shifting weight to relieve pressure intermittently
4. Good nutrition and hygiene
5. Clothing that absorbs moisture

Temperature Regulation Disorders

Causes
1. Exposure to hot sun/heat or cold in absence of temperature control or sweating mechanisms
2. Inadequate fluid intake/excessive water loss

Prevention
1. Wear adequate clothing for protection in hot and cold weather (insulation)
2. Replace fluids -- drink water
3. Assist with heat convection -- cool towels over body surfaces or spray bottle
4. Minimize exposure -- seek shade and cover

STUDY QUESTIONS

1. Define the C.N.S.

2. At what spinal level will all hand intrinsic muscles be usable?

3. At what spinal level are the hip flexors and quadriceps innervated?

4. Develop an exercise program for a T-7 SCI student.

5. Why is the standing position important to a SCI student?

VISUAL IMPAIRMENTS

Normal vision is technically referred to as 20/20. This means that a person can see at 20 feet what most people can see at 20 feet. A person is considered legally blind when vision is 20/200 in the better eye after correction. This means that what the impaired person can see at 20 feet, most people can see at 200 feet.

All definitions of blindness refer to how well the individual can see even with the best of corrective lenses. A person is said to be "legally blind" if his/her overall visual acuity does not exceed 20/200 in the better eye. This is also described as a total lack of sight or inability to perceive light. A person who is partially sighted or visually impaired (V.I.) falls into the category of visual acuity at 20/70 or less with correction. Over 75% of so called blind persons in the United States have some usable vision.

Visual impairments take many forms. Some may see a tiny spot of the visual field if the diameter is 20 degrees or less. Even though the spot of vision is 20/20, they may be considered legally blind. Fuzzy vision, peripheral vision, tunnel vision make the description of visual impairment difficult to understand.

COMMON TYPES AND ETIOLOGY

1. **Macula Degeneration** -- The macula is located in the central portion of the retina. Degeneration affects central vision, but the person maintains good peripheral vision. Usually this condition does not progress to total blindness.
2. **Glaucoma** -- Excessive high pressure within the eyeball, creating tunnel vision.
3. **Cataracts** -- A clouding of the cornea. The incidence of blindness from cataracts has decreased due to surgical techniques.
4. **Retinitis Pigmentosa** -- An inherited condition in which the rod-shaped cells in the retina degenerate. This disorder leads to total blindness.
5. **Diabetic Retinopathy** -- Since diabetes can induce vascular changes, the retina is particularly susceptible to hemorrhage and loss of vision.
6. Blindness can be caused by lack of blood supply to the visual cortex located in the occipital lobe. Blindness occasionally occurs in stroke cases where the person is only capable of seeing out of one side of each eye (hemianopsia).
7. **Refractory Errors** -- This includes farsightedness, nearsightedness, and astigmatism.
8. Blindness can be a result of venereal disease, the aging process, trauma causing detached retina, tumors, or exposure to bright light (e.g., sun, welding light).

It is important to remember that most persons with visual impairments are not totally blind. Some will have good tunnel vision while others will possess cloudy vision.

CHARACTERISTICS

The functional ability of a person who is blind or visually impaired varies with each individual, depending upon age of onset and whether the blindness is total or partial. A person who is visually impaired or has some perception of form and light may be completely independent with full use of his/her other senses. With proper training in the use of braille, large type books, tape recorders, new technological equipment and good mobility skills, individuals who are blind can be as functionally independent as their community will allow. Individuals who have been totally blind since birth do not have any visual memory, and, therefore, learn to use their other senses to perceive what others see. Some visually impaired or blind individuals may display annoying mannerisms such as eye-poking or rocking. This is usually due to a need for physical stimulation.

SIGHTED GUIDE TECHNIQUES

1. Making contact -- Lightly brush forearms with the student so he/she can find the back of your arm, proximal to the elbow. Keep your elbow flexed to 90 degrees.
2. Familiarize the student to the environment. When you give directions, give them according to the way student is facing -- left or right.
3. Pause before any stairs or curbs. Describe the height of the step up.
4. When approaching a door, inform the person whether the door is "away" or "toward" him/her and if it opens to the left or right.
5. When seating, put student's hand down on the back of the chair or back student up into the seat until the calves touch.
6. If going through a narrow passageway, keep your elbow flexed, but internally rotate your shoulder, placing the arm behind the back. The student will then slide the hand from the back of your bicep to the middle of the forearm and step directly behind you.

INDICATED EXERCISE PROGRAM

It is recommended that each visually impaired student have a medical verification completed by an ophthalmologist. These doctors have differing philosophies regarding physical activities for the visually impaired (e.g., bending over during exercise, putting the face in the water when swimming). Therefore, a phone call to the attending eye care specialist would be useful, especially in the case of diabetic retinopathy.

1. Encourage cardiovascular endurance. The visually impaired rarely get an opportunity to engage in aerobic activities due to amount of supervision or guiding required. Utilize stationary cycling, tandem cycling, folk and square dance, aerobic dance, swimming, and jogging.
2. Provide individual sport activities/leisure skills that have life-long carry-over value.
3. Postural exercises may need to be prescribed for lordosis, ptosis, kyphosis.
4. Goal ball is a very popular sport created for blind athletes. It is a modified form of soccer played while positioned on the hands and knees. It is played indoors with two teams and an audible ball.

STUDY QUESTIONS

1. Adapting a Basic Skill (low organized) Game:
   Choose a basic skill game that a student with partial vision (correctable to 20/200) could play with sighted teammates if modifications were made. Describe the ways in which the game could be adapted to ensure successful participation by the handicapped individual.

2. Motor Exploration:
   Develop three motor exploration activities that will promote spatial awareness in visually handicapped students.

REFERENCES

American Heart Association. Subcommittee on Exercise/Cardiac Rehabilitation (1981). Statement on Exercise. Circulation, 64, 1302A.

Basmajian, J. V. (1977). Therapeutic Exercise. Baltimore: Waverly Press.

Bleck, E. E. (1975). Physically Handicapped Children -- A Medical Atlas for Teachers. San Francisco: Grune & Stratton.

Bullock, E. A. (1974). Later stages of rehabilitation in hemiplegics. Physiotherapy, 60, 370-374.

Butler, R. & Lewis, M. (1973). Aging and Mental Health. St. Louis: C. V. Mosby Co.

Cooper, I. S. (1979). Living with Chronic Neurologic Disease. New York: Norton and Co.

Daniels, A. & Davies, E. (1977). Adapted Physical Education (3rd edition). New York: Harper & Row Publishers.

De Anza College. Adapted Physical Education Manual. Palo Alto, CA.

Epilepsy Foundation of America (1981). Epilepsy handbook for teachers and nurses. 1612 30th Street, San Diego, CA, 92101.

Frankel, L. & Richard, B. B. (1977). Be Alive As Long As You Live. Charleston: Preventicare Publications.

French, R. & Jansma, P. (1982). <u>Special Physical Education</u>. Columbus: Merrill Publishing.

Glaser, R. M., Sawka, M. N., Durbin, R. J., Foley, D. M., & Suryaprasad, A. G. (1981). Exercise program for wheelchair activity. <u>American Journal of Physical Medicine</u>, 60(2), 67-75.

Haring, N. (1982). <u>Exceptional Children and Youth</u> (3rd edition). Columbus: Merrill Publishing.

Hollander, J. (1976). The Arthritis Handbook. West Point: Merck Hape and Dohme Publishing.

Jennett, B. (1975). Outcome after severe brain damage. A practical scale. <u>Lancet</u>, 1, 480-483.

Lavigne, J. Home exercises for patients with Parkinson's Disease. The American Parkinson Disease Association.

Mason, E., & Dando, H. (1975). <u>Corrected Therapy and Adapted Physical Education</u>. Chillicothe, Ohio: American Corrective Therapy Association, Inc.

Moore, R. (1981). Handout for Therapeutic Exercise, San Diego State University, San Diego, CA.

Pollock, M. L., Miller, H. S., Linnerud, A. C., Laughridge, E., Coleman, E., & Alexander, E. (1974). Arm pedaling as an endurance training regimen for the disabled. <u>Archives of Physical Medicine and Rehabilitation</u>, 55, 252-261.

Sager, K. (1984). Exercises to activate seniors. <u>Physician and Sportsmedicine</u>, 12(5), 144-151.

Talbot, D., Pearson, V., & Loeper, J. (1978). <u>Disuse Syndrome: The Preventable Disability</u>. Minneapolis: Sister Kenney Institute.

Schauf, C. L. & Davis, F. A. (1974). Impulse conduction in multiple sclerosis: A theoretical basis for modification by temperature and pharmacological agents. <u>Journal of Neurology, Neurosurgery, and Psychology</u>, 37, 152-161.

CHAPTER 14

SPORTS PARTICIPATION

STROKE TECHNIQUE FOR WHEELCHAIR SPORTS
James Burke, Coordinator, Disabled Youth Sports Program
California State University, Long Beach

Before active involvement in wheelchair mobility may begin, one must instruct the essentials of a stroke. This can be taught in a three-step progression:
1. Grasp the push rims or the push rims and tires on the wheel at the point below the shoulders.
2. Push the wheels forward with both hands moving at the same time evenly and fluidly.
3. Maintain contact with the push rims after forward stroke is finished by sliding hands up the push rims to the starting position. By maintaining contact with the push rims, one increases the efficiency of the stroke.

TEACHING PROGRESSION

1. Pushing a straight line.
   a. On a flat surface, stroke wheels with both hands at the same time in a long fluid motion. If hands do not stroke at the same time, the chair will move erratically.
   b. On sloped surfaces, push harder on the wheel which is lowest on the slope. This will counteract the effects of the slope.
2. Turning the chair.
   a. Turing right or left may be accomplished by applying pressure on the push rim which faces the direction you wish to move in, and stroking the opposite wheel more aggressively.
   b. In a faster situation, one may need to slow the chair before turning. This can be accomplished by applying pressure equally to both push rims. As the turn approaches, simply press harder on the wheel which faces the direction you wish to move in, and stroke the opposite wheel.
3. Cutting (sharp turns) in a wheelchair. A technique used often in wheelchair basketball and tennis.
   Grab the push rims or the push rim and tire which face the direction you wish to cut

in first, then very aggressively push the opposite wheel. This progression must be done extremely quickly to be effective.

4. Ascending and descending ramps.
   a. When ascending a ramp of any height, one must move his/her center of gravity forward to maintain constant contact of all four wheels on the surface. The stroke here becomes shorter and quicker.
   b. When descending a ramp, one must lean back against the back rest of the chair. This will keep the bulk of the individual's body weight to the rear of the chair, and help in maintaining contact with all four wheels of the chair to the surface.
5. The Wheelie. Fear of falling backwards out of the chair often affects the proper learning of this skill.
   a. First it is important for the student to feel the point beyond where balance is established, and the point below balance. A spotter whom the student trusts actively finds these points.
   b. Wheelie progression.
      1) With the student in a wheelie beyond the balance point, the spotter should ask the student to lean torso forward.
      2) With the student in a wheelie below the balance point, the spotter should ask the student to lean back.
      3) The student should try now to control the wheelie with the spotter preventing a fall, by using the wheels. By very quickly pushing the wheels forward and leaning back, one may be able to bring front casters off the ground. By leaning forward and pulling the wheels back toward the body, one may bring the front casters toward the ground.
      4) A combination of these movements will enable the student to hold his/her wheelie.

THE CHARACTERISTICS OF A SPORTS WHEELCHAIR

WHEELS --May be cambered to increase stability of the chair without sacrificing its turning ability.

--The axle may be moved forward or backward to adjust the turning angle of the chair or to increase its stability. The closer the axles are to the front of the chair, the easier it is to turn. This position does reduce stability.

--The axle plate or axle position may be raised or lowered. This can assist the posture of the student. A student with poor sitting balance will benefit by lowering the wheelchair seat. This is accomplished by raising the axle or axle plates.

--The hubs of most sport chairs are equipped with quick release axles. They allow the wheels to be removed easily.

BACKREST --Most sport chairs have backrests with push handles available on request. This is entirely up to the individual.

--Most backrests are adjustable. They can be lowered or raised depending on the posture of the student.

FRAME --Folding frame chairs are very useful to a person who must transfer to and from a car. The ride in a folding chair is usually not as smooth as a rigid frame chair.

--Rigid frame chairs do sacrifice convenience and practicality. The ride in a rigid chair is much smoother. There is less play in a rigid frame. Folding chairs are rarely used in athletics because of the superiority of the rigid chair's ride.

CASTERS --There are forked casters and pin casters. Forked casters are smoother and negotiate obstacles better. Pin casters turn much faster and are more desirable on a playing court.

WHEELCHAIR BASKETBALL

A. <u>RULES</u>. (Source: National Wheelchair Basketball Association)
"Wheelchair basketball is played in accordance with NCAA rules with very few exceptions. These exceptions are:

1. <u>Player eligibility</u> is limited to those individuals who, because of permanent severe leg disability or paralysis of the lower portion of the body, would be prevented from playing stand-up basketball.
2. <u>Wheelchair</u>. The height of the seat must not exceed 21 inches from the floor. Foot platforms must be 4 and 7/8ths inches from the floor with seat cushions permitted only for therapeutic reasons. Each chair must be equipped with a heel strap of 1 and 1/2 inch width. The chair is considered a part of the player. General rules of contact in regular and stand-up basketball (charging, blocking, etc.) apply to wheelchair basketball.
3. <u>Jump Ball</u>. For any jump ball, each jumper shall remain firmly seated in his chair. He cannot lift his buttocks off the seat by use of arm, leg or force of movement. The jumper must be in the jumping circle at a 45 degree angle to his own basket.
4. <u>Dribbling</u>. A player may wheel the chair and bounce the ball simultaneously just as a man may run and bounce the ball simultaneously in regular basketball. In addition, a man with the ball in his possession can take no more than two consecutive pushes, with one or both hands, in either direction. If he has taken two pushes, he must shoot, pass or bounce the ball before pushing again. The

latter can be repeated again as there isn't any double dribble violation. Three or more consecutive pushes with the ball in his possession constitutes a traveling violation.

5. Loss of Ball. If a man in possession of the ball makes any physical contact with the floor or tilts his chair so far forward that the footrests touch or as far backwards that the safety casters touch the floor, it is a violation and the ball is awarded to the other team.

6. Falling Out of a Chair. If a competitor falls out of his chair, or if his chair becomes inoperable during play, the officials will immediately suspend play if there is any chance of danger to the fallen player. If not, the officials will withhold their whistles until the particular play in progress has been completed. If a player falls out of his chair to gain possession of the ball, the ball is awarded to the opposing team.

7. Time Limits. An offensive player cannot remain more than 5 seconds in the free throw lane while his team is in possession of the ball in his front court.

8. Out of Bounds. A player is considered out of bounds when he or any part of his wheelchair touches the floor on or outside the boundary.

9. Physical Advantage Foul. Because of the varying causes and degrees of disability among participants, a basic rule of keeping firmly seated in the wheelchair at all times and not using a functional leg or leg stump for physical advantage over an opponent, is strictly enforced. An infraction of this rule (rebound, jump ball, etc.) constitutes a physical advantage foul. It is so recorded in the official score book. Three such fouls disqualify a player from the game. A free throw is awarded and the ball is given to the opposing team, out of bounds.

10. Back Court Foul. A defensive player who commits a personal foul in his opponent's back court shall be charged with a back court foul. The offended player shall be awarded two (2) free throws.

B. EQUIPMENT.
   1. Axles of the wheelchairs should be moved forward.
   2. Footrests should consist of rowbars with rollers in order to prevent a player from being dumped.
   3. Wheelchair seats are deep and angled (knees are higher than hips) to facilitate balance.

C. BASIC GAME STRATEGY.
   1. Offense. On offense work for the inside shot. The outside shot (12-15 ft. range) has a much lower success percentage. To get in position for the inside shot, set picks and screens.

2. Defense. Man-to-man defense is generally preferable for defense because it is easier to screen out for position. Younger, more inexperienced teams may use a zone defense.

D. SKILLS TO BE MASTERED.
  1. Wheelchair Mobility. (See section on Wheelchair Mobility.)
  2. Dribbling.
    a. Basic hand placement: fingers are spread and the elbow is stationary. Action is in the wrist and fingers.
    b. Practice stationary dribbling 6-8 times without looking, using both right and left hands.
    c. Dribble a half circle in front of the chair, let to right and right to left. Practice this maneuver with both right and left hands. Balance may pose a problem for some individuals.
    d. Basic dribble: involves one bounce, then placement of ball in lap and 2 pushes.
    e. Continuous dribble while pushing: dribble up and down the court with one hand. Use a high bounce with one hand push for long distances. Cross-lateral dribble involves continuous dribbling using both the right and left hands.
  3. Ball pick up using the rim of the wheelchair.
    Partner rolls the ball down the court. The ball is approached and scooped up against the wheel rim, bringing it up to the top where it can be placed in the lap and dribbled. Practice should take place with both the right and left hands.
  4. Passing/receiving from a stationary wheelchair. (Note reaction of wheelchair).
    a. Two-handed chest pass.
    b. Baseball pass, right and left (sidearm).
    c. Shovel pass (underhand).
    d. Bounce pass.
    e. Overhead lob.
    f. Hook pass.
  5. Passing/receiving from a moving wheelchair.
    a. Forward moving.
    b. Backward moving (more advanced skill).
  6. Precaution.
    No passing from a turning wheelchair. This is regarded as a low percentage pass and is considered a safety risk.
  7. Wheelchair positioning to receive pass.

8. <u>Shooting and release of ball</u>.
   a. Wheelchair positioning for angles.
   b. Free throw.
   c. Lay ups, right and left side.
   d. Two-handed set shot.
   e. One-handed set shot (stationary and moving to position).
   f. Moving lay up, left and right side, using 2-man (in lines) with rebound recovery.
   g. Fast break (3-man).

E. <u>DRILLS</u>.

1. Wheelchair mobility. (See section on Wheelchair Mobility.)
2. Half court sprints.
3. Speed pushing (in lines with athletes at 10 ft. intervals): free throw to baseline, half court to baseline, free throw at opposite end to baseline, baseline to baseline. Include pivots in this drill, alternating turning right and left.
4. Push backwards across court lengths to refine symmetry of push, not for speed.
5. Relay races.
6. Shuttle runs.
7. Sprint races.
8. Slalom courses with stops and turns (right and left), spins, backward pushing, and sprints. May include dual and team races, as well as "follow-the-leader".
9. Cutting in and out of traffic cones.
10. Pass at a wall target while sitting stationary.
11. Pass at a wall target with a moving wheelchair (forward and lateral movement; no backward movement due to safety hazard).
12. Stationary passing and receiving (all types).
13. Incorporate mobile receiver with stationary passer and vice versa.
14. Moving passers and receivers with two moving lines with partners passing and receiving.
15. Caterpillar.
16. Shoot around: athletes shooting in pairs.
17. Shooting from a moving wheelchair.
18. Timing, wheelchair push/dribble/lay up.
19. Wheelchair moving shot (2 hands, 1 hand).

WHEELCHAIR TENNIS

A. <u>RULES</u>.

1. Two bounces are used in wheelchair tennis. A ball may hit the ground twice before being returned. The second bounce can land anywhere. Only the first bounce must land in the playing court. Also, the athlete may choose to hit the ball on either bounce.
2. The services must be accomplished with the rear wheels behind the baseline. Chair faults will be implemented if the rear wheels touch or cross the baseline. before the racket makes contact with the ball.
3. Open and "C" division servers may not bounce the ball on the ground for service. In the "Novice" division a bounce serve may be used.
4. The wheelchair shall be forbidden to touch the net or the ground within an opponent's court at anytime while the ball is in play.
5. If the ball touches the player or his chair, the player loses the point. This holds true only if the player is in the playing court. In essence, the chair is considered to be part of the person.
6. If the person is out-of-bounds and is struck by the ball, the ball is called out only if the player makes no attempt to hit the ball or tries to get away from the ball. If the ball hits the player's racket, then the ball is good. If the player is inside the playing court or is touching the line and the ball hits him, then the ball is good even if the player feels the ball would go out.
7. A player cannot intentionally jump out of his chair to hit or retrieve a ball, nor can he stand up in his chair to serve a ball. This rule is a judgment call and is to be determined by a court umpire. If a player unintentionally leaves the chair to make a play, no penalty is assessed.
8. In order to protect playing surfaces, the tournament officials may not allow a person to participate with black tires or anything which will mark the court.
9. A "maintenance delay" is a delay in the progress of a match due to a malfunction of a wheelchair, prosthesis or assistive device. Such delay must be requested by the player, granted by the umpire at the match, and shall not exceed 5 minutes. Only two such delays may be granted for each player for each match.

B. <u>SKILLS TO BE MASTERED</u>.

1. <u>Wheelchair Mobility</u>.
Since lack of maneuverability is one of the common problems in wheelchair tennis, it is important that athletes develop skill in moving to and from various court positions.

259

2. Forward Mobility.
To move forwards to a ball, both wheels of the chair are pushed evenly. The wheel on the side of the racket hand can be pushed either by using the base of the thumb or by pushing with the lower forearm.
3. Backwards Mobility.
To move backwards from a ball, both wheels of the chair are pulled evenly.
4. Lateral Mobility.
   a. To move to the left, push the right wheel and either hold or pull the left wheel.
   b. To move to the right, push the left wheel and either hold or pull the right wheel.
   c. Turning can be achieved faster when traveling backwards since the small steering wheels are then at the opposite or back end of the chair to the direction of travel.
   d. After playing a backhand shot (for a right-handed person), the right-hand side of the chair faces the net. To straighten up quickly, pull the right wheel with the left hand, and then push the left wheel with the left hand. The first movement can be done while executing the stroke or follow-through.
5. Stopping.
Sudden stopping of forward momentum is necessary to be able to quickly return to the best position on court, and it is achieved by leaning slightly backwards in the chair while gripping both wheels.
6. Forehand Grip and Swing.
7. Backhand Grip and Swing.
8. Overhand and Underhand Serve.
9. Volley.

C. DRILLS.

1. Familiarization with equipment (racket, ball, and wheelchair).
2. Wheelchair mobility and court positions.
3. Forehand Swing.
   a. Practice swing without ball.
   b. Assistants toss the tennis ball from the service line to the athletes positioned on the baseline (same side of court). Athletes should be positioned on the right, middle and left sides of the baseline.
   c. Assistants toss the tennis ball across the net to the athletes positioned on the baseline (opposite side of court).
   d. Assistants hit the tennis ball across the net to the athletes positioned on the baseline (opposite side of court).
   e. Assistants rally cross-court with athletes across the net from baseline.

    f. Assistants rally down the line with athletes across the net from baseline.

    g. Assistants alternate cross-court and down-the-line with athletes from across the net.

    h. Athletes rally with one another from across the net.

4. <u>Backhand Swing</u>.

    Follow same drills for #3.

5. <u>Overhand and Underhand Serve</u>.

    a. Use a side on "stance" for the serve as this gives the ball better direction and the action of the arm is stronger in this position.

    b. Practice the ball toss without the racket.

    c. Serves should first be practiced without the ball.

    d. The conventional overhand serve may need to be adapted due to the design of the wheelchair (full backswing may not be possible). Start by putting the racket down the back and then bring it forward over the head with the arm fully extended, making contact with the ball directly over the chair. The serve ends with a shortened follow through. The underhand serve can be used with beginners or those with limited arm strength. Practice serving on the service line first, then move to the baseline.

    e. Practice serving into either of the opposite service areas.

GOALBALL FOR VISUALLY IMPAIRED STUDENTS

A. <u>FRAMEWORK FOR GOALBALL</u>.

A game is played by three players on each of two teams. The game is conducted on the floor of a gymnasium within a rectangular court which is divided into two halves by a center line. The goals are erected at both ends. The game is to be played with a bell ball. The object of the game is for each team to roll the ball across the opponent's goal line, while the other team attempts to prevent this from happening.

B. <u>SKILLS TO BE MASTERED -- OFFENSE</u>.

1. <u>Throwing</u>. (stems from bowling style roll/throw)

    a. Legs: 1 to 5 step approach (depending on where they are on the court.

    b. Two-handed hold on the ball, backswing.

    c. From backswing, beginning forward movement of shoulder joint, plenty of follow-through after ball release.

    d. Must coordinate with foot movement.

2. <u>Passing</u>.

    a. Moving the ball between three players after one player has thrown ball two times consecutively.

b. Note: Communication between players on offense consists of verbal, finger-snapping, tapping on the floor, etc.
3. Localizing.
    a. Ability to distinguish ball noise from distracting sounds.
    b. Able to distinguish other players' positions on the court.

C. SKILLS TO BE MASTERED -- DEFENSE.
1. Lunge: Diving movement from a two-footed erect standing or squatting position to a prone position. Incorporates full body extension.
2. Auditory.
    a. Ability to track the sound of the ball.
    b. Ability to utilize cues from teammates.
    c. Auditory discrimination.
    d. Ability to lunge in the right direction at the right time.
    e. Ability to coordinate specific defensive patterns with teammates; i.e., lunging in same direction, etc.

D. SKILLS TO BE MASTERED -- ORIENTATION.
All lines on court are marked off by rope covered with tape so the goalball players can orient themselves in their area of the court. Players must know where they are on the court by feeling the lines or the goal case around them.

E. SKILLS TO BE MASTERED -- MOBILITY.
When players are on the court, they play in specific areas. Two back players are located at the 1.50m lines, and one center player is stationed at the .50m line (see court diagram in Appendices).

F. SAFETY CONSIDERATIONS.
1. Bicycle helmet for head.
2. Knee and elbow pads.
3. Cups and supporters for males.
4. Hip and thigh pads especially for women.
5. Full finger gloves to protect fingers.
6. Education of players concerning the rules to help with safety.

G. WARM UP DRILLS.
1. Offense.
    a. Throwing at target without blindfold.
    b. Throwing for distance from 10 to 60 feet.
    c. Practice various cues, passing ball to person giving cues.
    d. Practice all above with blindfold on.

3. Defense.
   a. Lunge
      1) Practice appropriate prone extension without blindfold.
      2) Practice lunging at moving ball.
      3) Practice appropriate prone extension with blindfold.
      4) Practice lunging at slow pitched ball.
      5) Increase speed of pitch and distance thrown.
      6) Practice throws from cross court and different types of throws.
   b. Auditory
      1) Practice with blindfold off, listen as ball approaches.
      2) Practice with blindfold on, throwing the ball slow at first, making sure athletes are moving in the right direction.
      3) Speed up as players improve.
   c. Connect skills by having players practice 1, 2 or 3 players at a time both offense and defense.
   d. Players need to be in constant communication with each other. They need to pay attention to how many throws in a row a player has (the maximum is 2). Have a lead person on the court.
4. Game Drills.
   a. Using a beach ball, have athletes throw the ball at a target. Start at 10 feet and work back to 60 feet.
   b. Same drill as above, only use a large rubber ball.
   c. Throw beach ball/rubber ball at goal area from 10 to 60 feet and different locations.
   d. Practice basic lunge: begin with squat position, lunge to the right or the left. Make sure body is in prone position and fully extended. Have athletes slide into the lunge to avoid bruising the hips.
   e. Lunge while trying to stop the beach ball/rubber ball. Vary the speed and direction (assistants throw the ball).
   f. Have the players track the ball by listening. Have them tell assistants where it is.
   g. Introduce various signals (verbal, finger-snapping, tapping on floor). Have players practice giving signals and have other players point to where the signal is coming from.
   h. Have players in position on the court. Give one player the ball and have another player give a signal to pass the ball. The player with the ball tries to pass to the players giving the signal. Repeat with each player getting a chance to give signal and receive passes.

i. Put players into lanes. Player A will throw the ball to try and score on Player B. Player B will lunge to stop the ball. Player B recovers the ball and throws the ball trying to score. Start 20 feet apart and use easy throws. Increase the distance to 60 feet. Switch players. Use a large rubber ball (regulation as stated in the rules).

j. Place players in various positions on the court. Have them feel lines around them. Tell them what part of the court they are on. Switch positions until each player has been in all three positions.

k. Switching positions, have players tell assistants where they are on the court.

l. Set players up for two-on-two play.

m. Team A will throw the ball to try and score on Team B. Team B will lunge to stop the ball. Team B will recover the ball and throw it to score. Start 40 feet apart and use easy throws. Increase the distance to 60 feet. Switch teams. Practice drill with goalball.

n. Mini two-on-two tournament using goalball.

o. Practice three-person offense using passing and orientation.

p. Practice three-person defense with the assistant throwing the ball.

q. Play three-on-three scrimmage. Switch players to different positions and teams.

r. Play best two out of three games with regulation rules.

WEIGHT ROUTINES

A. WEIGHT ROUTINES FOR AMBULATORY ATHLETES (including Blind)*

1. Wrist Flexion
2. Wrist Extension
3. Elbow Flexion
4. Elbow Extension
5. Shoulder Flexion, Abduction, Extension
6. Overhead Press
7. Upright Rows
8. Lat Pull (front and back)
9. Bench Press
10. Shoulder Horizontal Abduction (prone)
11. Shoulder Horizontal Adduction (supine-hook)
12. Abdominal Curls
13. Hip Hikers (supine-hook)
14. Leg Press

15. Hip Abduction (side-lying)
16. Hip Adduction (side-lying)
17. Hip Extension (prone-kneeling)
18. Knee Flexion
19. Knee Extension
20. Heel Raises (plantarflexion)
21. Dorsiflexion

* *Using the Universal Machine, free weights, wrist & ankle weights, and pulleys.*

B. <u>EXERCISE PRECAUTIONS FOR BLIND ATHLETES</u>**

1. Do not bend over from the waist.
2. No push-ups (unless accompanied by medical release from physician).
3. Avoid quick, sharp movements of the head.

** *When visual impairment has resulted from bleeding in the eye (e.g., diabetes), retinal hemorrhage, or detached retina.*

C. <u>WEIGHT ROUTINE FOR WHEELCHAIR ATHLETES</u>***

1. Lat pull
2. Bench Press
3. Military Press
4. Pect Deck (Freedom Machine)
5. Pulleys (Freedom Machine)
   a. Upright Rowing (bottom pulley)
   b. Upright Rowing (middle pulley)
   c. Shoulder Abduction
   d. Shoulder Horizontal Abduction (middle pulley)
   e. Shoulder Horizontal Abduction (bottom pulley)
   f. Shoulder Adduction
   g. Shoulder Horizontal Adduction (middle pulley)
   h. Shoulder Horizontal Adduction (bottom pulley)
   i. Spine Extension
   j. Spine Flexion
   k. Lateral Spine Flexion
   l. Lat Pull (front and side)
   m. Elbow Extension
   n. Elbow Flexion
   o. Bench Press

p. Shoulder Horizontal Adduction (bent-over)
q. Shoulder Flexion
r. Shoulder Extension
6. Rickshaw Exerciser
   a. Bench Press (bent-over)
   b. Dips
   c. Shoulder Depression with Externally Rotated Shoulder (for quads)

*** *Using the Freedom Machine, pulleys, Rickshaw, free weights, wrist weights. The Freedom Machine has 5 lb. increments with the exception of the military press (20 lb.). Counterweights may be used on any of the stations.*

CHAPTER 15

EMERGENCY PROCEDURES

The outline provided below identifies responsibilities which facilitate efficient and orderly conduct during an emergency. The procedures are designed to stabilize the client until advance medical personnel arrives. A team approach should be utilized by assigning responsibilities to assistants. The protocol should be established and practiced prior to implementing the exercise program. Emergency drills should be practiced one to two times per semester. It is suggested that each area of the facility have its own emergency team, as well as the procedures and assignments posted on a bulletin board (in full view of the class).

ASSIGN A QUALIFIED ASSISTANT TO EACH SPECIFIC EMERGENCY ASSIGNMENT LISTED BELOW.

1. Begin cardiopulmonary resuscitation (CPR)/first aid.
   a. Evaluate the victim and begin CPR as needed.
   b. Take over initial effort to revive the victim if a non-designated person is first to reach the victim.
2. Assist with CPR -- ventilation.
3. Call paramedics.
   a. Every assistant in the program should be familiar with the emergency telephone procedure. However, only one assistant per class should be assigned to make the call. In most cities dialing 911 will reach an emergency dispatcher.
   b. The following information should be provided:
      1) Name and telephone number of person calling.
      2) Description of the emergency.
      3) Exact location of the emergency.
4. Pull the medical file.
   An assistant should have the medical file available when the paramedics arrive. This will alert them to the type of disability and the types of medication the student is taking.
5. Evacuate all uninvolved individuals from the room (in the case of a serious emergency).
6. Assist the CPR team (stand-by).
   Remain by the resuscitation/first aid team in case any additional assistance or

supplies are needed.
7. <u>Parking lot stand-by</u>.
   Guide the paramedics to the facility or room where the victim is located.

FIRST AID

It is not within the scope of this manual to provide procedures for first aid, artificial respiration or cardiopulmonary resuscitation. Rather, it is suggested that the program director, instructors and at least two assistants (per class) obtain certification in basic first aid and cardiopulmonary resuscitation. Check your local American Red Cross for a schedule of certification classes.

CONTRAINDICATIONS TO EXERCISE TESTING

It is recommended that the instructor carefully review the medical history of a student to determine the safety of conducting a submaximal graded exercise test. Possible contraindications to testing include: (American College of Sportsmedicine, 1983)

1. Unstable angina or angina pectoris at rest.
2. Acute infectious diseases.
3. Thrombophlebitis.
4. Arrhythmias.
5. History suggesting excessive medication (i.e., digitalis, psychtropics, diuretics).
6. Untreated severe systematic or pulmonary hypertension.
7. Uncontrolled metabolic diseases (e.g., diabetes).
8. Resting blood pressure exceeding 140/90.

INDICATIONS FOR TERMINATION OF AN EXERCISE
OR A GRADED EXERCISE TEST

Abnormal distress during exercise may indicate underlying pathology which may require further medical evaluation. The presence of the following symptoms during any exercise or graded exercise test necessitates discontinuing the activity until further medical consultation/evaluation has been obtained. These indications have been provided by the American College of Sportsmedicine (1983).

A. Signs and symptoms of exercise intolerance.

1. Dizziness or near syncope.
2. Pain or pressure in the chest, arm or throat (angina); this may be immediate or delayed.
3. Nausea or vomiting.
4. Severe fatigue; prolonged fatigue after 24 hours.
5. Severe claudication or other pain in the lower extremities.
6. Mental confusion; glassy stare.
7. Sudden lack of coordination; unsteadiness.
8. General pallor, cold sweat; blueness.
9. Lack of rapid erythematous return of skin color after brief firm compression.

B. Abnormal blood pressure responses.

1. Systolic blood pressure does not rise with increasing intensity of the exercise.
2. A drop of 10 mm Hg or more in successive recordings.
3. An increase in systolic blood pressure of greater than 250 mm Hg.
4. A rise in diastolic blood pressure of greater than 120 mm Hg. It is recommended by the authors that a graded exercise test (even submaximal) not be conducted on a person with a resting diastolic blood pressure greater than 110 mm Hg.

C. Abnormal heart rate responses.

1. A heart rate exceeding 100% of predicted (age-adjusted) maximum heart rate (standard deviation = 10 beats/minute).
2. Sudden rapid or irregular heartbeats; sudden slow pulse.
3. Poor chronotropic response.

D. Respiratory responses.

1. Marked dyspnea.
2. Assistance of the accessory neck and shoulder muscles for respiration (exception: spinal cord injury).

The remaining symptoms listed below usually do not require any medical attention and may be remedied by some modification of the exercise program.

1. Excessively high recovery heart rate (i.e., heart rate near target level even 5 to 10 minutes after cessation of exercise).

Remedy: Select an exercise intensity at the lower end of the target zone (e.g., 60% of predicted maximum).

2. Dyspnea lasting more than 10 minutes after cessation of exercise.
   Remedy: Same as #1. Make sure it is possible to carry on a conversation during exercise.

3. Prolonged fatigue/soreness, even 24 hours later.
   Remedy; Reduce intensity of the exercise (e.g., workload, weight to be lifted, amount of stretch achieved).

4. Pain on the front or sides of the lower leg (shin splints).
   Remedy: Reevaluate type of shoes worn during exercise. Swim or use stationary bicycle instead of jogging. Exercise on surface which absorbs more shock.

5. Insomnia which was not present prior to participation in the exercise program.
   Remedy: Reduce the intensity of duration of the exercise program.

6. Diaphragm spasm (side stitch). Pain around lower rib cage.
   Remedy: Lean forward while sitting or standing.

7. Muscle cramps due to over-exertion.
   Remedy: Place muscle on stretch and hold until cramp subsides.

MEDICATIONS

If a student is taking medications, the following information should be recorded in the student's medical file for each drug:

1. Name of Drug.
2. Purpose.
3. Dose.
4. Side Effects.

This information should be readily accessible in case of an emergency. In addition, it is important to inform the assistant of any side effects from the medications which may affect performance (e.g., beta- blockers may keep the heart rate depressed during aerobic exercise) or affect behavior (e.g., seizure medication such as phenobarbital may induce drowsiness). The appearance of side effects varies among individuals and depends upon the dose. The side effects associated with anticonvulsant drugs are typically mild and occur only at the beginning of therapy (San Diego County Epilepsy Society, 1981). Common medications and their purposes are listed below (Larson & Snobl, 1978):

1. Urinary Tract Antibiotics -- Macrodantin, Gantrisin, Geocillin, Keflex, Septra, Ampicillin, Tetracycline.

2. Urinary Acidifiers -- Ascorbic acid (Vitamin C) and Mandelamine are used together to acidify and sterilize the urine.

3. Spasticity -- Valium (CNS depressant), Dantrium, Lioresal.
4. Pain -- Aspirin, Darvon, Dolene, Tylenol.
5. Seizures -- Dilantin, Phenobarbital, Mysoline, Tegretol, Mebaral, Diamox, Depakene.
6. Laxatives -- Modane, Dulcolax.
7. Stool Softeners -- Colace, Surfax.

REFERENCES

American College of Sportsmedicine (1983). Reference guide for workshop/ certification programs in preventive/rehabilitative exercise.

Bleck, E. E. & Nagel, D. A. (1975). Physically Handicapped Children - A Medical Atlas for Teachers. New York: Grune & Stratton.

Epilepsy Society (1981). Epilepsy Handbook for Teachers and Nurses. 1612 30th Street, San Diego, CA, 92102.

Fox, S. M., Naughton, S. P. & Haskell, W. L. (1971). Physical activity and the prevention of coronary heart disease. Annuals of Clinical Research, 3, 404.

Larson, M. R. & Snobl, D. E. (1978). Attendant Care Manual. Minnesota: Rehabilitation Service, Southwest State University.

FOR INFORMATION ON:

Seizure Management, see Chapter 13: Epilepsy.
Autonomic Dysreflexion, see Chapter 13: Spinal Cord Injury.
Diabetic Reaction, see Chapter 13: Diabetes.

ABBREVIATIONS

The following abbreviations are typically found on medical histories, physical evaluations, prescriptions, and exercise programs for disabled students. This acceptable format expedites the process of illing in forms and results in consistency among personnel. Some of the abbreviations have been created by the authors and found to be useful in writing exercise programs. The instructor and assistants should become familiar with these abbreviations and their meanings.

@	at
A	Active exercise
A-A	Active-assistive exercise
abd	abduction
add	adduction
ADL	Activities of Daily Living
AK	Above knee
AMA	against medical advice
amb	ambulatory
ant.	anterior
AODM	Adult Onset Diabetes Mellitus
A.P.	anterior-posterior
a-ROM	active range of motion
ASHD	Arteriosclerotic heart disease
b.i.d.	twice a day
BK	Below knee
B.M.R.	Basal metabolic rate
BP	blood presure
bpm	beats per minute
$\overline{c}$	with
CCU	Coronary Care Unit
cm	centimeter
C.N.	cranial nerves
CNS	Central nervous system
C/O	complains of

COPD	chronic obstructive pulmonary disease
CPR	cardiopulmonary resuscitation
C-R	contract-relax
C-Spine	cervical spine
C.T.	Corrective Therapy
CV	cardiovascular
CVA	cerebrovascular accident
Δ	change in
D.C.	discontinue
disch.	discharge
DM	diabetes mellitus
DOE	dyspnea on exertion
Dx	diagnosis
↓	decrease
E.C.G.	electrocardiogram
E.E.G.	electroencephalogram
E.M.G.	electromyogram
etiol.	etiology
F.B.S.	fasting blood sugar
FWB	full weight bearing
Fx	fracture
gm	gram
H-R	hold-relax
ht.	height
Hx	history
I.C.U.	Intensive Care Unit
I.E.P.	Individualized Education Program
↑	increase
I.V.	intravenous
Ⓛ or Lt.	left
LBBB	left bundle branch block
LBP	low back pain
<	less than
LE	lower extremity
LOM	limitation of motion
L-S Spine	lumbosacral spine
MBC	maximum breathing capacity
meds	medications
mg	milligram
M.I.	myocardial infarction
>	more than

$\overline{o}$	none
O2	oxygen
OBS	organic brain syndrome
Op	operation
O.T.	Occupational Therapy
oz.	ounce
$\overline{p}$	after
II bars	parallel bars
PNF	Proprioceptive Neuromuscular Facilitation
Post-op	post-operative
PRE	Progressive Resistive Exercise
p-ROM	passive range of motion
pt.	patient
P.T.	Physical Therapy
PVC	premature ventricular contraction
PWB	partial weight bearing
q.d.	every day or daily
q.h.	every hour
RHR	resting heart rate
ROM	range of motion
rpm	revolutions per minute
® or Rt.	right
Rx	prescription
$\overline{s}$	without
SCI	spinal cord injury
2°	secondary to
SOB	shortness of breath
S-R	slow reversals
THR	target heart rate
t.i.d.	three times per day
V.A.	Veteran's Administration
V.C.	Vital Capacity
WC	wheelchair
WNL	within normal limits
wt.	weight
x	times
y.o.	years old

SUMMARY OF MUSCLES INVOLVED IN ANATOMICAL MOVEMENT

Prime Movers (*) and Assistant Movers (•)

SCAPULA
Elevation (C-1 to -5)
* Trapezius I & II
* Levator scapulae
* Rhomboids Sternocleidomastoid
Upward Rotation (C-2 to C-8)
* Serratus Anterior
* Trapezius

Depression (C-4 to T-1)
* Trapezius IV
* Pectoralis minor
• Latissimus dorsi
Downward Rotation (C-3 to T-1)
* Rhomboids
* Pectoralis minor
• Levator scapulae

GLENOHUMERAL JOINT (shoulder)
Flexion (C-5 to T-1)
* Anterior Deltoid
* Pectoralis Minor
• Biceps Brachii
• Coracobrachialis
Abduction (C-5 to T-1)
* Middle Deltoid
* Supraspinatus
• Anterior Deltoid
• Triceps Brachii

Extension (C-5 to T-1)
* Latissimus Dorsi
* Teres Major
• Triceps Brachii
• Posterior Deltoid
Adduction (C-5 to T-1)
* Pectoralis Major
* Latissimus Dorsi
* Teres Major
• Biceps Brachii - short head
• Triceps Brachii - short head

Internal Rotation (C-5 to T-1)
* Subscapularis
* Teres Major
• Anterior Deltoid
• Pectoralis Minor
• Biceps Brachii

External Rotation (C-4 to C-6)
* Infraspinatus
* Teres Minor
• Posterior Deltoid

GLENOHUMERAL JOINT (continued)
Horizontal Adduction (C-5 to T-1)
* * Anterior Deltoid
* * Pectoralis Major
* * Pectoralis Minor
* * Coracobrachialis
* • Biceps Brachii

Horizontal Abduction (C-4 to C-8)
* * Middle Deltoid
* * Posterior Deltoid
* * Infraspinatus
* * Teres Minor
* • Latissimus Dorsi
* • Teres Major

GINGLYMUS JOINT (elbow)
Flexion (C-5 to T-1)
* * Biceps Brachii
* * Brachialis
* * Brachioradialis
* • Flexor Carpi Radialis
* • Flexor Carpi Ulnaris

Pronation (C-6 to T-1)
* * Pronator Quadratus
* • Flexor Carpi Radialis
* • Pronator Teres

Extension (C-6 to T-1)
* * Triceps Brachii
* • Anconeus
* • Extensor Carpi Radialis
* • Extensor Carpi Radialis Brevis
* • Extensor Carpi Ulnaris

Supination (C-5 to T-1)
* * Supinator
* • Extensor Carpi Radialis Longus
* • Extensor Pollicis Longus
* • Adductor Pollicis Longus
* • Biceps Brachii

RADIOCARPAL JOINT (wrist)
Flexion (C-7 to T-1)
* * Flexor Carpi Radialis
* * Flexor Carpi Ulnaris
* • Palmaris Longus
* • Flexor Digitorum Profundus
* • Flexor Digitorum Superficialis

Extension (C-6 to C-7)
* * Extensor Carpi Radialis Longus
* * Extensor Carpi Radialis Brevis
* * Extensor Carpi Ulnaris
* • Extensor Digitorum
* • Extensor Indicis
* • Extensor Digii Minimi

TRUNK
Spinal Flexion (T-5 to T-12)
* * Rectus Abdominis
* • Transversus Abdominis
* • External/Internal Obliques

Spinal Extension
* * Sacrospinalis (Erector Spinae)

HIP JOINT

Flexion (L-1 to S-3)
- * Iliopsoas
- * Rectus Femoris
- * Pectineus
- • Tensor Fascia Latae
- • Gracilis
- • Adductor Longus
- • Adductor Magnus

Abduction (L-4 to S-1)
- * Gluteus Medius
- • Iliopsoas
- • Sartorius
- • Rectus Femoris
- • Tensor Fasciae Latae
- • Gluteus Minimus

Internal Rotation (L-4 to S-2)
- * Gluteus Minimus
- • Tensor Fasciae Latae
- • Semitendinosus
- • Semimembranosus
- • Muscles listed under adduction

Extension (L-4 to S-3)
- * Gluteus Maximus
- * Biceps Femoris
- * Semitendinosus
- * Semimembranosus
- • Gluteus Medius
- • Gluteus Minimus

Adduction (L-1 to S-4)
- * Pectineus
- * Gracilis
- * Adductor Longus
- * Adductor Brevis
- * Adductor Magnus

External Rotation (L-1 to S-3)
- * Gluteus Maximus
- • Sartorius
- • Iliopsoas
- • Biceps Femoris
- • Six external rotators are also assisting

KNEE JOINTS

Flexion (L-2 to S-3)
- * Semitendinosus
- * Semimembranosus
- * Biceps Femoris
- • Sartorius
- • Gracilis
- • Gastrocnemius
- • Plantaria

Internal Rotation (L-2 to S-5)
- * Semitendinosus
- * Semimembranosus
- • Sartorius
- • Gracilis
- • Popliteus (also unlocks knee)

Extension (L-2 to L-4)
- * Rectus Femoris
- * Vastus Lateralis
- * Vastus Intermedius
- * Vastus Medialis

External Rotation (L-5 to S-3)
- • Biceps Femoris

278

TALOCRURAL JOINT (ankle)

Dorsiflexion (L-4 to S-1)
* * Tibialis Anterior
* * Extensor Digitorum Longus
* • Perioneus Tertius
* • Extensor Hallucis Longus

Plantarflexion (L-4 to S-2)
* * Gastrocnemius
* * Soleus
* • Plantaris
* • Peroneus Longus
* • Flexor Digitorum Longus
* • Flexor Hallucis Longus
* • Tibialis Posterior

Inversion (L-4 to L-5)
* * Tibialis Anterior
* * Tibialis Posterior
* • Flexor Digitorum Longus
* • Flexor Hallucis Longus
* • Extensor Hallucis Longus

Eversion (L-4 to S-1)
* * Extensor Digitorum Longus
* * Peroneus Tertius
* * Peroneus Longus
* * Peroneus Brevis

RESPIRATORY MUSCLES

Inspiration (resting)
* * Diaphragm
* * External Intercostals
* * Internal Intercostals
* • Erector Spinae

Expiration (forced)
* * Transverse Abdominis
* * Rectus Abdominis
* • External Intercostals
* • Internal Intercostals
* • Quadratus Lumborum
* * External Obliques
* * Internal Obliques
* • Muscles of the neck and shoulder

Inspiration (forced)
* * Diaphragm
* * External Intervostals
* * Internal Intercostals

POSTURE GRID

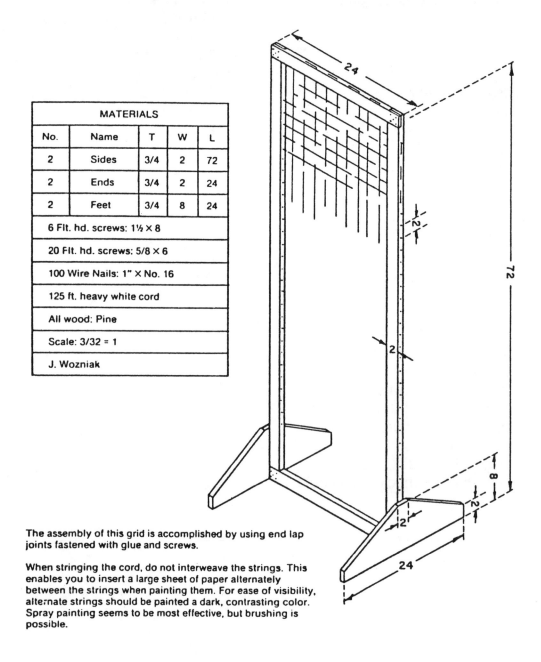

MATERIALS				
No.	Name	T	W	L
2	Sides	3/4	2	72
2	Ends	3/4	2	24
2	Feet	3/4	8	24

6 Flt. hd. screws: 1½ × 8

20 Flt. hd. screws: 5/8 × 6

100 Wire Nails: 1" × No. 16

125 ft. heavy white cord

All wood: Pine

Scale: 3/32 = 1

J. Wozniak

The assembly of this grid is accomplished by using end lap joints fastened with glue and screws.

When stringing the cord, do not interweave the strings. This enables you to insert a large sheet of paper alternately between the strings when painting them. For ease of visibility, alternate strings should be painted a dark, contrasting color. Spray painting seems to be most effective, but brushing is possible.

(Photo courtesy of J. Wozniak, LaCrosse, Wis.).

SIT-AND-REACH APPARATUS

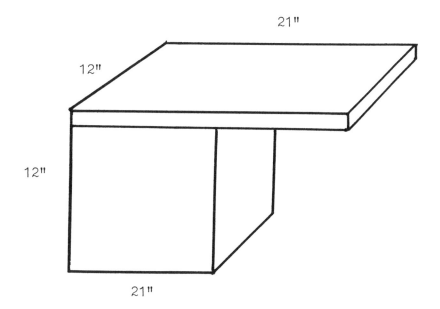

QUAD GLOVES

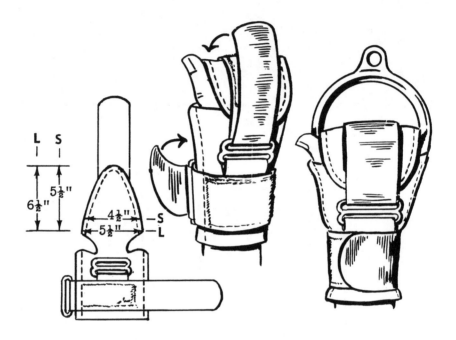

ANECDOTAL RECORD
FOR THE STUDENT WITH EPILEPSY*

WHAT DID THE STUDENT DO BEFORE THE SEIZURE (PRECIPITATING EVENTS, IF ANY)?

_____

_____

WHAT DID THE STUDENT DO DURING THE SEIZURE (SIDES AND PARTS OF THE BODY MOST AFFECTED DURING THE SEIZURE)?

_____

_____

_____

HOW DID THE STUDENT ACT AFTER THE SEIZURE? _____

_____

_____

DURATION OF SEIZURE: _____ TIME OF DAY: _____

REACTION OF OTHER STUDENTS: _____

_____

_____

ANY INJURIES SUSTAINED AS A RESULT OF THE SEIZURE? _____

_____

_____

DOES THE STUDENT EXHIBIT ANY UNUSUAL ACTIVITY THAT COULD BE A RESULTING SIDE EFFECT OF ANTICONVULSANT MEDICATION (DROWSINESS, INATTENTION, IRRITABILITY, ETC.)?

_____

_____

ADDITIONAL COMMENTS: _____*(This area should be used for answering*_____

_____*questions listed under "Observing the Seizure.")*_____

* This kind of record should be kept with the knowledge and written consent of student and parents, and should be sent to parents or physician after each seizure.